PRAISE F

HOSTELS CANADA

"No other guidebook I've seen provides hostel descriptions as accurate and insightful as *Hostels Canada*. . . . Whether you're a party animal or a quiet conversationalist this book makes it easy to find the hostel that's right for you."

—Darren Overby, Editor, *The Internet Guide to Hostelling*

"An invaluable resource for backpackers and other independent travelers. . . . A down to earth guide with personality and spunk."

—Jim Fortney, Editor, *Big World Magazine*

"Budget-conscious travelers will welcome this book."

—*Library Journal*

". . . an indispensable reference for thrifty travelers of all kinds."

—*American Bookseller*

"[The books in this series] are super-useful! What to do, how to get there, and what it's like, all rolled into one. You can't get this information all in one place anywhere else!"

—Peter Leblanc, Program Director, Hostelling International (Seattle)

HELP US KEEP THIS GUIDE UP TO DATE

Every effort has been made by the authors and editors to make this guide as accurate and useful as possible. However, many things can change after a guide is published—establishments close, phone numbers change, facilities come under new management, etc.

We would love to hear from you concerning your experiences with this guide and how you feel it could be made better and be kept up to date. While we may not be able to respond to all comments and suggestions, we'll take them to heart and we'll also make certain to share them with the authors. Please send your comments and suggestions to the following address:

The Globe Pequot Press
Reader Response/Editorial Department
P.O. Box 480
Guilford, CT 06437

Or you may e-mail us at:

editorial@globe-pequot.com

Thanks for your input, and happy travels!

HOSTELS SERIES

HOSTELS CANADA

The Only Comprehensive, Unofficial, Opinionated Guide

Second Edition

Paul Karr

with Martha Coombs

Guilford, Connecticut

Cover and text design: M.A. Dubé
Maps: M.A. Dubé
Editorial and research assistance: Evan Halper
Photography: Martha Coombs, Paul Karr, Tomomi Shibuya

Library of Congress Cataloging-in-Publication Data

Karr, Paul.
Hostels Canada : the only comprehensive, unofficial, opinionated guide / Paul Karr, with Martha Coombs. —2nd ed.
p. cm. — (Hostels series)
Includes index.
ISBN 0-7627-0616-3
1. Tourist camps, hostels, etc.—Canada—Guidebooks. I. Coombs, Martha. II. Title. III. Series.

TX907.5.C2 K37 2000
647.9471'06—dc21 99-086265

Printed on recycled and permanent paper
Manufactured in the United States of America
Second Edition/First Printing

CONTENTS

ACKNOWLEDGMENTS

Paul Karr thanks Martha for her companionship and editorial assistance. What a wonderful travel partner and writer you are!

Thanks to friends and family who gave bed, board, or companionship during the travels—the Karr, Couture, and Bottinger families in New Hampshire; Tom Paquette and Chris Allen in Maine, for continued inspiration and camaraderie; and Kimeiko Hotta in Toronto, for friendship, support, and good wine at all the right moments. Special thanks to Evan and Bob Halper in New York for assistance and good counsel.

Thanks to Tomomi Shibuya for her special help at a crucial juncture. Also, thanks to the good folks at Magellan's for kindly helping to sponsor the work a second time around with travel supplies; to Hostelling International for continued encouragement and assistance; to VIA Rail, for cheerful cooperation and some fine train riding through Canada; to Tilden, the finest auto-rental company we have ever worked with; to Prince of Fundy Cruises; to Hal Rennie at Nova Scotia Tourism; and to everyone else who provided information, shelter, or a kind word.

Thanks to those hostel managers and staff who answered questions or gave us a place to work on this book when we needed it most.

And thanks, finally, to a world (literally) of new friends met or made on the road—Atsuko, Mutsuno, Céline, Jérome, Katrin, Silke, Martin, and all the rest. So many of you have taught me about your corner of the world or otherwise made this work enjoyable and useful.

Martha Coombs thanks Paul, for his guidance, enduring friendship, and great gestalts, as well as Robert, Céline, Edna, Gilles, Mike, and my Korean friends from Jasper. Thanks to Mr. Reilly for helping me choose the right words.

We both thank the fine people of Canada.

The prices and rates listed in this guidebook were confirmed at press time. We recommend, however, that you call establishments before traveling to obtain current information.

HOW TO USE THIS BOOK

What you're holding in your hands is the first-ever attempt of its kind: a complete listing and rating of hostels in Canada. Dozens of hostellers from countries all over the globe were interviewed in the course of putting this guide together, and their comments and thoughts run throughout its pages. Who knows? You yourself might be quoted somewhere inside.

We wrote this guide for two pretty simple reasons.

First, we wanted to bring hostelling to a wider audience. Hostels continue to grow in popularity, particularly with older travelers, but most North Americans still don't think of them as options when planning a local trip. We wanted to change that, because—at its best—the hostelling experience brings people of greatly differing origins, faiths, and points of view together in a convivial setting. You learn about these people as well as about the place in which the hostel is situated in a very personal way that no textbook could ever provide.

Second, we wanted very much to give people our honest opinions of the hostels described here. You wouldn't send your best friend to a fleabag, and we don't want readers traveling great distances only to be confronted with filthy kitchens, nasty managers, or dangerous neighborhoods. At least, we thought, we could warn you about unsafe or unpleasant situations ahead of time.

On the other hand, of course, we would also tip off our friends to the truly wonderful hostels—the ones with treehouses, cafes, free breakfasts, the ones with real family spirit. So that's what we've done. Time after time on the road, we have heard fellow travelers complaining that the guidebooks they bought simply listed places to stay but didn't rate them. Well, now we've done it—and we haven't pulled a single punch or held back a bit of praise.

How We Wrote This Book

The authors, along with a cadre of assistants, fanned out across Canada from 1997 to 1999. Sometimes we identified ourselves in advance as authors; sometimes we just popped in for surprise visits. We counted rooms, turned taps, tested beds. And we talked with managers and staff.

We also took the time to interview plenty of hostellers in private and get their honest opinions about the places where they were staying or had already stayed.

The results are contained within this book: actual hosteller quotes, opinions, ratings, and more.

What Is a Hostel?

If you've picked up this book, you probably know what a hostel is. On the other hand, a surprising number of people interviewed for this book weren't sure at all what it means.

So let's check your knowledge with a little pop quiz. Sharpen your pencil and put on your thinking cap, then dive in.

1. A hostel is:

A. a hospital.

B. a hospice.

C. a hotel.

D. a drunk tank.

E. none of the above.

(Correct answer worth 20 points)

2. A hostel is:

A. a place where international travelers bunk up.

B. a cheap sleep.

C. an experiment in living semicommunally.

D. all of the above.

(Correct answer worth 20 points)

3. You just turned 30. Word on the street has it that you'll get turned away for being that age. Do you tell the person at the hostel desk the grim news?

A. No, because a hostel is restricted to students under 30.

B. No, because a hostel is restricted to elderly folks over 65.

C. No, because they don't care about your mid-life crisis.

(Correct answer worth 10 points)

4. You spy a shelf labeled FREE FOOD! in the hostel kitchen. What do you do?

A. Begin stuffing pomegranates in your pockets.

B. Ask the manager how Food ended up in jail.

C. Run for your life.

(Correct answer worth 5 points)

5. Essay question: Why do you want to stay in a hostel? (Extra credit; worth up to 45 points)

Done? Great! *And the envelope, please . . .*

1. E. None of the above. The word *hostel* is German, and it means "country inn for youngsters" (or something like that). In parts of

Canada, the word *auberge* is used instead; that means "rustic inn," approximately. The word is not related to "hostile," as in "hostilities." In fact, we've found that most Canadian managers are downright friendly.

2. D. All of the above. You got that one, right?

3. C. No age limits or restrictions here!

4. A. Free means free.

5. Give yourself 15 points for every use of the word friends, international, or cool, okay? But don't give yourself more than 45. Yes, we mean it. Don't make us turn this car around right now. We will. No kidding.

What? All you wrote was "It's cheap"? Okay, okay, give yourself 20 points.

So how did you do?

100 points:	Born to be wild
80–100:	Get your motor runnin'
40–80:	Head out on the highway
20–40:	Lookin' for adventure
0–20:	Hope you don't come my way

Don't be embarrassed if you flunked this little quiz. Even some hostel operators get confused and blur the lines, too. You'll sometimes find a campground, retreat center, or college setting aside a couple bunks and calling itself a hostel. In those cases, we've used our best judgment about whether a place is or isn't a hostel.

Also, we've excluded some joints—no matter how well meaning—if they (A) exclude men or women, (B) serve primarily as a university residence hall (with a very few special exceptions), or (C) serve you a heavy side of religious doctrine with the eggs in the morning.

In a few cases, our visits didn't satisfy us either way; those places were left out, were set aside for a future edition, or are briefly described here but not rated.

The bottom line? If it is in this book, it probably is a hostel. If it isn't, it's probably not, and don't let anyone tell you otherwise. There. 'Nuff said.

Understanding the Ratings

All the listings information in this book was current as of press time. Here's the beginning of a sample entry in the book, from a hostel in Regina (that's the capital of Saskatchewan province, by the way). It's a fairly typical entry:

TURGEON INTERNATIONAL HOSTEL

2310 McIntyre Street, Regina, Saskatchewan S4P 2S2

(306) 791–8165

Rates: $13.00 Canadian (about $9.00 U.S.) per Hostelling International member; family rooms, $27.00 Canadian (about $18 U.S.)
Credit cards: MC, VISA
Office hours: 7:00–10:00 A.M.; 5:00–11:00 P.M.
Season: February 1–December 24
Beds: 38
Private/family rooms: 1
Single rooms: None
Private bathrooms: None
Affiliation: Hostelling International Canada
Extras: Library, laundry, TV, grill, picnic tables, piano

10% S

First things first. See those little pictures? Those are icons, and they signify something important we wanted you to know about the hostel. A key to the icons used in this book is printed on the facing page.

The overall hostel rating consists of those hip-looking thumbs sitting atop each entry. It's pretty simple: Thumbs up means good. Thumbs down means bad.

We've used these thumbs to compare the hostels to one another. Only a select number of hostels earned the top rating of two thumbs up, and a few were considered unpleasant enough to merit two thumbs down. You can use this rating as a general assessment of a hostel.

Sometimes we didn't give any thumbs at all, such as to a hostel that was a mixed-bag experience. Or for one reason or another—bad weather, bad luck, bad timing, remoteness, an inability to get ahold of the staff, or our own ambivalence or confusion about the place—maybe we just didn't feel we collected enough information to properly rate that hostel for you.

That said, here's a key to what these ratings mean:

 Cream of the crop; fun, clean, and pleasant

 Nice; average to above-average

 Mixed bag; so-so; jury's still out

 Not recommended

 Bad news

Not rated

KEY TO ICONS

 Attractive natural setting

 Ecologically aware hostel

 Superior kitchen facilities or cafe

 Offbeat or eccentric place

 Superior bathroom facilities

 Romantic private rooms

 Comfortable beds

 Among our very favorite hostels

 A particularly good value

 Wheelchair-accessible

 Good for business travelers

 Especially well suited for families

 Good for active travelers

 Visual arts at hostel or nearby

 Music at hostel or nearby

The rest of the information is pretty much self-explanatory:

The **address** is usually the hostel's street address (occasionally it's the mailing address, with the town name in parentheses).

The **phone number** is the primary number.

E-mail is the staff's e-mail address, for those who want to get information or book a room by computer.

Web site indicates a hostel's World Wide Web address.

Rates are the cost per person to stay at the hostel—expect to pay somewhere around $15 Canadian per person as a rule (that's about $10 U.S.), more in cities or popular tourist areas. For private or family rooms, we've listed the total price for two people to stay in the room; usually it's higher than the cost of two singles, sometimes considerably so. Single or triple room rates will vary; ask ahead if you're unsure what you'll pay.

Note that these rates sometimes vary by season or by membership in a hostelling group such as Hostelling International-Canada (HI-C); we have tried to include a range of prices, where applicable. Most HI-C member hostels, for instance, charge $3.00–$4.00 Canadian (about $2.00–$3.00 U.S.) extra per day if you don't belong to one of Hostelling International's worldwide affiliates.

Also, some hostels charge about $1.00 Canadian (about $0.70 U.S.) to supply sheets and towels if you haven't brought your own. (Sleeping bags, no matter how clean you think they are, are often frowned upon.) Finally, federal, provincial, or local taxes may also add slightly to the rates quoted here.

Credit cards can be a good way to pay for a bed in a foreign country (you get the best exchange rates on your home currency). Here we list all the cards accepted by the hostel. More and more hostels are taking them. But remember, even if no credit cards are listed, things may have changed since we checked. When in doubt, call ahead and ask. Here are the credit-card abbreviations used in Hostels Canada:

AMEX: **American Express**
DISC: **Discover Card**
JCB: **Japan Credit Bureau**
MC: **Master Card**
VISA: **Visa**

Also note that many Canadian hostels take a Canadian-issued debit card called INTERAC. We haven't identified these places, but if you have one in your wallet, by all means ask the desk clerk. Go ahead. Make their day.

Office hours indicates the hours when staff are at the front desk and answer the phones, or at least would consider answering the phones. Keep in mind that nothing is fixed in stone, however. Some hostel staffs will happily field calls in the middle of the night if you're reasonable, while others can't stand it. Try to call within the listed hours.

A good rule of thumb to follow: The smaller a place, the harder it is for the owner-manager to drag out of bed at four in the morning just because you lost your way. Big-city hostels, however, frequently operate just like hotels—somebody's always on duty or, at least, on call.

Season indicates what part of the year a hostel is open—if it's closed part of the year. (No "Season" entry means all-year service.) We've made our best effort at listing the season of each hostel, but schedules sometimes change according to weather or a manager's vacation plans. Call if you're unsure whether a hostel will be open when you want to stay there.

Private/family rooms are rooms for a couple, a family with children, or (sometimes) a single traveler. Once in a while it's nice to have your own room on the road: It's more private, more secure, and your snoring won't bother anyone. Unlike Euro-hostels, many Canadian hostels offer at least one private room. But often it's hard to get; call in advance if you know you want one.

Single rooms are rooms with one twin bed.

Private bathrooms are bathrooms that belong to a certain private room; nobody else (in theory) can use 'em. This luxury is pretty unusual in any sort of hostel, but you've got a better shot in Canada than anywhere except the United States.

Affiliation indicates whether a hostel is affiliated with Hostelling International-Canada or any of several smaller hostel groups in Canada. For more information about what these organizations do, see "A Word About Affiliations" (page 10).

Extras lists some of the other amenities that come with a stay at the hostel. A dollar sign in parentheses after an item indicates that you must pay more for it. However, some—but not all—will be free; there's an amazing variety of services, and almost as big a variety in managers' willingness to do nice things for nothing. Laundries, for instance, are almost never free, and there's usually a charge for meals, lockers, bicycle or other equipment rentals, and other odds and ends. On the other hand, some hostels maintain free information desks. Some give you free meals, too.

At the end of each entry, we've given you a little more information about the hostel to make your stay a little more informed—and fun. Here's the last part of the hostel entry that began above:

Best bet for a bite: Heliotrope

What hostellers say: "One of the best!"

Insiders' tip: Wascana Centre parks

Gestalt: Regal beagle

Safety: A

Hospitality: A

Cleanliness: A

Party index:

What does all that stuff mean?

Best bet for a bite tells you where to find food in the area; often we'll direct you to the cheapest and closest supermarket. But sometimes, in the interest of variety—and good eatin'—we'll point you toward a health-food store, a place rich with local color, or even a fancy place that we loved. Maybe even to the hostel itself.

What hostellers say relates what hostellers told us about a hostel—or what we imagine they would say.

Insiders' tip is a juicy secret about the area, something we didn't know until we got to the hostel.

Gestalt is the general feeling of a place, our (sometimes humorous) way of describing what it's about.

Safety describes urban hostels only; it rates both the safety of the neighborhood and the security precautions taken by the hostel staff. The grades go like this:

A: No worries
B: Pretty safe
C: Somewhat dodgy
D: Use great caution
F: Dial 911

Hospitality grades the hostel staff's friendliness toward hostellers (and travel writers).

A: Friends for life
B: Smile city
C: Take a chill pill
D: Hostile hostel
F: Very hostile

Cleanliness rates (what else?) the general cleanliness of a place. Bear in mind that this can change—rapidly—depending on the time of year, turnover in staff, and so forth. So use the grades only as a general guide.

A: Immaculate
B: Spic-'n'-span
C: Gettin' grungy
D: Animal House
F: Don't let the bed bugs bite

The Party index is our way of tipping you off about the general scene at the hostel:

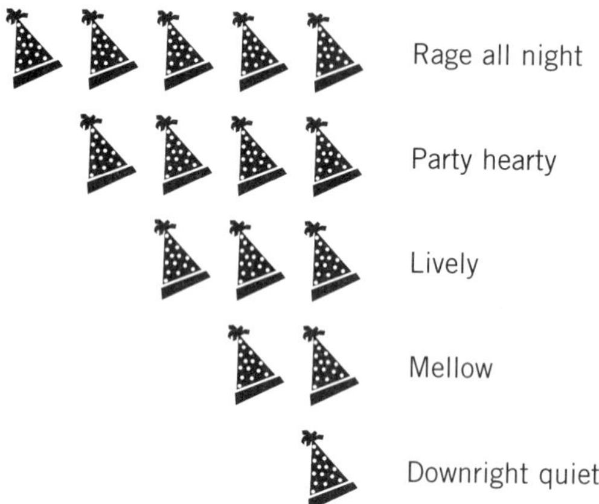

Finally, **How to get there** includes directions to hostels by car, bus, train, plane, or, in some cases, even ferry. Often the directions are complicated; in those cases, managers have asked (or we recommend) that you call the hostel itself for more precise directions.

A SHORT HISTORY OF HOSTELLING

Hostelling as we know it started around 1907, when Richard Schirmann, an assistant schoolteacher in Altena, Germany, decided to make one of the empty classrooms a space for visiting students to sleep. That was not a completely unique idea, as Austrian inns and taverns had been offering reduced rates and bunk space to students since 1885. But Schirmann would develop much grander plans. He was about to start a movement.

His idea was to get students out of the industrial cities and into the countryside. Schirmann was a strong believer that walking and bicycling tours in the fresh air were essential to adolescent development and learning. But such excursions were impossible without a place to spend the night. His logic was simple: Since rural schoolhouses were deserted during weekends and holidays, why not make use of those spaces?

The caretakers of the school he chose in Altena agreed to serve as houseparents, and some ground rules were established. Students were responsible for piling up the tables and benches in the classroom and laying out thin straw sacks on the floor. At some ungodly early morning hour, the students were to stack the straw mats back up and organize the classroom as they found it. Boys and girls slept in separate rooms but were treated as equals. Detractors cried scandal, speculating about what was going on in those schoolrooms after dark.

The experiment worked—sort of. Altena became a haven for student excursions into the countryside, but finding shelter in other communities proved to be difficult. Late one night in the summer of 1909, Schirmann decided that it was time to expand his movement beyond Altena. His goal was to establish a network of hostels within walking distance of one another; and, beginning in a schoolhouse with straw mats, Schirmann eventually acquired the use of a castle. It still stands—the Ur-hostel, if you will—in Altena, and it's still used as a hostel, believe it or not.

After World War I, the movement really began to spread. By 1928 there were more than 2,000 hostels worldwide. The first U.S. hostel opened in Northfield, Massachusetts, in 1934. Canadian hostelling began about the same time. The first Canadian hostel consisted of a 12-foot by 14-foot canvas tent in Alberta. That Bragg Creek hostel, called Wakesiah Lodge, cost on the order of 25 or 50 cents a night to stay, we're told. But the plumbing facilities were strictly, well, au naturel.

Calgary International Hostel
Calgary

(photo courtesy Hostelling International-Canada)

Still, the movement caught on in Canada almost as fast as it did in the United States. Today tens of thousands of hostellers stay at Hostelling International–affiliated hostels in Canada each year, hailing from everywhere from Alaska to Zaire; thousands more stay at independent hostels.

The goal of a single association of hostels located within a day's walk of one another will probably never be realized in Canada. In fact, a good number of them can't even be reached by public transportation, and more hostels seem to be dropping out from HI-C these days—a testament to Canadians' plucky self-determination, we think, not just a criticism of the umbrella organization's ways and means.

Still, you're likely to find a promising brew of cultural exchange and friendship over pots of ramen noodles and instant coffee almost anywhere you go in Canada. And believe us when we say that the Canadians, as a people, are among the friendliest folks on Earth. Your hostel manager will almost surely be kind-hearted.

In that sense, perhaps, Richard Schirmann's dream has been realized after all.

A Word About Affiliations

A majority of hostels in this book are affiliated with **Hostelling International-Canada** (HI-C); the rest we've labeled **independent hostels.**

Hostelling International-Canada has long been the backbone of hostelling in Canada. The organization is part of the International Youth Hostel Federation, which has 5,000 member hostels in seventy countries worldwide. Member hostels are held to a number of regulations, such as maximum number of beds per shower—even a minimum amount of space that must exist between top bunks and the ceiling.

Overall, the HI-Canada hostels tended to earn higher marks from our reviewers than independent hostels. They regularly own the nicest buildings and keep the floors cleanest. The organization's mission statement trumpets its contribution to "the education of young people," so be warned that some of its most popular hostels attract youth groups like molasses does flies. Families and senior travelers are also attracted to the Hostelling International network.

Liquor is supposed to be off limits at most of these places, and guests tend to be an orderly bunch. Many of the giant urban hostels are purpose-built facilities owned by the organization itself, often resembling well-equipped college dormitories. Some of these HI-C–owned hostels have developed impressive educational programs that incorporate volunteers from the local community and so forth.

The bulk of HI-Canada hostels, however, are independently owned. These joints are as varied in personality as their owners. A common thread that runs through them, though, is a respect for the educational dimension of hostelling. Owners reiterate again and again that hostels offer more than just a cheap sleep; they often join HI-Canada out of respect for the organization and its goals.

There is one last breed of HI-Canada hostels, the so-called home hostel—usually a spare bedroom or two in somebody's home. It goes without saying that your freedom (and partying) can be strictly limited at such places, but we've found that some of them are great if you can abide by the rules and enjoy getting to know your hosts. You'll definitely get more attention at these places.

Some owners opt not to join a hostelling organization. Membership costs are high, and they feel that the return on such an investment isn't enough. Such a decision, in and of itself, does not reflect on the quality of the hostel. It would be foolish to write a hostel off simply because it is not affiliated. On the other hand, there's no guarantee of quality, and the standards, upkeep, noise level, and beer flow tend to vary wildly from place to place.

HOW TO HOSTEL

Hostelling in Canada is, generally speaking, as easy as pie. Plan ahead a bit and use a little common sense, and you'll find that check-in goes pretty smoothly.

Reserving a Bed

Getting a good bunk will often be your first and biggest challenge, especially if it's high season. (Summer is usually high season, but in some parts of Canada—the Laurentians and the B.C. mountains, for instance—winter can be the toughest time to get a bed.) Hostellers often have an amazingly laissez-faire attitude about reservations; many simply waltz in at midnight expecting that a bed will work out.

Sometimes it does. Sometimes it doesn't.

Most every Hostelling International abode takes advance reservations of some form or another; so, if you know where you're going to be, use this service. Be aware that you'll often need a credit-card number to hold a bed; other hostels require that you send a deposit check in the mail. Some hostels maintain their own toll-free reservation numbers. We've included these numbers wherever they're available.

About a dozen HI-Canada hostels are also affiliated with the worldwide International Booking Network. You can make advance reservations for a very small fee by calling this service at (800) 663–5777; it connects you directly with the regional office of whatever local council is closest to the phone you're calling from.

Independent hostels are sometimes more lax about taking solid reservations, though they're also a lot more willing to find extra couch space or a spare mattress in case you're squeezed out. Calling a few days ahead to feel out the situation is always a good idea.

If you can't or won't reserve, the best thing to do is get there super-early. Office opens at 8:00 A.M.? Get there at 7:00. No room then, but checkout ends at 11:00 A.M.? Be back at 11:05 in case of cancellations or unexpected checkouts. The doors are closed again till 4:30 P.M.? No problem. Come back around 4:00 with a paperback and camp out on the porch. That's your only shot if you didn't reserve ahead, and hostellers are pretty respectful of the pecking order—it really is first come, first served. So come first.

Paying the Piper

Once you're in be prepared to pay for your night's stay immediately, before you're even assigned a bunk. Take note ahead of time which hostels take credit cards, checks, and so forth. Think you're being cheated on the bill? Remember that most hostels charge $1.00 or so Canadian ($0.70 U.S.) per night for linens if you haven't brought your own. (You always have the option of bringing your own, however, and we recommend it. See below.)

Other charges could include a surcharge for a private room and charges for phone calls from your room, if a phone is included (very unusual).

You might also need to leave a small deposit for your room key, usually about $5.00 Canadian (about $3.50 U.S.). You'll get it back when you check out—unless you lost the key in the meantime. Sometimes you will also be required to show some form of photo identification to check in. Very occasionally you'll even be forced to leave a passport or driver's license with the front desk. This is annoying and possibly illegal, but a few hostels still get away with it. Scream bloody murder, threaten to sue—but you might get shut out unless you play along.

Remember to pay ahead if you want a weekly stay, too. Often you can get deep discounts, though the down side is that you'll almost never get a partial refund if you decide you can't stand it and leave before the week is up.

If you're paying by the day, rebook promptly each morning. Hostel managers are very busy during the morning hours, keeping track of check-ins, checkouts, cleaning duties, and cash. Also, managers hate bugging guests all morning or all day about whether they'll be staying on. Don't put the staff through this. You'll make friends if you're early about notifying them of your plans.

Some hostel managers have the curiously softhearted habit of letting the rent slide for a few days. We can't figure why; when managers do this a day often becomes a week—or a month. Even if this courtesy is extended to you, don't use it, except in an emergency. You never know who they might hire to get that money out of you later.

Okay, so you've secured a bed and paid up. Now you have to get to it. This may be no easy task at some hostels, where staff and customers look and act like one and the same. A kindly manager will probably notice you bumbling around and take pity. As you're being shown to your room, you'll also likely get a short tour of the facilities and a briefing on the ground rules.

Knowing the Ground Rules

There's one universal ground rule at every hostel: You are responsible for serving and cleaning up after yourself. And there's a corollary rule: Be courteous. So, while you're welcome to use all the kitchen facilities, share the space with your fellow guests—don't spread your five-course meal over all the counter space and rangetop burners if other hungry folks are hanging around waiting for you to finish. And never, ever leave a sink full of dirty pots and pans behind. That's bad form.

Hostel guests are almost always asked to mark their name and check-in date on all the food they put in the refrigerator. Only the shelf marked FREE FOOD is up for grabs; everything else belongs to other hostellers, so don't touch it. (Hostellers get very touchy about people stealing their grub.) Some of the better-run hostels have spices and other kitchen essentials on hand. If you're not sure whether something is communal, ask. But don't assume that anything is up for grabs unless it is clearly marked as such.

Alcohol is still a major issue at some hostels. Hostelling International-Canada rules forbid it on the premises of HI-Canada hostels. We were not surprised to see this rule bent or broken in some places, but inquire with a smile on your face before you bring that brew inside. Independent hostels are a lot more forgiving; some—especially in Québec—even have bars.

Then there's the lockout, a source of bitter contention among hostel factions. A few rural and small-city HI-Canada hostels throw everybody out in the morning and don't let them back in until the early evening. Lockouts tend to run from around 10:00 A.M. to 4:00 P.M., during which time your bags might be inside your room—but *you* won't be.

The practice has its pros and cons. Managers usually justify a lockout by noting that it forces travelers to interact with the locals. The real reason is usually that the hostel can't or won't pay staff to hang around and babysit you all day. On the other hand, some hostels become semi-residential situations stuffed with couch potatoes. A lockout sure solves that problem.

In the reviews, we've identified those hostels that enforce lockouts. (Fortunately, the practice is much more common in the United States than in Canada.) Usually you wouldn't want to be hanging out in the hostel in the middle of the day anyway, but after several sleepless nights of travel, or when you're under the weather, daytime down time is certainly appreciated. So beware.

Some hostels also enforce a maximum limit on your stay—anywhere from three days, if the hostel is really popular, to about two weeks. You will instantly know if such a policy is in effect the moment you walk into a place. If there are lots of cigarette butts, slackers, or dirty clothes hanging around, it's the curse of the dreaded long-termers: folks who came for a day and stay for a lifetime just to avoid finding work. So a maximum-stay rule can be a very good thing. On the other hand, you might find yourself wanting to spend more than three days in some great place—and be shown the door instead.

Savvy budget travelers have learned how to get around this unfortunate situation, of course: They simply suck it up and spend a night at the Y or a convenient motel—then check back into the cheaper hostel first thing in the morning. But we didn't tell you to do that. Uh-uh.

Etiquette and Smarts

Again, to put it simply, use common sense. Hostellers are a refreshingly flexible bunch. All these people are able to make the system work by looking after one another; remember, in a hostel, you're a community member first and a consumer second. With that in mind, here are some guidelines for how to act:

- The first thing you should do after check-in is make your bed. When you're assigned a bed, stick to it. Don't spread your stuff out on nearby bunks, even if they are empty. Someone's going to be coming in late at night for one of 'em; you can bet the backpack on it.
- Be sure to lock your valuables in a locker or the trunk of your car. Good hostels offer lockers as a service; it might cost a little, but it's worth it.
- Set toiletries and anything else you need in a place where they are easily accessible. This avoids your having to paw through a bag later at night, potentially waking other guests from their slumber. The same goes for early morning departures: If you'll be taking off at the crack of dawn, take precautions not to disturb the whole place.
- If you're leaving early in the morning, try to make all arrangements with the manager before going to bed the night before. Retrieve your key deposit before the desk closes, if possible, and settle up any debts. Managers are usually accommodating and pleasant folks, but guests are expected to respect their privacy and peace of mind by not pushing things too far. (Dragging a manager out of bed at 4:00 A.M. is really pushing it.)
- Be sure to keep the bathroom tidy. A quick wiping of the shower floor with a paper towel after you use it is common courtesy.
- Finally, be sure to mind the quiet hours. Some hostels have curfews, but very few force lights-out. If you are up after hours, be respectful. Don't crank the television or radio volume too high.

Packing

Those dainty hand towels and dapper shaving kits and free soaps that you get at a hotel won't be anywhere in sight at the hostel. In fact, even some of the basic essentials may not be available, You're on your own, so bring everything you need to be comfortable.

There are only a few things you can expect the hostel to supply:

- a bed frame with a mattress and pillow;
- shower and toilet facilities;
- a working kitchen with communal pots, pans, and dishes;
- a common room with some Spartan furniture; and
- maybe a few heavy blankets.

Some of the more chic hostels we've identified in this guide may be full-service. Heck, we've stayed in hostels that provide the food for you to cook with—not to mention generous spice racks. But they are the exception to the rule.

Bring this stuff to keep your journey through hostel territory smooth and comfortable:

- A passport is strongly advised. Many urban hostels keep a very tight filter on who may check in. (The exception is Hostelling International-Canada affiliates, which are required by policy to admit all paying guests). A passport gives you a sense of legitimacy as a traveler. Be warned, however, that a few Canadian hostels simply will not allow Canadian visitors to stay; we have done our best to identify those in the write-ups.

- Hostelling International membership cards are a good thing to have on hand. They can be purchased at most member HI-Canada hostels; they cost $26.75 Canadian (about $18.00 U.S.) for one year, or $37.45 Canadian (about $25.00 U.S.) for a two-year card. This card identifies you as a certified super-hosteller and gets you the very cheapest rate for your bed in all HI-Canada (and also some unaffiliated) hostels. At $3.00–$5.00 Canadian ($2.00–$4.00 U.S.) savings per night, these savings can add up fast.

  Sometimes that membership card gets you deals at local restaurants, bike shops, and tours, too. And it will be easier to deal with the front desk at some of the more cautious hostels (even nonmember ones) if you can flash one of these cards.

- Red alert! Do not plan on using a sleeping bag in most hostels. A good number of places simply won't allow it—problems with ticks and other creatures dragged in from the great outdoors have propelled this prohibition into place. The alternative is a sleepsack, which is basically two sheets sewn together with a makeshift pillowcase. You can find them at most budget-travel stores, or make your own. Personally, we hate these confining wraps; we rarely get through the night in one without having it twist around our bodies so tight that we wake up wanting to charge it with manslaughter. Our preferred method is to bring our own set of sheets, though that might be too much extra stuff to pack if you're backpacking.

  Some hostels give you free linen; most of those that don't will rent sheets for about $1.00–$2.00 Canadian ($0.70–$1.50 U.S.) per night. You won't normally be charged for use of the standard army surplus blankets—or the musty charm that comes with them.

- Some people bring their own pillows, as those supplied tend to be on the frumpy side. Good idea if you're traveling by car and can fit them in. Also useful for pillow fights.

- We strongly suggest earplugs for light sleepers, especially for urban hostels—but also in case you get caught in a room with a heavy snorer.

- A small flashlight is a must. Not only for late-night reading, but also to find your bed without waking up the entire dorm.

- A little bit of spice is always nice, especially when you have had one too many plates of pasta. You'll find the spice prices in convenience stores way too high to stomach once you're on the road. Buy them cheap before you leave, and store them in small jars or plastic bags.

- Check to see which hostels have laundry facilities. It's much easier to do the wash while making dinner than to waste a day sitting around with the cast of *The Shining* at a local laundromat.
- Wearing flip-flops in the shower might help spare you a dreaded case of athlete's foot.
- Be sure that your towel is a quick-drying type. Otherwise, you'll wind up with mildew in your pack. And your food.

Money

The value of one Canadian dollar depends on a fluctuating exchange rate; at press time, it was worth about 70 cents U.S. In this book, we have given the approximate U.S. equivalents for room, meal, and other prices, using 70 cents as the exchange rate.

Changing money carries a fee if you do it in person; use your ATM card if possible. Change bureaus will charge you a higher fee than banks.

Speaking Canadian

Canada's an incredibly diverse place—there's a lot more than just trees and snow up there, believe us—so it makes sense that the country has developed its own unique sayings. Here are a few from English Canada:

Washroom is exactly the same as a bathroom.

Loonies (or looneys) are gold-colored one-dollar coins.

Toonies (or tooneys) are silver-and-gold–colored two-dollar coins.

Gas bar is a gas station.

French Canada—that's basically Québec, plus pockets of New Brunswick, Nova Scotia, and a bit of Manitoba—has its own special language, a localized French dialect called *joual.* In Québec province, especially, you'll notice that signs are often completely in French. Here are a few quick survival words:

Rue is a street.

Rue barré means road closed.

Nord is north.
Est is east.

Sud is south.
Ouest is west.

Gaz is gas.

Dépanneur is a convenience store (also an auto mechanic!).

Stationnement is parking.
Arrête means Stop.

Défense de stationner means No Parking.

Lac is a lake.

Cap is a cape.

Petit déjeuner is breakfast.
Dîner is dinner.

Déjeuner is lunch.

TRANSPORTATION

Take a careful look at your transportation options when planning a hostel journey. Public transportation in Canada is decent—much better than in many parts of the United States—so you should be able to hop from city to city by bus or train without a problem. You could have trouble getting to rural hostels without a car, but buses go many places you wouldn't expect, too.

By Plane

From the United States, there are two ways to get to Canada. Take a U.S. domestic flight to the coast you want, then hop a bus across the border. Or fly from the U.S. city directly to the Canadian city. Check with a travel agent and other sources first before deciding what to do; often it's cheaper to hop the bus to Canada, though, of course, it does take more time than a direct shot. Big-city Sunday newspapers are a great source for last-minute airfare deals, such as Atlanta to Vancouver or Miami to Minneapolis.

From Europe or farther afield, you'll want to consider whether or not you're going to the United States, as the rates can vary considerably. Paris to Montréal might be cheaper than Paris to New York, but Boston and New York are almost always the best bet for a cheap flight from London. Check carefully.

Within Canada, flying is surprisingly expensive. Your best bet is to check with the bigger carriers (such as Air BC, Air Canada, and Canadian Airlines) for special passes or deals; also scan the Sunday papers. Try to make longer flights between hubs if you can, then backtrack if necessary. You want to fly to Vancouver or Montréal, not Victoria or Québec, if you can help it: The money you spend on a bus or ferry will almost certainly be less than the extra plane fare to get to the smaller destination. *News flash:* Recently, Canada 3000 has offered incredibly cheap one-way flights within Canada.

If you really must fly from point to point within Canada and will be coming from outside of North America (sorry, Yanks), the **VUSA** pass—"Visiting the USA and Canada"—can be a big help. The pass lowers the cost for certain inter-Canada flights considerably, though you must buy it in your home country before leaving.

Cheap-ticket brokers (also called consolidators or bucket shops) are a great bet for saving money, but you have to be fast on your feet to keep up, as the deals appear and disappear literally daily. London and New York are major centers for bucket shops. (Both *Canada: The Rough Guide* and Lonely Planet's *Canada Travel*

Survival Kit include expanded material on the best hubs, connections, and consolidators from Australia to Ireland.)

Flying as a courier comes highly recommended by some folks who've tried it. Others are nervous about it. It works this way: You agree to carry luggage for a company in exchange for a very cheap round-trip ticket abroad. You must be flexible about your departure and return dates, you can't change those dates once assigned to you—and you can usually bring only carry-on luggage.

There isn't nearly as much demand for couriers from Canadian destinations to, say, Europe as there is from places like New York and Los Angeles; but it's still worth a shot.

By Car

Driving is an easy way to arrive in Canada from the United States. Border crossings are usually no trouble at all, and all you really need is the proper insurance papers from back home plus proof of citizenship. And some sort of driver's license, of course. Don't bring your radar detector, though; they're illegal in Canada.

Remember that speeds and distance are measured in kilometers in Canada. One kilometer (km) is 0.62 mile (mi.); 100 kilometers is about 62 miles. Here are some common speed limits you might see on Canadian road signs, with their U.S. equivalents:

50 kilometers per hour (km/h)	**31 miles per hour (mph)**
70 km/h	**43 mph**
80 km/h	**50 mph**
90 km/h	**56 mph**
100 km/h	**62 mph**

When deciphering a map, remember to check whether the distances are being given in miles or kilometers.

To convert kilometers to miles, multiply by 0.62.

To convert miles to kilometers, multiply by 1.6.

Of course, pay attention to **road signs.** Stop signs are red, octagonal, and obvious. Streetlights are another matter, depending often on local custom. A blinking green light means that a left turn is allowed; a solid green light may or may not allow such a turn. A blinking yellow light could mean either that it is about to turn red or green. Or it could mean that you can proceed, with caution, without stopping.

Gas is measured in liters, and there are roughly four liters to the U.S. gallon. (Gas prices are listed per liter; multiply by four to estimate the price per gallon you'll pay.) A ten-gallon fill-up generally costs around \$25–\$30 Canadian (about \$17–\$21 U.S.)—less in the Maritime provinces and possibly more in cities and parts of western Canada.

Penny-pinchers will want to make sure to fill up in the United States whenever possible—hop across the border if you need to. Gas prices are 50 to 75 percent higher in Canada.

Speeding is a serious thing up here, for some reason; police will nail you even for going a few kilometers over the limit, and fines can get hefty. Remember that when you're cruising west of Regina on your way to a bender somewhere in Moose Jaw.

Car-rental companies are a dime a dozen, and their rates can vary dramatically. The smaller companies that plaster hostels with flyers sometimes offer better deals than the larger conglomerates. The biggest hassle about renting a car is that it can run up to $500 Canadian (about $350 U.S.) to return it anyplace other than where you picked it up—a major headache. Also, you need a major credit card to rent from almost any company, and you must be above age twenty-one to rent a car from many.

In Canada, the lowest-cost choices seem to be Tilden (a Canadian division of the U.S. firm National), Discount (Canadian-owned), Budget (U.S.–based, with local franchises) and Rent-a-Wreck (less common). They're in all the big cities, as are other big American rental companies, like Enterprise, Avis, and Hertz. Smaller, local rental companies sometimes undercut the big guys, but they might charge more for mileage or refuse to do a one-way rental. National Interrent offered us the best service, we found.

Remember to check with your insurance company about whether driving rental cars in Canada is covered—often you are, even though the rental company will use pressure to get you to buy extra insurance for $8.00 to $10.00 Canadian ($6.00 to $7.00 U.S.) per day. Not covered? Buy the coverage. Just in case.

Auto Driveaway (800–346–2277) gets solid reviews from folks who have time to stick around and wait for a **driveaway**—a private car that needs driving. The company pairs you up with someone who needs a car to be moved from one city to someplace else, and this U.S. service includes Canada in its jurisdiction. All you have to do is put down a few hundred dollars for a deposit, pay for the gas, and leave the tank full when you deliver. Remember, however, that there is a time frame in which you must deliver the car, and you're not allowed to stray too far off a designated route.

Spring is a particularly good time to get such arrangements to Canada from, say, Florida, as thousands of Canadians fly back north with the sun. Hostel bulletin boards are a great source for this information: The local driveaway affiliate often faxes daily or weekly updates to hostel bulletin managers.

Other local companies often also provide the same service to smaller, more out-of-the-way destinations. Check the Yellow Pages under "Auto Transportation" or "Auto Driveaway."

Buying a used car is a popular (if risky) choice for many foreign travelers. Try to know a thing or two about cars if you're going to go this route, rather than spending hundreds of dollars for a set of wheels only to put twice that much into repairs during your cross-country journey. Remember that, at the very least, a Canadian auto registration and proof of Canadian insurance will be required before you hit the road. They can take a little time to obtain.

If you can't afford to drive, ALLOSTOP is a Canadian **ride-share** service that's gaining in popularity. It costs just $6.00 Canadian (about $4.00 U.S.) to join; once you become a member, you can share that six-hour ride from Montréal to Toronto for an incredibly low $26.00 Canadian (about $18.00 U.S.), get from New York City to Montréal for $50.00 Canadian (about $35.00 U.S.), and so forth. The bus or train fare would be considerably higher. In Montréal, call (514) 985–3032; in Toronto, call (416) 531–7668. Offices exist in places like Ottawa and Sherbrooke, too.

By Train

VIA Rail is Canada's national railway, stretching from sea to sea (Halifax to Vancouver, that is). It was once a more extensive network than it is today, but it still gets the job done nicely. Planning is crucial, however, since cross-country departures leave just once every two or three days. Miss the train and you'll be staring at Saskatoon for seventy-two long hours. If you can handle it, though, it's a good option—the Jasper-to-Kamloops stretch through the Canadian Rockies is particularly beautiful riding.

Local trains, running along busy corridors such as Montréal to Toronto or Toronto to Niagara Falls, leave much more often. And several useful side routes remain, such as the Western Canada service—running from Manitoba to Churchill and, on Vancouver Island, from Victoria up to Courtenay—and the Eastern Canada line, which begins in Montréal and proceeds east through the scenic Gaspé Peninsula to Halifax, Nova Scotia.

Ticket prices depend on your comfort level. Travel in coach class and the ticket prices are lower; reserving a bunk or a private sleeping cabin quickly increases the price, although special passes and discounts can reduce some of that cost. Check with your travel agent.

Province-hopping visitors should look into the Canrailpass, a terrific deal giving a rider twelve days of unlimited coach travel for between $339 and $569 Canadian (about $240 to $400 U.S.), depending on the time of year—summer is most expensive—and age of the rider. Young hostellers should make sure to flash that ISIC (International Student Identification Card), worth an instant 40 percent discount. Riders over age sixty get the lowest possible fare, plus an additional 10 percent off.

Amtrak (800–USA–RAIL) is the United States' passenger railroad network, and it's a good way to get near or into Canada—especially since several Amtrak lines (Seattle to Vancouver, New York to Montréal) connect seamlessly with VIA Rail lines. Hostellers who really like trains should get the NorthAmerican Railpass, a package deal similar to the Canrailpass but more comprehensive. It allows coach access to all of Amtrak's U.S. routes and all of VIA's Canadian ones; fifteen days of riding around North America within a one-month period costs $416 to $895 Canadian (about $290 to $630 U.S.), again depending on season and age.

Service in the busy coastal corridors gets much higher marks than it does on cross-country routes, and the train can be a surprisingly expensive option if you need a sleeping car. Still, seats are comfortable and the ride is usually smooth; so, if you're going from the States to Canada, planning your trek around the Amtrak schedule may not be a bad idea.

By Bus

Bus is, generally speaking, the cheapest way to travel. Service in Canada is good and regular, although a bus might come only once every few days in some of the country's more remote areas. Check ahead of time to be sure. We have included bus directions wherever possible to help you figure out what to do. Still confused? Call the hostel directly to clear up things ahead of time.

Also remember that it can take somewhat longer to get where you're going, especially if the bus stops a lot on the way. Be ready, too, for possible stopovers in bus stations in the middle of nowhere. Who needs it? Probably you, if you're broke, because tickets can be super-cheap. Some lines also offer even more affordable unlimited-travel passes.

Greyhound Canada (800–661–8747) is the dominant carrier in western Canada, while Voyageurs is big in Québec and Acadian Lines runs major routes in the Maritimes.

Smaller local lines, like Sherbus and Viens, fill in the rest of the gaps quite capably. They're the ones that will get you to most of those small-town hostels, so grab as many schedules at the airport or bus station as you can.

OTHER RESOURCES

There's surprisingly little out there about hostelling and hostels—that's why you're reading this, right?—but we did find a few sources. Most simply list phone numbers and addresses. Remember that hostels are constantly opening, closing, renovating, being sold, and changing their policies. So not everything written in a guidebook will always still be true by the time you read it. Be smart and call ahead to confirm prices, availability, and directions, rather than rolling into town expecting a bed—and getting a nasty surprise like a vacant lot instead. We know; it has happened to us.

With that in mind, here's what else is around:

Hostelling North America is the official U.S. and Canadian guidebook of Hostelling International. It provides much of the same basic information as this book, without the opinions, but little else besides maps to most of the member hostels. The directions are sometimes a bit difficult to follow. The North American handbook—some years it doesn't include Canada's hostels, but in 1997 it did—comes out early each year and is available free at HI-affiliated hostels.

Or contact Hostelling International directly. The American headquarters are located at 733 15th Avenue NW, Suite 840, Washington, D.C. 20005, and you can call 'em at (202) 783–6161. Canadian headquarters are situated at 400-205 Catherine Street, Ottawa, Ontario K2P 1C3, and can be reached toll-free from eastern provinces at (800) 663–5777 and at (613) 237–7884 from other locations.

Hostels U.S.A., (Globe Pequot, 1998, 2000), is perhaps the finest guide to hostelling ever written. And we know, because we wrote it. Seriously, though, there's more hostelling info than you can shake a stick at between those two covers, especially if you'll be heading to the States at some point. A great value for the price, and it fits neatly in your pack.

There are also some good World Wide Web sites worth checking out, especially the ones run by Hostelling International-Canada's regional chapters. Twirl your browser to these coordinates:

www.destination-ns.com/halifax/hostel
Based out of Halifax, this is the page of information for Nova Scotia's small collection of HI-Canada hostels.

www.tourismeJ.qc.ca
In French! Yep, it's the home site of Hi-Canada's Québec Council (Tourisme Jeunesse). Consult that Larousse's French–English dictionary.

www.magi.com/~hicoe
This is the Eastern Ontario Council's home page. It covers only a couple of hostels, but it does offer information about hostelling in general and can point you to other HI-Canada sites.

www.HostellingIntl.ca/alberta
This really great page covers all hostels in Alberta—and two more just over the border in eastern British Columbia. It includes maps, full rate information, and tons of information about the surrounding areas. It has a superb links collection, too, allowing you to zip around the world and learn about Hostelling International–affiliated hostels in Europe and beyond.

www.microage-tb.com/user/jonesl
This site is maintained by independent Canadian hostel guru Lloyd Jones from his base in Thunder Bay. It's updated pretty frequently and features photos of hostels. Be aware, though, that his site is also heavy on retreat centers, ecocenters, farms, and church buildings—places more conducive to levitation practice or Bible talks than hostelling. (If we haven't listed the place in this guidebook, it probably isn't a true hostel.)

www.hostels.com
The Internet Guide to Hostelling is a fairly comprehensive list of hostels worldwide, though it's incomplete in places and still inaccurate in others. A good place to get your feet wet.

Finally, there are regional councils of Hostelling International-Canada to steer you on your way:

Northern Alberta Council
10926-88th Avenue
Edmonton, Alberta T6G 0Z1
(780) 432–7798
Fax: (780) 433–7781
E-mail: *NAB@HostellingIntl.ca*

Southern Alberta Council
1414 Kensington Road NW, #203
Calgary, Alberta T2N 3P9
(403) 283–5551
Fax: (403) 283–6503
E-mail: *SAB@HostellingIntl.ca*

British Columbia Council
#402, 134 Abbott Street
Vancouver, British Columbia V6B 2K4
(800) 661–0020 (from British Columbia,
Alberta, and Washington State);

(800) 663–5777 (elsewhere in Canada);
(604) 684–7111 (locally)
Fax: (604) 684–7181
E-mail: *info@hihostels.bc.ca*

Manitoba Council
194A Sherbrook Street
Winnipeg, Manitoba R3C 2B6
(204) 784–1131
Fax: (204) 784–1133

New Brunswick Council
c/o Bill Leonard, Sr.
890 Mitchell Street
Fredericton, New Brunswick E3B 6C5
(506) 454–9326

Nova Scotia Council
Sport Nova Scotia Centre
5516 Spring Garden Road
Halifax, Nova Scotia B3J 3G6
(902) 425–5450
Fax: (902) 425–5606
E-mail: *hostellingintl@ns.sympatico.ca*

Eastern Ontario Council
c/o Ottawa International Hostel
75 Nicholas Street
Ottawa, Ontario K1N 7B9
(613) 235–2595
Fax: (613) 569–2131
E-mail: *hic_oer@yahoo.com*

Ontario Great Lakes Council
76 Church Street
Toronto, Ontario M5C 2G1
(416) 363–0697
Fax: (416) 368–6499

Prince Edward Island Council
P.O. Box 1718
Charlottetown, Prince Edward Island C1A 7N4
(902) 894–9696 (summer only);
(800) 663–5777 (winter)
Fax: (902) 628–6424 (year-round)

Québec Council (Tourisme Jeunesse)
4545 Pierre de-Coubertin
Montréal, Québec H1V 3R2
(514) 844–0287
Fax: (514) 844–5246
E-mail: *Info@tourismej.qc.ca*

Boutique Tourisme Jeunesse
Membership Services
4008 rue St.-Denis
Montréal, Quebec H1V 3R2
(514) 844–0287
Fax: (514) 844–5246

Booking Center
(514) 252–3117
(800) 461–8585
Fax: (514) 252–3119
E-mail: *info@tourismej.qc.ca*

Saskatchewan Council
2014-14th Avenue
Regina, Saskatchewan S4P 0X5
(306) 791–8160
Fax: (306) 721–2667
E-mail: *hihostels.sask@sk.sympatico.ca*

The Hostels

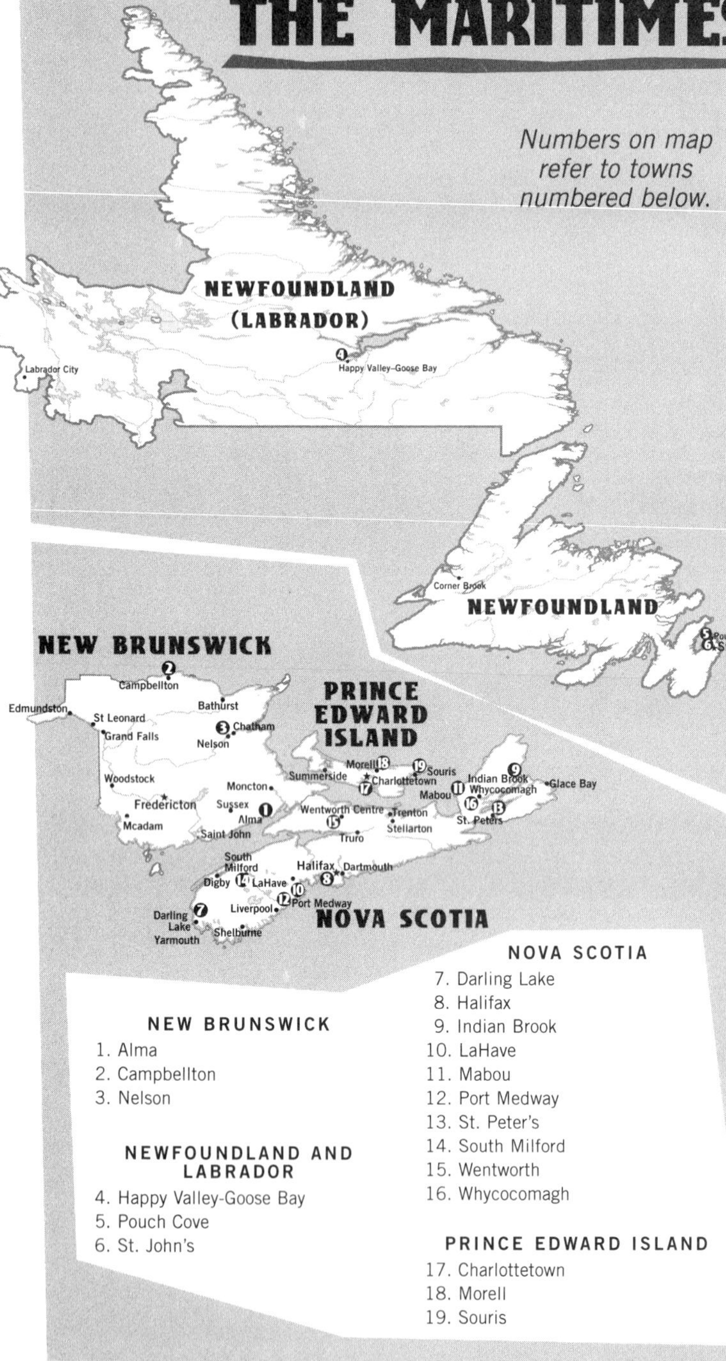
THE MARITIMES
Numbers on map refer to towns numbered below.
NEWFOUNDLAND (LABRADOR)
Labrador City
Happy Valley–Goose Bay
NEWFOUNDLAND
Corner Brook
Pouch Cove
St. John's
NEW BRUNSWICK
Campbellton
Edmundston
Bathurst
St Leonard
Chatham
Grand Falls
Nelson
Woodstock
Moncton
Fredericton
Sussex
Alma
Mcadam
Saint John
PRINCE EDWARD ISLAND
Morell
Souris
Summerside
Charlottetown
Indian Brook
Glace Bay
Mabou
Whycocomagh
Wentworth Centre
Trenton
St. Peters
Stellarton
Truro
South Milford
Halifax
Dartmouth
Digby
LaHave
Port Medway
Liverpool
Darling Lake
Yarmouth
Shelburne
NOVA SCOTIA
NEW BRUNSWICK
1. Alma
2. Campbellton
3. Nelson
NEWFOUNDLAND AND LABRADOR
4. Happy Valley-Goose Bay
5. Pouch Cove
6. St. John's
NOVA SCOTIA
7. Darling Lake
8. Halifax
9. Indian Brook
10. LaHave
11. Mabou
12. Port Medway
13. St. Peter's
14. South Milford
15. Wentworth
16. Whycocomagh
PRINCE EDWARD ISLAND
17. Charlottetown
18. Morell
19. Souris

NEW BRUNSWICK

Amorphously shaped and, for some reason, much maligned, New Brunswick is Canada's waif child. Yet it conceals astonishing coastal scenery, clear mountain streams, and gorgeous fall foliage.

Many travelers enter the province from Maine. Coming up beautiful coastal U.S. 1, you cross the border at St. Stephen-Calais, where you'll hardly notice a difference between sides of the line. From there it's not far to Saint John—a fine old town.

If you don't have a car, stitching together bus schedules is your best transportation option; this isn't big airport territory. The VIA Rail train line does pass through Campbellton, where there's an interesting little lighthouse hostel—and access to several more across Québec's Gaspé Peninsula.

FUNDY NATIONAL PARK HOSTEL 

General Delivery, Alma, New Brunswick EOA 1BO

(506) 887–2216

Rates: $9.00 Canadian (about $6.00 U.S.) per Hostelling International member
Credit cards: None
Office hours: 8:00 A.M.–1:00 P.M.; 5:00–10:00 P.M.
Season: Mid-May to mid-October
Beds: 24
Private/family rooms: None
Single rooms: None
Private bathrooms: None
Affiliation: Hostelling International-Canada
Extras: Bicycle rentals, laundry, storage

This hostel basically consists of rustic cabins in the woods, smack dab in a really interesting national park of rocks and trees, a setting that typifies the Maritime coast of Canada. Most hostellers come here to gawk at the huge range of tides—they drop and then rise nearly 17 meters (50 feet) because of the shape of the inlet (believe it or not, these are the highest tides in the world). Hiking is also good around here, and bikes can be rented at the hostel.

What hostellers say:
"Get the tide chart."

Gestalt:
Barrels o' Fundy

Party index:

This is definitely a good place to get away from it all. Just remember that accommodations here are really simple—and, since there are just twenty-four beds and the hostel operates a short season, you might want to book ahead. No private rooms are available, but access to a nearby lake and swimming pool may provide some consolation.

How to get there:

By car: From the south, take Route 1 or Canada Route 2 north to Penobsquis; turn right onto Route 114 and drive 40 km (25 mi.) to Fundy National Park in Alma. Turn right and take Point Wolfe Road to Devil's Half Acre. Hostel is on right. From the north, take Canada Route 2 south to Moncton; turn onto Route 114 south and drive 95 km (57 mi.) to Fundy National Park in Alma. Turn left and take Point Wolfe Road to Devil's Half Acre. Hostel is on right.

By train: VIA Rail stops in Moncton, 105 km (65 mi.) away. Call hostel for transit route.

CAMPBELLTON LIGHTHOUSE HOSTEL 

1 Ritchie Street, Campbellton, New Brunswick E3N 3G1

(506) 759–7044

Rates: $12.00 Canadian (about $8.00 U.S.) per person
Credit cards: None
Office hours: 8:00 A.M.–noon; 4:00 P.M.–midnight
Season: June 1–August 30
Beds: 20
Private/family rooms: None
Single rooms: None
Private bathrooms: None
Affiliation: Hostelling International-Canada
Extras: Lockers, laundry, camping sites, storage

This hostel, Canada's only lighthouse hostel, is positioned right on the Matapédia River, which soon widens into the beautiful Bay of Chaleurs and separates the Gaspé Peninsula from the rest of eastern Canada. (You can actually see the bridge to Québec from the hostel door.)

It's standard-issue all the way here: small bunkrooms and a perfunctory kitchen. And you'll be evicted between noon and 4:00 P.M. for cleaning and other hostel-management duties. Hey, what were you expecting, the Hilton? This is a lighthouse keeper's house, for gosh sakes! If you made it here, you just want a cheap sleep and a write-home-about-it experience before you head for the wild Gaspé. That you'll certainly get.

The main attractions around here have to do with the sea, of course, and the hundreds of brooks and rivers that interlace the surrounding countryside. There's whale watching along the coast; an annual salmon festival in town that celebrates the silvery, succulent fish; and a marine museum and other heritage sites nearby. Campbellton is big enough to have a couple of indoor attractions, too, such as a mall. But that's not what you come here for. You come to sleep beside the lighthouse.

Best bet for a bite: Save-Easy

What hostellers say: "You light up my life."

Insiders' tip: Salmon festival

Gestalt: Shiner

Hospitality: B

Party index:

How to get there:

By bus: Orleans/Acadian Lines bus line stops in Campbellton. From depot, call hostel for directions.

By car: Take Route 134 to Campbellton. From Route 134, turn onto Ritchie Street (toward riverfront). Hostel is located beside lighthouse.

By train: VIA Rail stops in Campbellton. From train station, call hostel for directions.

BEAUBEAR MANOR HOSTEL

62 Riverside Drive, Nelson, New Brunswick E0C 1T0

(506) 622–3036

Fax: (506) 622–3035

Rates: $18 Canadian (about $12 U.S.) per HI member
Credit cards: None
Office hours: 8:00 A.M.–10:00 P.M.
Beds: 24
Private/family rooms: 12
Single rooms: Yes; number varies; call for availability
Private bathrooms: Yes; number varies; call for availability
Affiliation: Hostelling International-Canada
Extras: Library, music rooms, free pickup, breakfast

10% ♫ ♥

This hostel was recently named one of the best in all of Canada by a magazine writer. We liked it, too.

The three-floor Beaubear Manor building is certainly steeped in history. Built above the Miramichi River in 1865, it was once home to the Governor General of New Brunswick. Today the hostel beds occupy about a dozen bedrooms on the top floor; private rooms are especially beautiful, with beds just like in the best home. Other floors house scads of old antiques and model ships, a music room, a really nice library, and a dining area where you can partake of a classy breakfast. Hostel manager Father Mersereaux (yes, *that* kind of Father), who's full of character, is extremely helpful with travel information—and he sometimes serves dinner in the classy dining room too.

Best bet for a bite: Local fish

Insiders' tip: Find that Ogham stone

Gestalt: Well manored

Hospitality: A

Cleanliness: A

Party index:

The surrounding Nelson-Miramichi area is noted mostly for its rivers, which are great for fly-fishing and salmon eating. And there's an old, old Celtic stone on the property—it dates back to the fourth century! Talk about your rolling stone gathering no moss . . .

How to get there:

By bus: Bus line stops in Miramichi, 3 km (2 mi.) away. From depot, call hostel for free pickup.

By car: From the south, take Route 126 to village of Chatham Head. Turn left on Riverside Drive just before river. Hostel is 3 km (2 mi.) down road, at #62. From the north, take Route 8 to town of Newcastle. Cross river on Route 126 into Chatham Head and make immediate right onto Riverside Road. Hostel is 3 km (2 mi.) down road, at #62.

By train: VIA Rail stops in Miramichi, 3 km (2 mi.) away. Call hostel from station for free pickup.

KEY TO ICONS

Attractive natural setting	Romantic private rooms	Good for business travelers
Ecologically aware hostel	Comfortable beds	Especially well suited for families
Superior kitchen facilities or cafe	Among our very favorite hostels	Good for active travelers
Offbeat or eccentric place	A particularly good value	Visual arts at hostel or nearby
Superior bathroom facilities	Wheelchair-accessible	Music at hostel or nearby

NEWFOUNDLAND AND LABRADOR

Storm-tossed and lonesome, the province of Newfoundland is way off the beaten track. After they return to civilization, awed visitors tend to babble about the astonishing scenery, midnight summer sunshine, Viking and native relics, and a deep friendliness in locals. It's definitely worth a visit if you want to get away from cities and people, to get back to nature and simplicity (and a lot of stone and water) for a while.

First things first. The province includes the Island of Newfoundland plus Labrador—which feels like an island but is actually a coastal spur of mainland attached to far eastern Québec.

To get to the Island of Newfoundland, you can take a long-distance ferry from North Sydney, Nova Scotia—that's way up at the northern tip of Cape Breton Island—to one of two docks. It's either a six-hour, expensive ferry ride, or a fourteen-hour, more expensive one. Haven't got a car? Some bus lines take the ferry.

Other travelers fly into St. John's, a city of 100,000 that has a decent-size airport but certainly isn't a super-cheap hop—unless you find a deal in Halifax. Check the Halifax papers and give a call to Canada 3000, a charter airline that sometimes offers good discounts.

To get to Labrador, follow the above set of directions and then take yet another ferry from Newfoundland. (As there isn't a town in Newfy with more than 7,000 souls, flying into its small airfields is very, very expensive.)

There aren't many people here, and so there aren't many hostels, either—or public transit. Most hostels are near the ferry docks; a couple are hundreds of miles away. A car is absolutely essential if you want to explore on a short timetable.

LABRADOR FRIENDSHIP CENTRE 

49 Grenfell Street, Happy Valley–Goose Bay, Labrador, Newfoundland A0P 1E0

(709) 896–8302

Rates: $25 Canadian (about $18 U.S.) per person
Credit cards: None
Office hours: 24 hours
Beds: 26
Private/family rooms: 2
Single rooms: None
Private bathrooms: 2
Affiliation: None
Extras: TV, meals

Okay, we'll admit it. This isn't truly a hostel. It's actually a nonprofit group that does the admirable work of giving aboriginal visitors from northern Labrador a place to stay while they seek out jobs and stable footing in the big city.

Gestalt: Happy Valley campers

Hospitality: C

Party index:

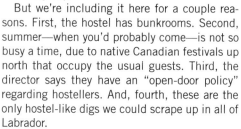

But we're including it here for a couple reasons. First, the hostel has bunkrooms. Second, summer—when you'd probably come—is not so busy a time, due to native Canadian festivals up north that occupy the usual guests. Third, the director says they have an "open-door policy" regarding hostellers. And, fourth, these are the only hostel-like digs we could scrape up in all of Labrador.

There. We feel better. Now, on to the facility. It's standard bunks, with a couple of private rooms thrown in. All the rooms have televisions. There's a common sitting room, and an on-site cafeteria serves three filling meals a day for a small charge.

Keep in mind, though, that most of the clientele here aren't from Germany or France—they're Inuit from the northern coast of Labrador. If that's your bag, you'll love the place.

How to get there:

By car: Call hostel for directions.

By plane: Airport in Happy Valley–Goose Bay. Call hostel for transit details.

POINTS EAST HOSTEL 

34 Sullivan Loop, Pouch Cove, Newfoundland A0A 3L0

(709) 335–8315

E-mail: edettmer@nf.sympatico.ca

Rates: $10.00–$20.00 Canadian (about $7.00–$14.00 U.S.) per person; private rooms $50.00 Canadian (about $35.00 U.S.)

Credit cards: None
Office hours: 24 hours
Beds: 11
Private/family rooms: 4
Single rooms: None
Private bathrooms: 1
Affiliation: None
Extras: Bikes, laundry, gardens, CD player, library

Basically, this place consists of accommodations in a big old house and a barn with a spectacular view of the Atlantic Ocean.

Owner-manager Elke Dettmer's home has four smallish guest bedrooms, which are usually rented out B&B style. One has a private washroom, while the other three share an enormous second one. In addition, Dettmer maintains a barn loft with three pull-out, hostel-style beds. Lodging here costs less than in the house.

You can cook breakfast yourself or eat communally from a meal prepared with Dettmer's vegetables, goat cheese, and eggs. Right next door in the village of Pouch (pronounced *pooch,* by the way) Cove is a general store for basic supplies. A fish-and-chips–style restaurant lies close at hand, too.

Dettmer is active in the building of the island's East Coast Trail—it begins here and stretches 300 wild km (185 mi.) along the ocean to Cape Race—and can thus direct you to that trail as well as lots of other hiking spots. Just make sure to catch her when she isn't giving tours to a visiting German group.

Best bet for a bite: In-house grub

What hostellers say: *"Wunderbar."*

Gestalt: Good Pouch

Hospitality: A

Cleanliness: A

Party index:

How to get there:

By car: In summer, take car ferry from North Sydney, Nova Scotia, to Argentia, Newfoundland (fourteen-hour trip, starting at $235 Canadian/$165 U.S. for car and two adults). Drive approximately 40 km (25 mi.) north on Route 100 to junction with Canada Route 1 (Trans-Canada Highway). Turn east on Route 1 and drive approximately 90 km (55 mi.) to St. John's. Take Kings Bridge Road to Torbay Road and drive 23 km (15 mi.) to just past Pouch Cove harbor; hostel is at corner of Sullivan Loop, on right.

By plane: Large airport in St. John's. From airport, call hostel for possible pickup; if unavailable, take taxi (about $20 Canadian/$14 U.S.) to hostel.

TRAVELLERS B&B HOSTEL

Box 29024, Torbay Road Post Office, St. John's,

Newfoundland A1A 5B5

(709) 437–5627

Rates: $25 Canadian (about $18 U.S.) per person; private room $40 Canadian (about $28 U.S.)
Credit cards: None
Office hours: Vary; call
Beds: 3
Private/family rooms: 1
Single rooms: 1

Private bathrooms: None
Extras: Laundry, bike, breakfast, shuttle

"Once you come in the door," says Donna O'Brien of her home-hostel, "you're part of the household."

The O'Briens had traveled to New Zealand and Australia. When they returned home they felt sad that they were no longer meeting the friendly extended family of hostellers one comes across on the road. Ping! A light bulb went on, and the Travellers B&B Hostel was born.

The single-story house sits on a nice, four-acre property on the quiet outskirts of St. John's. Trees surround the land, which also has two lambs and a calf. Inside, there's a kitchen for hostellers—though they won't need it much. Breakfast, included with the tab (that's the other "B"), consists of whatever the family's having. There's a nice sunroom for sitting around, too, and writing "Wow!" in your diary a lot.

Best bet for a bite: Home cookin'

What hostellers say: "Call me Ishmael. . . ."

Gestalt: Pleasant little 'berg

Safety: A

Hospitality: A

Cleanliness: A

Party index:

But you won't be sitting for long, we'd wager. If the weather's good during Newfoundland's brief, shining moment of summer, the options are endless. Biking. Hiking. And it's a fifteen-minute stroll to the coastline, with its high cliffs, pebbly beaches, and splendiferous views of icebergs and whales passing by in midsummer.

The city perks up too, becoming awfully lively for a while—lots of live music, for example, and outdoor concerts, an annual regatta, and on and on.

For a combination of city and country, this place is hard to beat. Just remember to bring the umbrella and raincoat: Newfoundland's weather can change quickly and fiercely.

How to get there:

By car: Call hostel for directions from St. John's. To get to St. John's in summer, take car ferry from North Sydney, Nova Scotia, to Argentia, Newfoundland (a fourteen-hour trip, starting at $235 Canadian/$165 U.S. for car and two adults). Drive approximately 40 km (25 mi.) north on Route 100 to junction with Canada Route 1 (Trans-Canada Highway). Turn east on Route 1 and drive approximately 90 km (55 mi.) to St. John's.

By plane: Airport in St. John's. Call hostel for pickup.

NOVA SCOTIA

Nova Scotia is as underappreciated as it is beautiful—not an easy trick. How to see it? Depends. If you're in a great hurry and are coming from the States, spring for the extra expense and take a ferry cruise from Portland or Bar Harbor, Maine, or from Saint John, New Brunswick; it will shorten the travel time considerably and give you an experience to write home about. But it can be pricey. To save money you'll have to drive all the way to Truro, and then all the way back south again, to see the best parts. (Check out a map now and see what we mean.)

Once there, if you're traveling by bus, there's only one way to go: Acadian Lines buses circle the peninsula. Drivers, however, can choose between the faster expressways (stretches of Routes 101 and 103) or little Route 3, which meanders—sometimes tortuously—along every breathtaking inch of that coast.

Train and plane travelers will almost certainly arrive in Halifax, which is Nova Scotia's capital and its most happenin' town by a long shot; it's a nice place to sample some quasi-urban culture and food that isn't fried fish before you hit the sticks. The airport is the largest in the province. And VIA Rail's Eastern Canada line—which comes in from Montréal and, by connection, the rest of Canada—runs to Halifax, too, a good way to get to Nova Scotia's biggest city.

To hit the most hostels, here's what we'd do. Take the overnight ferry from Portland, Maine—losing a bundle at the slot machines en route—then drive Route 3 from Yarmouth southeast along a gorgeous stretch of coast to Barrington, La Have, and/or Halifax. From there it's a long but beautiful stretch up the coast along Route 7 as far as Stillwater, where the road turns inland and angles north to Antigonish. From there, you can grab the Trans-Canada Highway for a quick ride to Cape Breton Island's gorgeous scenery. Too bad the island has only a few rather plain hostels.

You can use the Trans-Canada to leave Nova Scotia (if you want to leave), hitting the Wentworth hostel if you need a break; it's literally a stone's throw from the cross-country highway.

ICE HOUSE HOSTEL 

Highway 1, Darling Lake, Nova Scotia B5A 4A5

(902) 649–2818

E-mail: sprimrose@atzon.com

Rates: $8.50 Canadian (about $6.00 U.S.) per person
Credit cards: DISC, MC, VISA
Office hours: 24 hours
Season: May 1–November 30
Beds: 8

Private/family rooms: Yes; number varies
Single rooms: None
Private bathrooms: None
Affiliation: None
Extras: Pickup from bus, meals, swimming, canoe, rowboat, piano, organ, TV

Climb off the ferryboat from the United States and take a gander at downtown Yarmouth, Nova Scotia, and you might begin wondering what all the fuss is about. Yarmouth's a pleasant enough port-of-call, but no great shakes, and not particularly scenic.

Ah, but then begin to drive, bike, or bus west and north up Route 1. The T-shirt shops and quick-lube joints, you find, suddenly give out—replaced by a patchwork quilt of unspoiled coastal vistas and farms and sturdy, well-kept wooden houses. It's in the middle of this little dreamland that Bob Benson has set up his Ice House Hostel.

The hostel sits adjacent to Benson's pet project, an inn called Churchill Mansion (you can't miss his huge sign), and it's almost as good. A cottagelike former ice house with four beds—perfect for couples, this—stares out at big and beautiful Darling Lake. The hostellers get their pick of using the smart little kitchen or dining on the nightly seafood buffet: for $11.95 Canadian ($8.50 U.S.) you get to pick from three kinds of sea creature. In the morning, there's breakfast for $1.00–$4.00 Canadian ($.70–$3.00 U.S.) too, in a communal dining hall that's a welcome relief from many crowded hostel kitchen tables.

Best bet for a bite: Seafood buffet

What hostellers say: "Yum."

Insiders' tip: Beach in Port Maitland

Gestalt: Real darling

Hospitality: A

Cleanliness: A

Party index:

Hostellers get the run of the inn, too, which includes a piano, an organ, a record player, sitting rooms, and so forth. Bob asked us to mention that the nice rooms in his inn are also available for $34.00–$59.00 Canadian ($24.00–$41.00 U.S.) in case hostellers want additional privacy and comfort. But we said we couldn't, in good conscience, include that. So we won't.

What to do in Darling Lake? Well, not much, but there's one terrific park just a bit down the road in Port Maitland—miles of empty sand beach, changing facilities, camping, and great views, too. This is absolutely primo biking territory (as much of Nova Scotia is), so bring the two-wheelers. Or just stroll around the very rural area, chatting with the locals, who are so friendly it might bring tears to your jaded eyes.

How to get there:

By bus: Take Acadian Lines from Halifax or Annapolis Royal to Yarmouth. From depot, call hostel for pickup.

By car: From Yarmouth, drive north and west on Route 1 about 22 km (15 mi.). Make a left off Route 1 at CHURCHILL MANSION sign. Hostel is on left. From Digby or Annapolis Royal, drive south on Route 101 to Metaghan; exit main highway to Route 1 and drive 30 km (20 mi.) farther. Look for CHURCHILL MANSION sign on right. Turn right to hostel.

By train: VIA Rail to Halifax; take Acadian Lines bus from Halifax to Yarmouth. From station, call hostel for pickup.

HERITAGE HOUSE HOSTEL

1253 Barrington Street, Halifax, Nova Scotia B3J 1Y3

(902) 422–3863

Fax: (902) 422–3863

E-mail: hostellingintl@ns.sympatico.ca

Rates: $15–$20 Canadian (about $10–$14 U.S.) per Hostelling International member; private rooms $38 Canadian (about $27 U.S.) per Hostelling International member
Credit cards: MC, VISA
Office hours: 8:00 A.M.–11:00 P.M.
Beds: 70
Private/family rooms: 3
Single rooms: 2
Private bathrooms: 1
Affiliation: Hostelling International-Canada
Extras: Ironing board, travel store, TV, VCR, video-game rentals, laundry, parking

10% $

A neat and clean little city like Halifax deserves a neat and clean hostel like Heritage House Hostel. And that's what you get—more so, even, if you are lucky enough to land a bunk in the newer rooms.

The big and comfy common room is replete with couches, the big TV is impressive, but don't even think of bringing your tea and scones in here—you might be reprimanded by fellow hostellers who take the NO FOOD sign pretty seriously. There's also a small but truly efficient kitchen: two sinks, two wide-slot toasters, a microwave, and scads of tables. Eco-points, too, for the excellent and comprehensive recycling area. While waiting for your tea water to heat up, you can even peruse the stacks of old records in the dining room and spin your faves on the hi-fi! Way cool, daddy-o.

Heritage House Hostel
Halifax

(photo courtesy HI-Canada)

Most of the bunkrooms are located on the creakier but full-of-character second floor (bathroom space is nice, if a bit at a premium). Private rooms are on the first floor, one of which is swingin' enough to have its very own washroom (Canadian for bathroom).

Parking is a bit of a chore. The hostel has a few parking places out back, but they do fill up; if you lose, you're on a fairly busy street. It's very safe here, by the looks of things, so that's usually okay. But if you park in the adjunct YWCA lot, you'll probably find a polite (this is Nova Scotia, not New York) note explaining how they will be compelled to tow you if you park there again. So try to get in early.

The staff can help arrange various one- to three-day adventure tours of the province and beyond. If you want to take in the salt air close at hand, hoof it a few short blocks to the waterfront and hop a ferry for McNab's Island ($10.00–$11.00 Canadian/$7.00–$8.00 U.S.), an uninhabited spot with good views of Halifax.

What else to do in the eminently walkable "City of Trees"? Head up Spring Garden Road a few blocks to see a great and vibrant park. You want culture? Well, you're in a bit of luck here—Halifax is the culture capital of southern Nova Scotia. Unfortunately, "culture" often means "bar hopping": There seem to be an unusual preponderance of bars, live bands, and cheap student-type restaurants here, rather than much actually happening in the arts scene. Still, it's nice to see live music by real working bands rather than the latest lip-synchers.

Anyway, where else around these parts are you going to find a solid vegetarian restaurant on one street, good Vietnamese on the next, and the latest fashions and grinds of designer coffee? Nowhere else in Nova Scotia, certainly. If you want a taste of something really local, look for a donair, a kind of mystery-meat sandwich that appears everywhere around town. (We didn't dare try it.) Might as well sink your teeth into something daring here and now, 'cause once you leave the city limits, it's fried fish all the way, baby.

Sorry, we digress. Excellent hostel, and an especially terrific source for budget-travel tips for the rest of Eastern Canada—and beyond! Wade and his staff get the highest marks.

Best bet for a bite:
King Spring Roll

What hostellers say:
"Who's playing tonight?"

Insiders' tip:
Park early

Gestalt:
SuperHalifaxalistic

Safety: A

Hospitality: A

Cleanliness: A

Party index:

How to get there:

By bus: Bus lines stop in Halifax. From station, take #7 bus ($1.35 Canadian, about $1.00 U.S.) south to Barrington and South Streets. Walk 1 block north on Barrington. Hostel is on right, just after YWCA.

By car: Call hostel for directions.

By plane: Airport in Halifax. Take taxi ($30.00 Canadian, about $21.00 U.S.) or airport shuttle ($12.00 Canadian, about $9.00 U.S.) to Westin Hotel; walk up Hollis Street 1 block to Barrington; turn right, walk 1 block north. Hostel is on right, just after YWCA.

By train: VIA Rail stops in Halifax. From train station, walk up South or Hollis Street 1 block to Barrington; turn right, walk 1 block north. Hostel is on right, just after YWCA.

CAPE BRETON INTERNATIONAL HOSTEL

c/o Piper's Guest House, Indian Brook, Nova Scotia B0C 1H0
(902) 929–2233

Rates: $30–$35 Canadian (about $20–$24 U.S.) per person
Credit cards: MC, VISA
Office hours: 7:30 A.M.–10:00 P.M.
Season: May 1–October 1
Beds: 6
Private/family rooms: None
Single rooms: None
Private bathrooms: None
Affiliation: None
Extras: Laundry

Best bet for a bite: Fish fish fish

Gestalt: Paying the piper

Hospitality: C

Cleanliness: C

Party index:

This extremely simple hostel is the closest one to Cape Breton Highlands National Park, a wonderland of cliffs, valleys, and ocean. That's great. It's just too bad this isn't a great hostel.

The owners focus their efforts on a nice bed-and-breakfast. The hostel—a trailer that sleeps six happy hostellers—seems to have been thrown in as an afterthought. It's certainly more affordable than the inn or a motel, and it can be nice to sleep in a trailer in the woods. We appreciate the fact that it exists. But we just didn't get the feeling that hostellers are a priority here. There is a kitchen, however, to save you money after paying the high prices.

KEY TO ICONS

 Attractive natural setting

 Romantic private rooms

 Good for business travelers

 Ecologically aware hostel

 Comfortable beds

 Especially well suited for families

 Superior kitchen facilities or cafe

 Among our very favorite hostels

 Good for active travelers

 Offbeat or eccentric place

 A particularly good value

 Visual arts at hostel or nearby

 Superior bathroom facilities

 Wheelchair-accessible

 Music at hostel or nearby

How to get there:

By bus: Call hostel for transit route.

By car: From Truro, follow Route 104 east (Trans-Canada Highway) approximately 170 km (105 mi.) to Canso Strait Bridge. Cross bridge onto Cape Breton Island. In Port Hastings, switch to Route 105 north (still the Trans-Canada Highway) and drive 104 km (65 mi.) to South Gut St. Ann's. Bear left onto Cabot Trail. Drive north approximately 30 more km (20 mi.) to Indian Brook. Look for Piper's Guest House.

By plane: Airport in Sydney. From airport, call hostel for transit route.

LAHAVE MARINE HOSTEL 

P.O. Box 92, LaHave, Nova Scotia B0R 1C0

(902) 688–2908

Fax: (902) 688–1083

Rates: $11.00 Canadian (about $9.00 U.S.) per Hostelling International member

Credit cards: MC, VISA

Office hours: 9:00 A.M.–7:00 P.M.

Season: June 1–September 30

Beds: 8

Private/family rooms: 2

Single rooms: 1

Private bathrooms: None

Affiliation: Hostelling International-Canada

Extras: Laundry, SCUBA-equipment rental, piano, cafe

10% $     

There aren't too many hostels you ring up to make reservations and get a baker answering on the other end. Or suck down cups of self-serve organic java. But here, in out-of-the-way and beautiful little LaHave, you do.

This small hostel occupies the long, long upper floor of what was originally a marine outfitter. Boat building still takes place out back. But these days the building is mostly a cafe serving treats that are rare indeed in rural parts of the Maritimes: good coffee, sweets ranging from the Nanaimo bar to muffins, and inexpensive daily lunch specials. There's also a really nice seating area to hang out in while drinking in the slow end to a day, and odd groceries like pickled eggs and the Turkish chewing gum (it's actually the gum of a tree) that the boat-happy hostel owners picked up somewhere in their peregrinations.

On to the hostel. While taking a breath after hiking up the steep steps, an arty common room greets you. Decorated with a rustic branch chair, posters of Costa Rica, and a long wooden dining table, the homespun quality of the space proves that the owners do indeed live up here in the off season. (They live on their boat during the summer, ferrying baked goods to places like Newfoundland. No, we're not making this up.)

Best bet for a bite: In-house treats

What hostellers say: "Floats my boat."

Insiders' tip: Take the cable ferry

Gestalt: Hip hip LaHave!

Hospitality: A

Cleanliness: A

Party index:

But don't think your room is the one on the left; that room is reserved for the manager and looked just a bit too lived-in to belong to a backpacker. Actually, two separate doors allow entry into the actual hostel quarters, which are interestingly furnished with the owners' knicknacks from their land and sea trips around the world—soapstone carvings and the like.

Single travelers can pick a room with the solitary twin bed but will have to let others step through on their way to another bunkroom. And a strange bunkroom that is! One double bed is surrounded by two sets of bunks; both sets are frighteningly narrow. We suppose someone flips a toonie (the Canadian two-dollar coin) for the double. Next door, we found two full-size mattresses and another private room (unusually, it comes with just one full-size bed), which are probably in high demand when hostellers find their way here. Rooms are sunny, and some come with a view of LaHave's cute little main street.

The kitchen here is immaculate; there's plenty of space, and it's well equipped with pots and pans and cabinets. Everything is well marked. The bathroom includes a claw-foot bathtub and ironing board, but, for some reason, no shower.

As we said, the place does suffer from a bit of a confusing layout; doors and beds seem to be everywhere, making it possible that you'll have to walk through someone else's bedroom to get to your room. And the furniture all has a worn look to it.

Those are minor quibbles, though. This is an exceptionally friendly hostel, and you can't beat the incredible scenery in this part of the province's coast: green, green inlets coming right up to the blue, blue water. A little cable ferry even makes half-hourly crossings of the LaHave River, saving you a roundabout (though pretty) drive and revealing more of the coast's hidden pleasures. Once again, this is super biking territory—and you know you'll get your sugar fix at the end of the ride!

How to get there:

By car: From Halifax, drive Route 103 south and west about 100 km (60 mi.) to Bridgewater and turn off onto Route 331. Drive on 331 to LaHave, about 20 km (15 mi.). In center of LaHave, hostel is on left, inside LaHave Bakery. From Yarmouth, drive Route 103 east about 200 km (125 mi.) to Bridgewater and turn off on Route 331. Drive on 331 to LaHave, about 20 km (15 mi.). In center of LaHave, hostel is on left, inside bakery.

By train: VIA Rail stops in Halifax. From station, call hostel for transit route.

MABOU RIVER HOSTEL

19 Mabou Ridge Road (P.O. Box 255), Mabou,
Nova Scotia B0E 1X0
(888) 627–9744; (902) 945–2356
Fax: (902) 945–2258
E-mail: mabouriverhostel@ns.sympatico.ca
Rates: $18 Canadian per HI member ($12 U.S.)
Credit cards: MC, VISA
Office hours: 8:00 A.M.–10:00 P.M.
Beds: 25
Private/family rooms: Yes
Extras: Breakfast, bike rentals, meals ($), kitchen

A good location is the key to this small new place, located in a farmhouse up on wild Cape Breton Island at the top of Nova Scotia.

The place has a few private rooms plus the usual dorms, a kitchen, and some meal service; they rent bikes as well. It isn't the fanciest hostel around, but if you want rustic atmosphere it definitely delivers. (There are just twenty-five beds here, though, so book ahead in summertime to be safe just in case they're really busy.)

Mabou is locally famous as the town that produced the Rankin Family, a popular Canadian singing group combining Celtic, Canadian folk, and New Age influences to impressive effect. Religious types will want to look in on the shrine adjoining the hostel, a pilgrimage site of a different sort.

Gestalt: Mabou-tiful

Hospitality: A

Cleanliness: A

Party index:

How to get there:

By bus: Call hostel for transit route.

By car: Take Highway 19 north from the Canso Causeway; follow the Ceilidh Trail to ten minutes north of Port Hood, watching for signs to Mother of Sorrows Pioneer Shrine. Hostel is adjacent to shrine. From the north, take Highway 19 south to signs for shrine just before Mabou.

By plane: Airport in Sydney. Call hostel for transit route.

SCHOOL BUS HOSTEL 

Long Cove Road, Port Medway, Nova Scotia B3J 1Y3
(902) 677–2509

Rates: $10.00 Canadian (about $7.00 U.S.) per person
Office hours: 7:00 A.M.–11:00 P.M.
Credit cards: None
Season: June 1–September 30
Beds: 6
Private/family rooms: None
Single rooms: None
Private bathrooms: None
Affiliation: None
Extras: Natural A/C

If location were everything—as it supposedly is in real estate—this hostel would be a double thumbs-up all the way. Picture this: a gorgeous saltwater cove complete with its own lighthouse, with little fishermen's homes sprinkled about on the rocky crags.

Yet location *isn't* everything. And this hostel, which really does consist of the inside of one recycled school bus set up on blocks, just doesn't measure up in the all-important categories of convenience and accessibility to public transport.

In fact, we can't imagine what traveler would find this place. It's several kilometers down an unmarked, twisty lane that threatens to tear a car apart at the seams; bring the jacked-up truck or sport utility vehicle, or don't bother coming at all. Needless to say, there isn't a bus or train or plane for many miles. (By dory, however, we imagine the ride would be quite nice.)

Once improbably here, you likely won't have to fight for space. Six bunks occupy the rear quarters of the bus; light cooking equip-

KEY TO ICONS

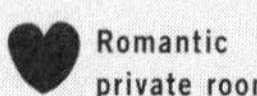

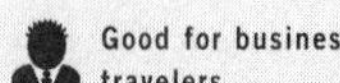

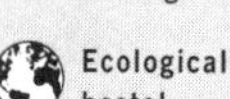

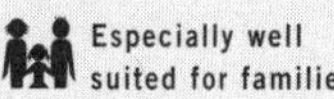

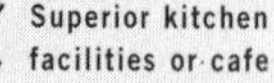

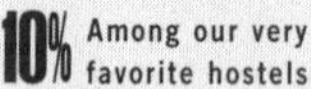

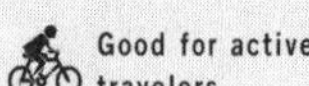

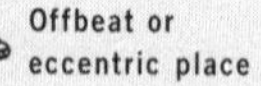

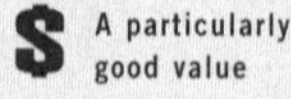

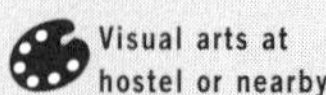

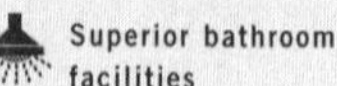

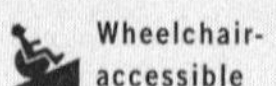

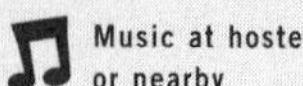

ment sits up front. The bunks are actually nicely installed, and they look pretty comfy. But the bathroom? An outhouse. Laundry? Forget it. Heat? Gas stove upon request, according to a note on the bus. Air-conditioning? Crank open those bus windows, 'cause the wind always blows in from the sea. Water comes from a jug. Showers aren't possible.

Heck, this ain't hostelling—it's camping. Really nice camping. But not hostelling.

The guests appear mostly to be cyclists exploring the wild, beautiful peninsulas along eastern Nova Scotia: mighty fine country to get lost in, we've got to admit it. And it is a bed. For food, we suppose you could dig clams around here—yes, really—or backtrack carefully out to the little Medway Market.

Come for the views, if you must, but make sure you know what you're getting yourself into: a ton of austere solitude. Next time we wanna sleep in a bus, we'll probably go Greyhound.

Best bet for a bite: Fishin' pole

What hostellers say: "We all live in a yellow submarine."

Insiders' tip: Bring food

Gestalt: Magic bus

Hospitality: A

Cleanliness: B

Party index:

How to get there:

By car: From Halifax, drive Route 103 south and west 130 km (about 80 mi.) to Port Medway turnoff. Then drive several kilometers east from main highway to village; at village center, turn right on Long Cove Road. Proceed several kilometers past one working school bus (but this is *not* the hostel) and keep going beyond pavement, down rough gravel road and around curves and over bumps, to very end. Hostel is on the left. Yes, in the bus. From Yarmouth, drive east on Route 103 about 165 km (about 100 mi.) to turnoff. Then follow directions above.

JOYCE'S MOTEL HOSTEL

Box 369, St. Peter's, Nova Scotia B0E 3B0

(902) 535–2404

Rates: $15 Canadian (about $10 U.S.) per person
Credit cards: MC, VISA
Office hours: 7:00 A.M.–11:00 P.M.
Season: May 15–October 31
Beds: 6
Private/family rooms: 1
Single rooms: None

Private bathrooms: None
Affiliation: None
Extras: Boat rental, bike rental, swimming pool, hiking trails, horseshoe pit

First things first. "Joyce" isn't the friendly woman who greets you in Cape Bretonese in the office of this hostel, situated about 50 km (about 30 mi.) east of the Canso Strait Bridge, which links Cape Breton Island to the rest of Nova Scotia. That would be Dianne Rutherford, co-owner of the place. (A Mr. Joyce once owned this complex of cabins, you see, and subsequent owners never bothered changing the name.)

Best bet for a bite: Fish fish fish

Insiders' tip: Back-road biking

Gestalt: Big birds

Hospitality: A

Cleanliness: A

Party index:

For starters, the cottages and hostel are situated in a really nice spot overlooking an arm of Bras D'Or Lake—the largest saltwater lake in the world, don'cha know—replete with fish life, animal life, and bird life. During summertime there are more bald eagles living here in a certain cove than you'll find in the entire United States, we're told. It's prime boating, too.

However, the place is handicapped by a rather strange setup. In one room, there are two bunks and a double bed. OK. But in the other, there's one double—and the stove! Yep, the kitchen's been built right into what otherwise would be a very nice little couples' room, which comes complete with a desk and chair for writing postcards and journal entries.

The layout here is just a bit too strange. Too bad, because the hosts are friendly people, and Cape Breton's a wonderful place to explore. Come to think of it, you can rent rooms at the motel pretty inexpensively—not a bad option at all, considering the million-dollar view, and one we'd take any day.

How to get there:

By bus: Take Acadian Lines to downtown St. Peter's; walk 1.6 km (1 mi.) east on Route 3. Hostel is on right, overlooking lake.

By car: Cross Canso Strait Bridge onto Cape Breton Island. Follow signs to Route 104 east; take Route 104 to end, then switch to Route 4. Pass through village of St. Peter's, crossing bridge, and drive 1.6 km (1 mi.) farther east. Hostel is on right, overlooking lake.

By plane: Airport in Sydney. Call for transit details.

RAVEN HAVEN HOSTEL 

South Milford, Nova Scotia, c/o Annapolis County Recreation Department, Box 100, Annapolis Royal, Nova Scotia BOS 1A0

(902) 532–7320

Fax: (902) 532–2096

Rates: $11.00 Canadian (about $8.00 U.S.) per Hostelling International members
Credit cards: VISA
Office hours: 1:00–10:00 P.M.
Season: June 15–September 1
Beds: 10
Private/family rooms: Yes; number varies; call for availability
Single rooms: None
Private bathrooms: None
Affiliation: Hostelling International-Canada
Extras: Canoe rentals, paddleboats, grill, store, takeout shop

This extremely basic summer-only hostel, which serves primarily as a campground on a nice little lake, is run by the Annapolis County Recreation Department and keeps very busy during its short season. Be prepared to rough it, though. Last year, there were no hot water or flush toilets on the premises—a serious disincentive to travelers. They've now been added—although there's no laundry, and there is no public transportation to get here.

Hostel housing consists of two cabins, each sporting two double beds and a single bunk—a perfect setup for families, especially once that new plumbing is finished. Each cabin also has a living room and a kitchen with full-size stove, big refrigerator, toaster, and other cookery. The campground's got a little takeout shop (they call it a canteen) offering pizza, ice cream, sweets, and other unchallenging food. They'll sell you basic grocery items like milk, bread, butter, tuna, and charcoal for the grills, too.

For slightly more variety, head up the road a bit to the Graywood General Store and get a sub or fried fish. Our real hot tip, though, is to arrive on Friday and hit the good waterfront farmer's market in nearby Annapolis Royal on Saturday mornings. There you can get fresh produce from the farms that dot the local hills. It's about 20 km (12 mi.) to town. Festivals throughout

Best bet for a bite: Graywood General Store

What hostellers say: "Nevermore."

Insiders' tip: Farmer's market in Annapolis Royal

Gestalt: Rough and ready

Hospitality: A

Cleanliness: B

Party index:

summer and fall celebrate scallop harvesting, cherry blossoms, and other food-related stuff.

Don't forget to use the beach here, which is supervised by a lifeguard (parents will like that). Also take a drive up north from Annapolis Royal through the Annapolis Valley. This area contains some of Nova Scotia's oldest and best-preserved homes, farm stands, even a university. Or venture inland to Kejimkujik National Park, a still-wild place full of outback hikes where you won't be trampled by camera-toting tourists. (If you really want to see other tourists, you'll see plenty in nearby Bear River, a Swiss village chock-full of lederhosen and attractions.)

How to get there:

By bus: Acadian Lines stops in area. From depot, call hostel for details.

By car: From Yarmouth or Digby, drive Route 101 north to Annapolis Royal and exit onto Route 8. Drive 27 km (17 mi.) to village of South Milford; turn right onto Virginia Road. Proceed to lakeside park/campground. From Halifax, take Route 102 out of town to junction with Route 101; exit onto Route 101 and follow it approximately 160 km (100 mi.) to Annapolis Royal, then exit onto Route 8. Drive 27 km (17 mi.) to village of South Milford; turn right onto Virginia Road. Proceed to lakeside park/campground. From Truro, follow Route 102 south approximately 85 km (55 mi.) to Route 101 outside Halifax. Exit onto Route 101 and follow it approximately 160 km (100 mi.) to Annapolis Royal, then exit onto Route 8. Drive 27 km (17 mi.) to village of South Milford; turn right onto Virginia Road. Proceed to lakeside park/campground.

By plane: Airport in Halifax. From airport, call hostel for transit route.

By train: VIA Rail stops in Halifax, about 170 km (105 mi.) away. From Halifax, call hostel for transit route.

WENTWORTH HOSTEL 

RR 1, Wentworth, Nova Scotia B0M 1Z0

(902) 548–2379

Fax: (902) 548–2389

Rates: $10.00 Canadian (about $7.00 U.S.) per person
Credit cards: None
Office hours: 8:00–10:00 A.M.; 5:00–11:00 P.M.
Beds: 24
Private/family rooms: 1
Single rooms: None
Private bathrooms: None
Affiliation: Hostelling International-Canada

Extras: Laundry

Wentworth's hostel is the sort of place Teddy Roosevelt would have loved. We can just see old T.R. now, hanging out here with his blunderbuss and maybe some snowshoes. Unfortunately, the building doesn't look like it's been fixed up—or swept out—since T.R.'s time. Still, this is an awfully nice patch of countryside, and it's conveniently located to break up your cross-Maritimes wanderings.

This extremely laid-back hostel occupies an old wooden building (it was once a lumber merchant's home and store, we're told) that has certainly seen better days—back when Wentworth Station was a railroad hub for this rather unremarkable chunk Nova Scotia. Now, thanks to a nearby ski hill, the place serves as a magnet for downhill schussers, usually from local schools. So, if it's real peace and quiet you seek, summertime finds this hostel—let's borrow the words of Sid Vicious and Johnny Rotten—pretty vacant.

Which made it hard to understand why the rooms, despite management claims to the contrary, weren't especially clean. Dirt and dust graced the standard bottom sheets that hostels commonly provide and, although linen rental is advertised, we were asked to use our sleeping bags—a practice discouraged in most hostels because of sanitary regulations. Bathrooms also hadn't been cleaned in a while, it seemed.

Best bet for a bite: Groceries in Truro

What hostellers say: "Peaceful and quiet."

Insiders' tip: Head for the look-off

Gestalt: Rustic never sleeps

Hospitality: A

Cleanliness: C

Party index:

On the up side, though, the kitchen was immaculate: well stocked with cooking equipment and two refrigerators, blessed with plenty of tabletop prep space. We found only one dining-room table, perplexing since the place often entertains large groups of hungry young'uns. There was plenty of room, however, in the common area, where you can peruse old *Northwest Territory Airline* magazines in three languages: French, English—and Inuit!

During the daytime, gorge yourself on 75 km (50 mi.) of trails, which the hostel has permission to use. One right out the backyard leads through pretty meadows to a nice view of the valley, which gets even nicer in multicolored autumn. Or watch the mountain-bike races they sometimes hold in the area.

At night, it's quiet as a mouse. You'll see thousands of stars, 'cause there just aren't any streetlights up here. Still restless? It's only an hour or two's drive to Five Islands Park (if it's sandstone cliffs on the ocean you want) or to Parrsboro (for some of Canada's best fossil hunting).

Maple-sugaring season fires up in the early spring, and local syrup makers offer tours of their sugarbushes as well as pancake breakfasts. Didn't we mention that? This hostel is smack in the middle of Nova Scotia's maple-sugar belt—certainly a bonus after a strenuous morning of skiing or hiking those trails.

Hostelling International-Canada may relocate this getting-run-down hostel within the next few years. So bear in mind that improvements are on the way. There's still no excuse for the uncleanliness, but spend as much time as you can outside and you might not notice too much.

How to get there:

By bus: Take Acadian Lines from Truro or Amherst to Wentworth; driver will drop at stop about 8 km (5 mi.) from hostel, sometimes closer upon request.

By car: Drive Canada Route 104 (Trans-Canada) to Wentworth. From north, go right onto Valley Road, travel 1 km (0.6 mi.), and make a left onto Wentworth Station Road. Proceed uphill to hostel on right. From south, make a left onto Valley Road, travel 1 km (0.6 mi.), and make a left onto Wentworth Station Road. Proceed uphill to hostel on right.

By train: VIA Rail stops in Truro, 200 km (125 mi.) away. Call hostel for transit details.

GLENMORE INTERNATIONAL HOSTEL

RR 1, Whycocomagh, Nova Scotia B0E 3M0

Phone: (902) 258–3622

Rates: $12.00 Canadian (about $9.00 U.S.) per person
Credit cards: None
Office hours: 24 hours
Beds: 11
Private/family rooms: 1
Single rooms: None
Private bathrooms: None
Affiliation: None
Extras: Laundry, boat tours, canoe rentals, ski rentals

By the look of things, the Glenmore Hostel has an awful lot in the works. When we checked in, the management was drawing up blueprints for new showers, a new dormitory, new cabins, new bikes to rent, a new hostel store. And they were planning to reapply to Hostelling International-Canada for membership. But none of those things were actually in place, so you'll want to call ahead of time and find out what kinds of progress they've made.

This awfully simple hostel might still appeal to you, though, because of its location: It isn't far at all from the breathtakingly scenic circular drive around the towering cliffs of the Cabot Trail. The road to the hostel continues through a nearby Native Canadian settlement, too, meaning that there are a few festivals you could hit in summertime.

Or, for a nice drive in autumn—and some genuine Bretonese (that's wistful Scottish) music fairs—press northward into the Margaree Valley, where maples turn flame red and orange at the end of the summer.

Closer to the hostel, Lake Ainslie has some decent sand beaches. There's a historic farmhouse and one-room schoolhouse nearby and an 1839 home sporting such items as a spinning wheel and carpentry tools. The hostel also offers schooner tours of the area; inquire on the premises.

This is a pretty rustic experience. It's not a fancy hostel at all, but at least it's in a nice part of the world.

Best bet for a bite: In Whycocomagh

What hostellers say: "Let's hit the Trail."

Insiders' tip: Schooner tours

Gestalt: Why-not

Hospitality: A

Cleanliness: B

Party index:

How to get there:

By bus: Acadian Lines runs from Halifax and other parts of Nova Scotia to Whycocomagh, 25 km (15 mi.) away. Call hostel for pickup.

By car: Cross Canso Straight Bridge and continue on Route 105 (Trans-Canada Highway) about 50 km (30 mi.) to Whycocomagh. Take Route 395 exit and drive north on 395 about 25 km (15 mi.). Count bridges. Immediately after third bridge, turn right onto Twin Rock Valley Road. Continue 3 km (1.7 mi.) to hostel.

By plane: Small airport in Sydney. From airport, take Acadian Lines ($40 Canadian/about $30 U.S.) to Whycocomagh, 25 km (15 mi.) away. Call hostel for pickup.

By train: VIA Rail stops in Truro, 200 km (125 mi.) away. From train station, take Acadian Lines bus to Whycocomagh, 25 km (15 mi.) away. Call hostel for pickup.

KEY TO ICONS

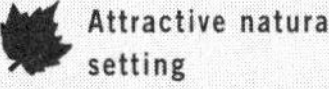

Good for business travelers

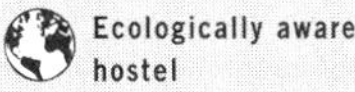

Comfortable beds

Especially well suited for families

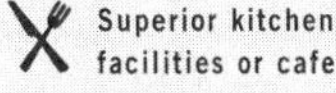

Among our very favorite hostels

Good for active travelers

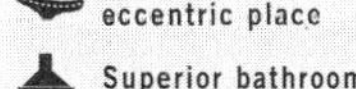

A particularly good value

Visual arts at hostel or nearby

Superior bathroom facilities

Wheelchair-accessible

Music at hostel or nearby

PRINCE EDWARD ISLAND

Prince Edward Island may be the place where English Canada has made its strongest stand—and it sure picked one heck of a great place to stand! It's a beautiful, rural place.

Surprisingly, though, there are just three hostels here. All are decent, though none knocked our socks off. It's easy to hit them all—you can do it in a couple of hours, in fact. Simply drive Route 1 as far as Charlottetown, switch to Route 2, and go north through Midgell and then on to Souris.

You can also arrive here by plane—in Charlottetown, which is pretty expensive—or by ferry from Nova Scotia, which is inconvenient without a car. Driving across the new bridge is already most people's choice, despite the approximately $38 Canadian (about $27 U.S.) toll you pay when leaving. The solution? Don't leave—we certainly didn't want to, once we'd seen the beaches, and you'll feel the same way.

CHARLOTTETOWN HOSTEL

153 Mount Edward Road, Charlottetown,

Prince Edward Island C1A 7N4

(902) 894–9696 (summer); (800) 663–5777 (winter)

Fax: (902) 628–6424

Rates: $14.00–$16.50 Canadian (about $10.00–$11.50 U.S.) per Hostelling International member
Credit cards: VISA
Office hours: 7:00–10:00 A.M.; 4:00 P.M.–midnight
Season: June 1–September 1
Beds: 52
Private/family rooms: 1
Single rooms: None
Private bathrooms: None
Affiliation: Hostelling International-Canada
Extras: Lockers, bike rentals

Look up the word *quaint* in your Japanese–English dictionary and you'll probably find the name "Prince Edward Island." For the uninitiated, sunny, verdant P.E.I. is home to Canada's favorite plucky, red-haired orphan, Anne of Green Gables. The popular novel of the same name and its sequels have spawned an unexplained following in Japan and draws *beaucoup* tourism dollars from that country. Charlottetown, the capital city of P.E.I., offers a bit of its pastoral island charm in the form of this hostel—a big green converted barn that Canada's hostelling association rents from the convent next door for a penny a year.

Nice idea—badly executed. For starters, the ceiling on the second floor is constructed in such a way that sound travels, specifically the blaring television, into the very rooms in which you sleep. If you are situated next to the men's bathroom, as we were, you are treated to the soothing sounds of all forms of water trickling.

Sound appealing? Read on. The lumpy mattresses were probably used at one time to cushion the former bovine inhabitants. Bottom sheets were unwashed as well. And, get this, you must pay $1.07 Canadian (about $0.80 U.S.) to use the blankets! A family room is slightly more comfy than the crowded dorms, at least.

The herdish morning bathroom scene should persuade you to take your shower in off-peak hours if staying more than a day. A smallish kitchen makes up for its lack of space with two toasters, a microwave, and lots of pots and pans; but you might be wanting for a place to sit, as many hostellers hang around practicing their English there long after dinnertime. How come? No common room, that's why. (The TV room doesn't really count; everybody here is glued to the set.) Other minuses? No laundry on the premises, an all-day lockout starting at 10:00 A.M., and the hostel is farther from town than it ought to be.

Best bet for a bite:
Farmer's market

What hostellers say:
"Moooo-ve over, buddy."

Insiders' tip:
Top floor's noisy

Gestalt:
Green stables

Hospitality: C

Cleanliness: C

Party index:

If you do feel like hoofing it, a nice little indoor farmer's market nearby opens its doors Wednesdays, Saturdays, and Sundays. If you miss out on the market, remember that all the large supermarkets on the island are closed on Sundays. Luckily, mom-and-pop stores abound, though you'll need a car to reach most of 'em. A sparkling clean laundromat sits at the bottom of the hill.

Charlottetown, by the way, isn't really all it could be. Really nice homes and parks mix with monstrosities (the arts center) and tacky discount shops. Our picks for a quick fix include several Lebanese places that looked okay, plus the quirky Cows ice-cream chain. How appropriate for a hostel so, er, rustic.

Okay, class, let's review. P.E.I.? Ahhhh. Hostel? Blahhhh.

How to get there:

By car: From New Brunswick, cross Confederation Bridge ($37.50 Canadian/$26 U.S. toll when returning to mainland) to Prince Edward Island. Follow Canada Route 1 about 55 km (35 mi.) to Charlottetown. Make a left onto Route 2 at intersection of

Longworth/Euston. Continue to Mount Edward Road, make a left, and go through two lights and up hill. At top of hill, make left at green hostel sign onto skinny dirt lane just before church.

By plane: Small airport in Charlottetown. Call hostel for transit details.

MIDGELL CENTRE HOSTEL 

Route 2, Morell, Prince Edward Island C0A 1S0

(902) 961–2963

Rates: $14 Canadian (about $10 U.S.) per person
Credit cards: None
Office hours: Vary; call for hours
Season: June 1–September 30
Beds: 20
Private/family rooms: Yes; number varies; call for availability
Single rooms: Yes; number varies; call for availability
Private bathrooms: None
Affiliation: None
Extras: Lawn games, grill, kitchen

A cluster of green buildings situated at the top of a hill, the Midgell (say *mih-JELL*) Centre originally served as overflow housing for Hostelling International-Canada's Charlottetown hostel. And if it's peace and quiet you're seeking, you'd be better off heading here first than going to the city, where chaos sometimes rules and nature is nowhere at hand.

Set in fields, the hostel is one of the cleanest we have seen, right down to the plastic covers protecting the beds and linens. Kitchen facilities are more than adequate, with about four kitchens in the

KEY TO ICONS

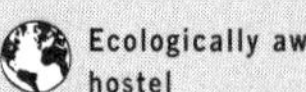

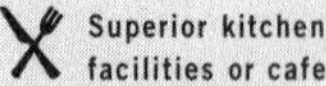

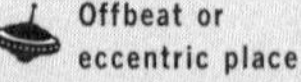

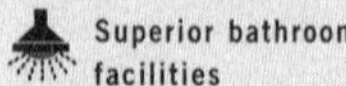

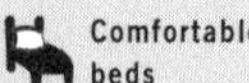

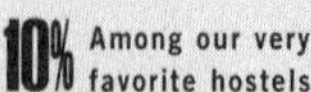

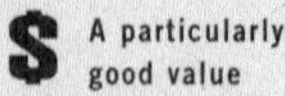

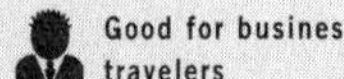

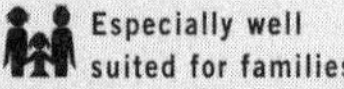

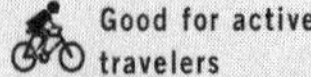

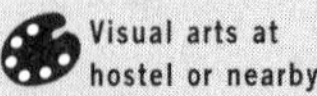

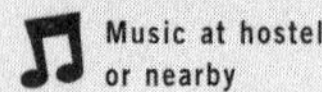

place. You often have your choice of where to sleep, too: Since this hostel-cum-retreat center generally caters to church and youth groups, you might hit a night when the place is empty. (Some of the full-size beds are designed to be dismantled into twin beds for such aforementioned occasions.) Also, many of the rooms are designated for group leaders and, as such, are private, with just one single bed—excellent for seekers of solitude.

Best bet for a bite: Oyster Bed Bridge general store

What hostellers say: "Have faith."

Insiders' tip: Sunset over St. Peters Bay

Gestalt: Cross road

Hospitality: A

Cleanliness: A

Party index:

The manager, Eileen Munn, is a spunky islander of Irish heritage whose brogue remains intact, especially when describing the Presbyterian origins of the Centre or typical local "P.E.I. directions." She and her daughter, a Mountie (Canadian horse-top cop) on leave for the summer from duty in the Northwest Territories, proudly explain how all the furniture on the premises was constructed by island volunteers. They're also terrific guides to their favorite spots for enjoying the quieter spots (like nearby Lakeside Beach) on P.E.I.

Don't worry much about the religious backdrop, by the way—the place's official name is Midgell Christian Nondenominational Association—because its managers are quick to point out that the facility adheres to its nondenominational dogma despite the crosses, Bibles, lecterns, and other religious fixtures that fill the place.

While blissing out to the fragrant odor of island cows, you can relax in any number of Adirondack chairs scattered about, broil some local salmon on the barbie, shoot some roadside hoop, or maybe even pull some stubborn weeds from the garden. If you're so inclined, pick from either of two laundry facilities on-site and scrub your clothes clean of that P.E.I. red clay.

The island is blessed with a fantastic bike trail that runs through this area, and the hostel is very close to it—so bring your two-wheeler, or rent one on the island, if possible. Or you might head for Prince Edward Island National Park and miles of wonderful beach. The lovely little fishing village of St. Peters Bay is another side trip worth doing, especially toward sundown. And backtrack for the hamlet of Oyster Bed Bridge to check out a great little country store.

In short, this place is a bit odd—but it really delivers convenience, economy, a natural setting, and the space to enjoy it.

How to get there:

By car: From Charlottetown, drive Route 2 east (use bypass around town if coming from off-island). Drive west approximately 45 km (30 mi.). Hostel is on right in cluster of green buildings.

A PLACE TO STAY INN HOSTEL 

9 Longworth Street, Souris, Prince Edward Island COA 2BO

(800) 655–7829; (902) 687–4626

Rates: $20 Canadian (about $14 U.S.) per person
Credit cards: VISA, MC
Office hours: 8:00 A.M.–11:00 P.M.
Beds: 14
Private/family rooms: None
Single rooms: None
Private bathrooms: None
Affiliation: None
Extras: Ironing board, bike rental, grill, TV, VCR, games, laundry, light breakfast

As we pulled in, Jay Hannan, who manages the hostel with his mother, Betty, quickly threw on a shirt and apologized for his appearance. "I wear many hats at this place," he said, explaining that he'd just been doing some yard work. He then politely assisted some guests, offered us something to quench our thirsts, and took us on a whirlwind tour of a rather quirky hostel.

Best bet for a bite: IGA

What hostellers say: "Two wheels good."

Insiders' tip: Singing sands at Basin Head

Gestalt: Inn luck

Hospitality: A

Cleanliness: A

Party index:

Until the Hannans purchased the property, the former convent sat vacant. It now serves as both an inn and a hostel. Jay had worked in a hostel in Alberta and decided that he, too, wanted to run a comfortable place for budget-conscious travelers; after scoping out several locations, he and his mom picked the village of Souris (pronounced *SOO-ree*—and, yes, it mean "mice") for their ferry connection to the Madeleine Islands and its choice position right on top of the half-island-long Confederation Bike Trail.

As such, the hostel really tries to cater to bike groups, although individual travelers are welcomed as well. Jay has constructed some nice bicycle storage units and rents two-wheelers for $20 Canadian (about $14 U.S.) a day.

Located in the basement, dorm rooms are small and airy, clean and comfortable. However, the decorating scheme could be a bit off-putting, as various shades of orange and green are not too easy on the eyes. Private rooms are sometimes available, and hostellers are occasionally bumped up to one of the inn rooms when things are slow.

The spacious layout leaves a lot of breathing room, with a well-designed kitchen, dining room, and common area (which comes with its own confessional!). Sweaty cyclists will rejoice at the large laundry room that comes complete with iron and ironing board. Nice for putting that crease back in the biking shorts.

Food options are a bit limited, although Souris is Gotham-sized compared to the other fishing villages up here on the untouristed northeast end of P.E.I. You'll pick from either of two grocery stores—though very quaint, Montréal this ain't; exotic provisions are definitely not the norm on P.E.I. No matter: The scenery around here is excellent, among the best anywhere on the island. Grab a camera or a bike and follow the lupine-lined roads to the sea.

How to get there:

By car: From Charlottetown, drive Route 2 about 80 km (50 mi.) east to Souris. Make a left just after the Esso station entering town, then a right onto Longworth Street at big red church. Hostel is on left.

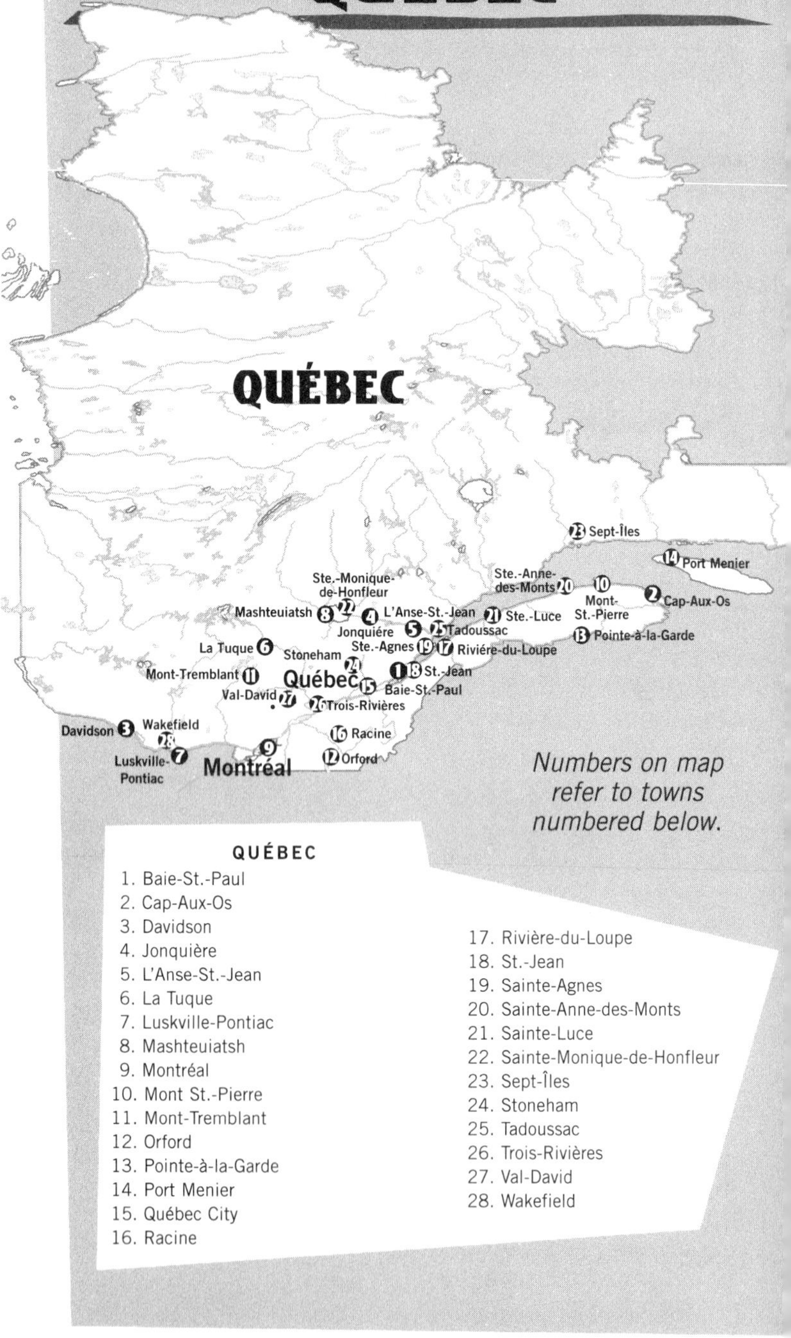

Numbers on map refer to towns numbered below.

QUÉBEC

1. Baie-St.-Paul
2. Cap-Aux-Os
3. Davidson
4. Jonquière
5. L'Anse-St.-Jean
6. La Tuque
7. Luskville-Pontiac
8. Mashteuiatsh
9. Montréal
10. Mont St.-Pierre
11. Mont-Tremblant
12. Orford
13. Pointe-à-la-Garde
14. Port Menier
15. Québec City
16. Racine
17. Rivière-du-Loupe
18. St.-Jean
19. Sainte-Agnes
20. Sainte-Anne-des-Monts
21. Sainte-Luce
22. Sainte-Monique-de-Honfleur
23. Sept-Îles
24. Stoneham
25. Tadoussac
26. Trois-Rivières
27. Val-David
28. Wakefield

QUÉBEC

It has often been said that the Province of Québec is like another country. But now that observation has taken on some irony: A vocal contingent is trying to make it just that—a nation apart from Canada.

Part of what's remarkable about the place is the tremendous difference between the towns here and similar-size towns just across the border in New England. The food in the Québecois towns is just so much better; the people are astonishingly social and tolerant; and everyone is so active that you can't go anywhere without falling all over mountain bikes, bike paths, ski trails, and in-line skates.

The local hostels reflect this Québecois love of both food and sport. Almost every hostel in the province includes a really good restaurant on the premises, and often there's a bar. Cycles, canoes, and kayaks are readily available for rental. The settings are breathtaking, the rules aren't too strict, and everyone ends up having tons of fun. As a group, this area's hostels are perhaps the best in eastern Canada.

To hit the most and best hostels in Québec, decide what you want to see ahead of time—this is a big place! For small-town friendliness, gentle hills and waters, and great backroads biking, we love driving the quiet byways of the Cantons de l'Est (Eastern Townships) that lie south of Montréal and Québec City. The food is out of this world, and two of the best hostels are nestled within 50 km (about 30 mi.) of each other. Get there by taking Route 55 from Québec City or, from Montréal, Route 10 or 104.

If you want rugged ocean views and great hiking, chart a course along Route 132 around the Gaspé Peninsula, which sticks out into the Atlantic like the bow of a ship. For gorgeous mountain scenery, jump on Route 15 north *(nord)* for the Laurentians. The hikes and lakes are excellent here, and the hostels are good, too.

KEY TO ICONS

Attractive natural setting	Romantic private rooms	Good for business travelers
Ecologically aware hostel	Comfortable beds	Especially well suited for families
Superior kitchen facilities or cafe	10% Among our very favorite hostels	Good for active travelers
Offbeat or eccentric place	$ A particularly good value	Visual arts at hostel or nearby
Superior bathroom facilities	Wheelchair-accessible	Music at hostel or nearby

For big-city flash, Québec City and Montréal present two different but equally wonderful experiences. Compact, romantic Québec City is the more French of the two, a bit snazzier; more of a place to eat, shop, and snuggle—and the only place to be in midwinter for the big carnival. Friendlier (and lots bigger) Montréal hums with hundreds of good ethnic restaurants, great festivals, and almost too much to see and do. Hostels in both cities are, again, terrific.

Finally, note that the province's hostels have a toll-free phone number for booking dorm beds *only*: It's (800) 461–8585.

AUBERGE LE BALCON VERTE (GREEN BALCONY HOSTEL)

Box 442, Route 362, Baie-St.-Paul, Québec G0A 1B0

(418) 435–5587

Rates: $16 Canadian (about $11 U.S.) per person; private rooms $28 (about $40 U.S.)
Credit cards: MC, VISA
Office hours: 8:00 A.M.–1:00 A.M.
Season: June 16–September 1
Beds: 70
Private/family rooms: 11
Single rooms: None
Private bathrooms: None
Affiliation: None
Extras: Bar, cafeteria, laundry

Named "Green Balcony" not only because of its green paint but also because the surrounding view is so green—in summertime, anyway—this hostel's a pretty happening place in an unlikely spot: a scenic artists' colony northeast of Québec City.

Private rooms here are especially suited for families, consisting of a double bed plus a single bunk. Sometimes the manager, Gilbert, even arranges entertainment—talent shows featuring the guests, children's programs, and the like. A bit hokey if you're here to party or seek solitude, but wonderfully welcome if you're trying to enrich the little ones.

There are some nice restaurants around, but the hostel touts its own in-house meals, which always include a vegetarian offering. Supper (as in dinner) costs $7.50 Canadian (about $5.00 U.S.) and is "never the same twice in a month," Gilbert points out proudly. Breakfast runs you $3.60 Canadian (about $2.50 U.S.) and consists of a bacon-and-eggs type of meal. Lunch is not served, but there are a bar and lounge.

It's only a forty-five–minute drive to the whales of the Saguenay River, and less to nearby Grands-Jardins Park, with its lakes and mountains. Baie-St.-Paul is best known, however, for its dense concentration of visual artists. There are more than a dozen galleries in the little town, enough to keep you occupied for hours if that's your bag.

How to get there:

By bus: Voyageurs runs from Québec to Baie-St.-Paul. Call hostel for details.

By car: From Québec City, drive 95 km (60 mi.) east *(est)* on Route 138 to Baie-St.-Paul. Pass through town and look for church; at church, follow sign to Route 362. Look for AUBERGE sign on left; turn at sign and climb driveway to hostel.

By plane: Airport in Québec City. Call hostel for transit route.

By train: VIA Rail stops in Québec City. Call hostel for transit route.

Best bet for a bite: On-site

What hostellers say: "So-so."

Insiders' tip: Gallery hopping

Gestalt: Green acres

Hospitality: A

Party index:

AUBERGE DE CAP-AUX-OS 

2095 Boulevard Grande-Grève, Cap-Aux-Os, Québec G0E 1J0

(418) 892–5153

Fax: (418) 892–5292

Web site: www.tourismeJ.qc.ca

Rates: $15 Canadian (about $10 U.S.) per person; private rooms $35 (about $25 U.S.)
Credit cards: MC, VISA
Office hours: 24 hours
Beds: 56
Private/family rooms: 4
Single rooms: None
Private bathrooms: 4
Affiliation: Hostelling International-Canada
Extras: Cafeteria, bicycle rentals, binoculars, tours, snowshoe rentals, skate and ski rentals

This hostel is located in the eye-popping Gaspé region of Québec, a wild peninsula of caribou, geese, whales, and lots of other critters. So wild is this area that, during the summer, the hostel can offer tours to observe black bears one day and whales the next. This hostel rents binoculars—a necessity and a blessing in such a place.

Top-of-the-line equipment is available for rent, too. Gilles Shaw, the enthusiastic manager, is most excited about recently purchased backcountry touring skis, which will enable hostellers to get out into the bush in wintertime. The hostel also arranges coastal tours and presents slide shows on selected topics.

Hostellers sleep on comfy, handmade hardwood bunks. Most dorm rooms have just four beds—a nice switch from the huge dorm rooms you sometimes get, though two single-sex dorm rooms here do contain eight beds each. There are also four private rooms in the place.

From mid-June to mid-September, lobster suppers are served for $15.00 Canadian (about $10.00 U.S.) that include not only the buttery crustacean but also rice, salad, garlic bread, dessert, and tea or coffee. Other meals feature freshly caught crab, codfish, and so forth. These meals cost on average of $8.50 Canadian (about $6.00 U.S.) and include soup. Not up for it? An Omni supermarket nearby supplies all the staples.

Best bet for a bite: On-site

What hostellers say: "Amazing."

Insiders' tip: Hike that park

Gestalt: Gasp! Hey! See!

Hospitality: A

Party index:

Extended stays are not uncommon, both because this is a long haul from points south and because of the wealth of activities here. Forillon National Park alone is home to a wide variety of terrain, everything from 200-meter (600-foot) limestone cliffs and seal watching on the rugged coast to forests, peat bogs, dunes, and more in the inland sections.

Yes, we've heard good reports about both the hostel and the park. So we can wholeheartedly recommended it as a good base for the Gaspé.

How to get there:

By bus: Bus line stops at hostel door in summertime. In off-season, bus stops in Gaspé 25 km (15 mi.) away. Call hostel for possible pickup; if unavailable, take taxi (about $20 Canadian/$14 U.S.) to hostel door.

By car: Call hostel for directions to Gaspé Peninsula and village of Cap-Aux-Os. Hostel is at #2095.

By train: VIA Rail stops in Gaspé, 25 km (15 mi.) away. Call hostel for possible pickup; if unavailable, take taxi (about $20 Canadian/$14 U.S.) to hostel door.

THE POINTE HOSTEL

c/o Esprit Rafting, Thomas Lefevbre Road, Davidson, Québec JOX 1RO

(800) 596–7238; (819) 683–3241

E-mail: esprit@iosphere.net

Rates: $15–$20 Canadian (about $11–$15 U.S.) per Hostelling International member

Credit cards: AMEX, MC, VISA
Office hours: 24 hours
Season: April to October
Beds: 38
Private/family rooms: Yes
Single rooms: None
Private bathrooms: None
Affiliation: Hostelling International-Canada
Extras: Laundry, tours, canoe rentals, hammock, meals ($)

Situated on a beautiful five-acre point of land on the Ottawa River, this establishment's main business is whitewater rafting and tours. But the newly certified hostel is sure to be a welcome addition for travelers heading west up the river in search of adventure.

The hostel consists of two buildings: a main building with the tour headquarters and hostel kitchen and showers, plus the actual accommodations (that is, the bunks) in a separate lodge. Rooms vary in bed size. A sitting room has facilities for game playing and a fireplace, too.

You'll certainly spend lots of time outdoors here; the staff offers canoe trips, canoe rentals, kayaking lessons, water-rescue instruction, and (of course) the famous rafting runs. There's a small general store in Davidson for essentials and a few restaurants for budget-busting splurges.

All in all, a laid-back place where you'll feel at home lounging around on the deck, snoozing in the hammock, walking among the pine trees, or fishing the river.

Best bet for a bite: Catch of the day

What hostellers say: "Splash!"

Gestalt: Rapids City

Hospitality: A

Cleanliness: A

Party index:

How to get there:

By bus: Pontiac bus lines run from Ottawa to Fort Colounge, 5 km (3 mi.) away. Call hostel for pickup.

By car: From Ottawa, drive across bridge to Hull, Québec, and turn east *(est)* onto Highway 148. Drive approximately 110 km (70 mi.) to village of Davidson and make a left on Thomas Lefevbre Road. Continue 3 km (2 mi.) to Esprit Rafting.

By plane: Airport in Ottawa. Pontiac bus line to Fort Colounge, 5 km (3 mi.) away and call hostel for pickup. Or call hostel for pickup in Ottawa ($15 Canadian/about $10 U.S.).

By train: VIA Rail stops in Ottawa. From train station, take train into city to bus station. Then take Pontiac bus line to Fort Colounge, 5 km (3 mi.) away, and call hostel for pickup. Or call hostel for pickup in Ottawa ($15 Canadian/about $10 U.S.).

L'AUBERGE JEUNESSE DE VIEUX ST.-PIERRE (OLD ST. PETER'S HOSTEL)

4933 chemin St.-Andre, Jonquière, Québec G7X 3G3
(418) 547–0845

Rates: $15.40 Canadian (about $11.00 U.S.) per person
Credit cards: MC, VISA
Office hours: 24 hours
Beds: 10
Private/family rooms: 3
Single rooms: None
Private bathrooms: None
Affiliation: None
Extras: Laundry, meals, picnics, TV

Note: This hostel has recently downsized and changed locations due to a fire.

North of Québec City, hordes of French hostellers have staked out the hostels of the Saguenay/Lac St.-Jean region. They go wild for this area; so much so that a work-exchange program has been set up between the hostel organizations of France and Québec.

We discovered this well into a conversation with the French summer manager of this place. She was busy impressing us with her encyclopedic knowledge of the hostel's programs and facilities, and we asked if she was a local. *Mais non!*

This hostel is especially good for outdoorsy types, since the staff will help you arrange a wide range of tours and outings. There is everything from a half-day Shipshaw River rafting expedition to lake and river cruises, ice-fishing trips, forest camp tours, and—thank goodness for this—snowshoes. Oh, and did we mention the sled-dog trip with a musher? If you're into history, the nearby village of Val-Jalbert provides you with a glimpse of how folks lived before flip phones and the Internet.

Best bet for a bite:
Here and now

Gestalt:
Fjord tough

Hospitality: A

Cleanliness: B

Party index:

After all this day-tripping you'll need sustenance, and the on-site restaurant makes an effort to provide hearty, low-cost meals representing the local cuisine. Typically featured is the ubiquitous Québecois meat pie known as tourtière, as well as salmon pâté and a dessert using local fruit. These scrumptious meals generally go for $7.00–$8.00 Canadian (about $5.00–$6.00 U.S.). Breakfast ($4.00 Canadian/about $3.00 U.S.) is more standard, but still big enough—cereal, pancakes, toast, fruit, orange juice, and so forth. There's no midday meal here, however.

After supper, the managers light a campfire each night, weather permitting. As the fire catches and glows, stories and strains of music from guests' guitars fill the air. Yes, there's a television here, too, for those of you (like us) who can't live without your fix of *ALF* reruns.

This is a fun place, and it gets extra points for a bathroom specially designed for folks in a wheelchair and just generally easy-access accommodations.

How to get there:

By bus: Voyageur bus line stops near hostel. Call hostel from depot for details or for pickup.

By car: From Québec City, drive north *(nord)* on Route 175 approximately 220 km (140 mi.) to just outside Chicoutimi. At junction of Route 170, turn left onto 170 and drive 12 km (7 mi.) north *(nord)* to Jonquière; in town, use the elevated highway to the left. Turn right at light after bridge; hostel is 4 km (2.5 mi.) from turn.

By train: VIA Rail stops in Jonquière. Call hostel from depot for details or for pickup.

AUBERGE CHEZ MONIKA (THE HOSTEL AT MONIKA'S PLACE)

12 Les Plateaux, L'Anse-St.-Jean, Québec G0V 1G0

(418) 272–3115

Rates: $10.00 Canadian (about $7.00 U.S.) per person; private rooms $20.00 (about $14.00 U.S.)
Office hours: Vary; call
Credit cards: None
Beds: 10
Private/family rooms: 3
Single rooms: None
Private bathrooms: None
Affiliation: None
Extras: Kayaks, gardens, horses

For a peaceful antidote to the madding crowds of other Lac St. Jean–Saguenay region hostels, Chez Monika delivers an offbeat pastoral experience.

In fact, more Québecois families are finding their way here to escape the party-time ambience of some nearby young-adult–oriented hostels. Family activities offered by Monika, such as horseback riding (it's also an equestrian center), provide hours of relaxation and an opportunity to explore the surrounding area more closely. Other possible activities include sea kayaking and hiking the two trails that leave from the hostel property. And the village of

Best bet for a bite: Chicoutimi or bust

What hostellers say: "Show me the garden."

Gestalt: Garden party

Hospitality: B

Cleanliness: B

Party index:

L'Anse-St.-Jean is quietly growing into a quaint little tourist destination.

Kids are especially enchanted by the castlelike design of the wooden building; it looks like something out of a Cinderella story. There's a tower with small vertical windows that creates a "special energy," claims Monika. That gives you some hint about what sort of place this is: a bit starry-eyed. Monika's medicinal garden, for instance, attracts budding aromatherapists (she'll be happy to take you on a tour of them and explain the uses for the herbs). And she often refers to "the community" here.

So understand what this is. A decidedly offbeat retreat, but one that's beautifully situated nonetheless.

How to get there:

By bus: From Montréal and Québec City, Voyageurs bus line stops once a day in L'Anse-St.-Jean. Ask driver for drop-off at Plateau Chez Monika; leave baggage at bottom of hill for pickup and walk uphill to hostel.

By car: From Québec City, drive Route 138 approximately 185 km (115 mi.) to St.-Siméon. Turn left on Route 170 and drive north *(nord)* toward Chicoutimi. Continue about 75 km (45 mi.) north *(nord)* to sign for Centre Équestre le Plateau (L'Anse-St.-John Equestrian Center). Turn right and drive 4 km (2.5 mi.) down road. Hostel is at end of road.

By plane: Airport in Québec City. From airport, take bus to Voyageurs' bus terminal. Voyageurs bus line stops once a day in L'Anse-St.-Jean. Ask driver for drop-off at Plateau Chez Monika; leave baggage at bottom of hill for pickup and walk uphill to hostel.

By train: VIA Rail stops in Québec City. Voyageurs bus line stops once a day in L'Anse-St.-Jean. Ask driver for drop-off at Plateau Chez Monika; leave baggage at bottom of hill for pickup and walk uphill to hostel.

AUBERGE LA RÉSIDENCE

352 avenue Brown La Tuque, Québec G9X 2W4

(819) 523–9267

Fax: (819) 523–3678

E-mail: nbilodeau@tr.cgocable.ca

Rates: $14.00 Canadian (about $9.00 U.S.) per Hostelling International member

Credit cards: VISA
Beds: 40
Private/ family rooms: Yes
Office hours: Call hostel for hours
Affiliation: Hostelling International-Canada
Extras: Kitchen, game room, campfire area, volleyball, lockers, laundry, pickups

This plain two-story hostel is just a way station for hostellers heading between the St. Lawrence Valley and big Lake St.-Jean. But it's a decent bed for the night, surrounded by big woods and the St.-Maurice River.

The hostel's forty beds include some private digs, plus access to a kitchen, game room, campfire ring, volleyball net, and a laundry. There are lockers for your stuff. And the staff will pick you up from the tiny local train station if you need a lift.

Area attactions boil down to the river, the Lumberjack Museum, or the walls of your room. Also remember that winter is high season up here due to area ski hills.

Gestalt: Tuque of earl

Hospitality: A

Cleanliness: A

Party index:

How to get there:

By bus: Call hostel for transit route.

By car: From Highway 55, take St.-Michel Street to Brown Street and continue to hostel on right.

By train: From La Tuque Station, call hostel for free pickup.

WANAKI (OTTAWA) RIVER HOSTEL

133 Avenue des Plages, Luskville-Pontiac, Québec J0X 2G0
(819) 455–9295
E-mail: kfisher@magi.com
Web site: www.bb.com/612.html
Rates: $15 Canadian (about $10 U.S.) per person
Credit cards: None
Office hours: Vary; call
Beds: 10 (summer); 6 (winter)
Private/family rooms: Yes; number varies; call for availability
Single rooms: None
Private bathrooms: None
Affiliation: None
Extras: Fireplaces, laundry, TV, VCR, hot tub, exercise room, meals

This B&B with a few hostel rooms sits on a sandy beach overlooking a bend of the Ottawa River. Hostellers get use of the resort's kitchen, shower, bathroom, and fireplaces. An additional fee is charged for laundry and the big hot tub. Meals are also available; price "depends on what is asked for," according to owner Ken Fisher.

Best bet for a bite: Right here, right now

Gestalt: King fisher

Hospitality: A

Cleanliness: A

Party index:

Inside the lodge, a bunkroom contains six beds (three of 'em bunks); outside, another unheated cabin—for summer hostelling only—contains two beds and a screened-in porch with two more.

River rafting is big in these parts. The hostel's also close to a marina, golf course, and boat launch, if you happen to have brought your yacht, golf clubs, or speedboat. Fat chance, right? Well, fear not. There's also a waterfall in town, and it's not far to Gatineau Park and kilometer after kilometer of skiing, hiking, and biking trails.

How to get there:

By bus: Bus lines stop in Ottawa. Call hostel for best transit route.

By car: From Montréal, drive west *(ouest)* on Route 40 to junction of Route 417. Exit onto 417 and continue west to Ottawa. Take exit 18 and go north *(nord)* on Nicholas to Laurier; turn right and go to King Edward Drive. Follow King Edward across bridge into Hull, Québec, and get onto Route 5 north *(nord)*. Go north 2 km (1.2 mi.), then take St. Raymond exit. From exit, turn left and drive west *(ouest)* 3.5 km (2 mi.), keeping right at Chemin Pink; turn right onto Chemin de la Montagne and drive 18 km (11 mi.) to the end; turn right on Route 148 and go 0.3 km (0.2 mi.). Make a left onto Chemin des Dominicains, go 2 km (1.2 mi.) to Chemin de la

KEY TO ICONS

 Attractive natural setting

 Romantic private rooms

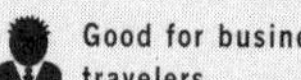 Good for business travelers

 Ecologically aware hostel

  Comfortable beds

 Especially well suited for families

 Superior kitchen facilities or cafe

10% Among our very favorite hostels

 Good for active travelers

  Offbeat or eccentric place

 A particularly good value

Visual arts at hostel or nearby

 Superior bathroom facilities

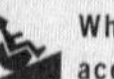 Wheelchair-accessible

 Music at hostel or nearby

Sapinière, and make a left. Go 1.6 km (1 mi.) more to Avenue des Plages, turn right, and continue to end of street. Hostel is at top of hill, off circle.

By plane: Airport in Ottawa. Call hostel for best transit route.

By train: VIA Rail stops in Ottawa. Call hostel for best transit route.

AUBERGE IKUKUM (GRANDMOTHER'S HOSTEL)

241 Ouiatchouan, Point Bleu (Mashteuiatsh), Québec G0W 2H0

(418) 275–0697

Rates: $25 Canadian (about $18 U.S.) per person; private rooms $50 (about $35 U.S.)
Credit cards: None
Office hours: 8:00 A.M.–11:00 P.M.
Season: Varies; call
Beds: 25
Private/family rooms: 5
Single rooms: None
Private bathrooms: None
Affiliation: None
Extras: Meals, educational programs

We've gotten reports that the facilities at this hostel have fallen into a bit of disrepair in recent years. Still, this is an absolutely unique hostel, we hear—maybe the place to go if you're keen on learning about Native Canadian lifestyles.

Situated almost directly on the south shore of enormous Lake St. Jean, this hostel is run by a native of France who felt compelled to move here and has since been hired to promote the "reality of life"—her description—in this town populated mostly by Montaignais (Native Canadians).

In any event, what you get here is a big house that accepts people who are willing to quietly observe normal everyday life among the Montaignais. Believe it or not, you can even go out on a beaver hunt or a forage for wild berries and nuts. You can also eat these wild foods at the hostel table if you make a dinner reservation.

Best bet for a bite: Out in the woods

Gestalt: Leave it to beaver

Hospitality: B

Cleanliness: C

Party index:

Concessions are made to the Western way of life, however, in the form of a television, VCR, and lots of elbow room. The hostel reportedly has two dining rooms, a big self-service kitchen, and acres of surrounding forest.

Guylaine du Hamelle, the manager—not the grandmother for whom the hostel is named, by the way—also says she has plans to hold retreats here in the future to promote "international cultural understanding." Again, that's her description.

This place is off the beaten track, and we've heard mixed reports. So buyer beware.

How to get there:

By car: Call hostel for directions.

By train: VIA Rail stops in Jonquière. Call hostel for transit route.

AUBERGE ALTERNATIVE OF OLD MONTRÉAL (ALTERNATIVE HOSTEL OF OLD MONTRÉAL)

358 Rue St.-Pierre, Montréal, Québec H2Y 2M1

(514) 282–8069

Rates: $17 Canadian (about $12 U.S.) per person; private rooms $40–$45 (about $28–$32 U.S.)

Credit cards: MC

Office hours: 8:00 A.M.–11:00 P.M. (summer); 9:00 A.M.–10:00 P.M. (winter)

Beds: 44

Private/family rooms: 2

Single rooms: None

Private bathrooms: None

Affiliation: None

Extras: Laundry, lockers, Internet access, kitchen

Usually a hostel is either fun or big. But here, finally, is one that's both: sizable, yet still friendly and somewhat clean, though recent visitors have noted a slightly scrungier feel to the place. It is one of the better hostels in Montréal; a big, high-ceilinged space with views aplenty of the touristy Old Montréal area. It should win some sort of architectural prize for North America's most interesting hostel layout. Just be prepared to walk lots of stairs: This is vertical hostelling at its finest.

The two owners—a Tasmanian and a Québecker, and how's that for covering the globe?—bought half a burned-out stone building right in the city's historic district, then set about refurbishing it from top to bottom. They sure have done a nice job: freshly painted walls in soothing, offbeat pastel colors; scrubbed-clean wooden floors;

MONTRÉAL-AREA HOSTELS: A Summary

	RATING	PROS	CONS	COST	PAGE
Auberge de Montréal		hoppin' place	big	\$18.00	p. 76
Gîte du Parc Lafontaine		great rooms	busy street	\$19.00	p. 78
Auberge Chez Jean		laid-back	sometimes packed	\$17.00	p. 74
Hôtel de Paris		fun crowd	crowded fun	\$18.00	p. 80
Vacances de Quartre Saisons		great location	grafitti	\$11.50–\$12.50	p. 82
Auberge Alternative		fun	blah location	\$17.00	p. 72

handmade bunks; and big windows with southern exposures to let in lots of sun. Out those windows you'll see an old fire station and the historic Place d'Youville square, which, in the summer, teems all day with horse-and-buggy rides and strollers.

The kitchen area and living room are among the most unique such spaces we've seen—one whole open floor dedicated to checking in, hanging out, cooking up, and winding down. It features two big refrigerators and two rangetops, and there are only a few bunks on this busy floor. And don't forget the nice laundry, equipped with a new washer and dryer.

The next floor up consists mainly of a huge coed bunkroom, with twenty bunks tucked against one another at angles (you have to see it to know what we mean). Plus a small quad-room dormitory for women. Each bed comes with its own locker underneath, too—a thoughtful security touch by the owners.

Best bet for a bite: Chinatown

What hostellers say: "Hey! Another parking ticket!"

Gestalt: Alt.hostel

Safety: B

Hospitality: A

Cleanliness: C

Party index:

Finally, on a top floor, a smaller bunkroom accommodates the inevitable summer overflow. There's a great little private room, too—very romantic—with views of a side street, and more sunny windows. The views from here, of course, are the best, and the manager often opens those windows in summer to get a nice cross-breeze going.

What to do? That's a drawback, unless you're into big old blocky stone buildings—then you'll love this neck of the woods. It's not too far to Old Montréal's public square, where street theater abounds, or to the waterfront and its big flea market and IMAX cinema. Chinatown, which in Montréal is just an alley or two, is just a short walk away and the best destination for cheap eats. Otherwise you'll need to hop Metro subway to see the best of Montréal. (If you're hungry in a pinch, the staff will sell you juice, tea, yogurt, coffee, and other basics. And coming soon: breakfast delivery each morning from a local bakery, for a small charge.)

Bathrooms are a bit short, it's true. And a twenty-bed bunkroom isn't nirvana to some folks, especially guys who get stuck there. (The small dorm is always reserved for women.) In addition, the manager was honest enough to report that a few smash-and-grab thefts from parked cars have taken place at night—so clean out those valuables when you unpack. And the wooden bunks seem to attract creepy crawling critters.

This is a fun joint, though, there's no denying it.

How to get there:

By bus: Bus lines stop in Montréal. From bus station, take Metro subway to Victoria Square stop. From station, walk south on Rue Square Victoria, which turns into Rue McGill in 6 blocks. Turn left on Rue Saint-Paul and walk 1 block to Rue St.-Pierre. Turn left up St.-Pierre; hostel entrance is around corner, on left. Enter door and walk upstairs to reception area.

By car: Call hostel for directions.

By plane: Two large airports in Montréal. Call hostel for transit route.

By train: VIA Rail stops in Montréal. From train station, take Metro subway to Victoria Square stop. From station, walk south on Rue Square Victoria, which turns into Rue McGill in 6 blocks. Turn left on Rue Saint-Paul and walk 1 block to Rue St.-Pierre. Turn left up St.-Pierre; hostel entrance is around corner, on left. Enter door and walk upstairs to reception area.

AUBERGE CHEZ JEAN (THE HOSTEL AT JEAN'S PLACE)

4136 Rue Henri-Julien, Montréal, Québec H2W 2K3

(514) 843–8279

Rates: $17 Canadian (about $12 U.S.) per person
Credit cards: None
Office hours: Vary; call

Season: Varies; call
Beds: Number varies; call
Private/family rooms: Yes; call for availability
Single rooms: Yes; number varies; call for availability
Private bathrooms: None
Affiliation: None
Extras: Jacuzzi, TV, VCR, breakfast, triple bed, cat, laundry

A little bit of San Francisco in the middle of Montréal? You've found it at Chez Jean, an improbable and funky little place tucked on a side street in the heart of an interesting city's most interesting neighborhood.

Jean himself seems like enough of a character that he ought to have a hostel named after him. He first started the hostel, he says, about ten years ago, when a tenant in the ground floor of his town house started coming up short on the rent. It's not clear whether Jean gave him the boot (seems unlikely) or started charging less, but it was the seed for his conversion of the house into a full-time crash pad.

And what a pad it is. There is a serious Haight-Ashbury feel going on here: mattresses splayed out on the floor for crashers-in-the-know, spiral outdoor metal staircases winding God-knows-where, a very laid-back crowd of mostly French revelers. The ageless Jean roars up on a motorcycle. Showers, kitchenettes, and patios appear and disappear like something out of an Escher print; you step out onto a terrace on the top floor and catch a great view of Montréal's famous mountaintop cross.

You never know what will happen next around here, but the mood stays incredibly convivial. There's even a really nice Jacuzzi. Don't miss the unique-for-a-hostel triple bed, either: Snuggle up with two really good friends (or cute strangers).

Best bet for a bite:
Schwartz's

What hostellers say:
"Cool, man."

Insiders' tip:
Triple bed

Gestalt:
Van go!

Safety: B

Hospitality: A

Cleanliness: C

Party index:

Hungry? You'll never go without in this neighborhood. There must be as many restaurants (and kinds of restaurants) within 10 blocks of Jean's as there are in any comparable city neighborhood in North America. Try anything. Thrift shops are everywhere on Boulevard Saint-Laurent and other major streets, too, making quick image makeovers a snap.

To top it all off, the ageless Jean and his young staff are all super-friendly, and they give excellent advice about where to eat, dance, hike, and so forth. The owner has a soft spot for the bedless, too—in overflow situations, he offers up two vans and the rooftop as emergency sleep sites! He's been known to rent one of the vans, too, for tooling around the city, and he even publishes a newsletter so that hostellers can keep in touch with friends.

Jean is a trusting guy, and you're sleeping on his floor, so you'll want to treat him with courtesy in return. Don't come banging on the door at 3:00 A.M. Also, if you're bothered by a lack of privacy, this definitely isn't the place for you; in midsummer, there are people hanging out all over the place, and sheets serve as room dividers in extreme cases. This is probably not the place to put up Mom and Dad when they're visiting for the weekend.

But if you can hang loose with the best of 'em, then this is your Montréal mecca.

How to get there:

By bus: Bus lines stop downtown. From terminal, take Metro subway to Mont-Royal stop. Walk down Rue Mont-Royal to Henri-Julien; turn left and walk 1 block to Rachel. Cross Rachel and continue 50 yards down Henri-Julien. Hostel is on right, upstairs, at #4136.

By car: Call hostel for directions.

By plane: Two large airports in Montréal. Call hostel for transit route.

By train: VIA Rail and Amtrak stop downtown. From train station, take Metro subway to Mont-Royal stop. Walk down Rue Mont-Royal to Henri-Julien; turn left and walk 1 block to Rachel. Cross Rachel and continue 50 yards down Henri-Julien. Hostel is on right, upstairs, at #4136.

AUBERGE DE MONTRÉAL (MONTRÉAL HOSTEL)

1030 Mackay Street, Montréal, Québec H3G 2H1

(800) 663–3317; (514) 843–3317

E-mail: info@hostellingmontreal.com

Web site: www.hostellingmontreal.com

Rates: $18 Canadian (about $12 U.S.) per Hostelling International member
Credit cards: MC, VISA, AMEX, DINER'S CLUB
Office hours: 24 hours
Beds: 243
Private/family rooms: 12
Single rooms: None
Private bathrooms: 12
Affiliation: Hostelling International-Canada
Extras: Lockers, laundry, cafe, TV, games, tours, kitchen, Internet access

Auberge de Montréal
Montréal
(photo courtesy HI-Canada)

As hostels in big cities go, it just doesn't get much better than this. Montréal's Hostelling International hostel, which bills itself as "the real one," manages to cram several hundred bodies into a smallish-looking hostel on the corner of an afterthought of a street—and to keep things running smoothly—while offering enough amenities to make even grizzled hostel-vets weep with joy.

The hostel recently moved from another (much better) location, in order to handle the crush of summer visitors. It is staffed with an unfailingly courteous, helpful, and firm staff who keep the masses in line while doling out great advice. Bunkrooms are clean, if somewhat packed; at least each dorm room has its own bathroom. The common rooms stay active with story-swapping travelers. As befits the French-Canadians, who take their food very seriously, the kitchen's also good-sized—and management has even opened a cafe, serving everything from croissants in the morning to local brew and sandwiches later on in the day.

What else? How about a nice little laundromat, daily free tours of the city, events like rafting trips and pub crawls? It's clean. It's fun. What else do you want?

We could find just a few things to complain about: mainly, the location. As Montréal neighborhoods go, the hostel's neighborhood

Best bet for a bite:
Ben's on Metcalfe

What hostellers say:
"Efficient and well run."

Insiders' tip:
Rooftop pool bar nearby

Gestalt:
French bliss

Safety: A

Hospitality: A

Cleanliness: A

Party index:

is a good news/bad news situation—very close to the largest museum, the Canadiens' new hockey rink, the overly touristy Old Port, and scads of university students at McGill and Concordia. That's good, we suppose.

But as for that university food, well, forget about it. You're stranded in an urban wasteland of lame pubs and through-the-roof bistros and fast food. Ask about how to get to the covered marketplace a few blocks away, and buy some fruit and bread. Or take the Metro subway to the really interesting Boulevard Saint-Laurent district, where the food's better and cheaper, and feast away.

Other possible diversions include Underground Montréal, the city's cavernous mall-née-subway system, and a nearby hotel (we'll let you discover its location) where, if you buy a drink at the bar, you get free access to a rooftop pool—perfect for those steamy summer days.

How to get there:

By bus: Bus lines stop downtown. From station, take Metro subway to Lucien L'Allier stop. Walk to Overdale; hostel is at corner of Overdale and Mackay.

By car: Drive Route 15 to Route 10; cross Cartier Bridge and exit onto University Street, then go left onto René-Lévesque. Drive several blocks and make a left onto Mackay; hostel is at corner of Mackay and Overdale.

By plane: Two large airports in Montréal. Call hostel for transit details.

By train: VIA Rail stops in Montréal. From station, walk south to René-Lévesque, then turn right and walk down René-Lévesque to Mackay. Make a left at Mackay; hostel is at corner of Mackay and Overdale.

GÎTE DU PARC LAFONTAINE (LAFONTAINE PARK HOSTEL)

1250 Sherbrooke Est, Montréal, Québec H2L 1M1,
and 185 Sherbrooke
(514) 522-3910

Rates: $19 Canadian ($13 U.S.) per person; private rooms $45–$55 ($32–$39 U.S.)
Credit cards: None
Office hours: Vary
Season: Summer only
Beds: 33
Private/family rooms: 3
Single rooms: None
Private bathrooms: 3
Affiliation: None
Extras: Continental breakfast, laundry, tours

10% $

You might find it a bit odd at first that this summers-only hostel—a rambling house on a very busy downtown street—is positioned right next to Montréal's biggest public library. But fear not: This isn't really a place for bookworms. Instead, the city's best hostel offers a homey place to kick back and learn about the city from the inside out.

First things first: This is a family affair. Manager Carl Gagné—who roamed the world as a hosteller before returning to his native French Canada—runs the hostel with his sister and mother, and it really does feel like a home around here. There's a light continental breakfast of toast and good jellies. Everyone at the hostel is unfailingly courteous and helpful—and you might pick up some French, too, as it's the primary language used around the house.

The family has obviously put a lot of work into upgrading this place. Private rooms in particular are well appointed, washed in pastel shades of peach or lime (or wilder), and done up in great furniture and linens. There are bathrooms aplenty, and each room—bunk or private—comes with a sink for washing your face and brushing your teeth.

Best bet for a bite:
rue Ontario

What hostellers say:
"Trés bien!"

Insiders' tip:
Fireworks fest in summer

Gestalt:
Parc centrale

Safety: A

Hospitality: A

Cleanliness: A

Party index:

The small hostel kitchen is nicely done, and we applaud the fact that you can use it only between 5:00 and 8:00 P.M. (There's so much to see and eat around here that nobody uses it anyway.) The lights even go out at 23.00 (that's 11:00 P.M. to you and me, Yank), but you can still sneak back in later with your key. Just don't try to use the common room at that hour.

Outside the doors, you've got Lafontaine Parc across the street to see first. Something's going on there every night in the summer.

From Carl's back terrace you can view Montréal's annual fireworks festival (it lasts for weeks, and it's spectacular). Or trundle up to Rue Saint-Dénis for fashionable grub or nearby Rue Ontario for a grittier, multiethnic urban experience. Still hungry? A little open-air produce market opens its doors every day just a few blocks away, at the corner of Ontario and Amherst.

News flash: these folks recently added a nice second building to the hostel complex, closer to town and equally nice. This town house features more good dorms, a location near popular Prince-Arthur Street (a pedestrian walkway where you bring your own wine to the restaurants), and even a kitchenette unit for groups or couples.

How to get there:

By bus: Bus lines stop in downtown Montréal. From bus station, walk north on Berri to Ontario; turn right onto Ontario and walk to Beaudry. Turn left and walk 1 block uphill to corner of Sherbrooke. Hostel is at corner, on right.

By car: Take Route 10 across Jacques Cartier Bridge into Montréal. Route 10 becomes University Street; proceed north to Sherbrooke, turn right, and drive east just past library. Hostel is at corner of Bleury, across from large park.

By plane: Two large airports in Montréal. Take shuttle from Dorval ($9.60 Canadian; about $7.00 U.S.) with hostel voucher—or Mirabel ($14.50 Canadian; about $10.00 U.S.) to hostel door.

By train: VIA Rail and Amtrak stop downtown. From train station, take Metro subway to Sherbrooke stop; walk down Berri to Sherbrooke Street, cross street and go east to corner of Beaudry.

HÔTEL DE PARIS HOSTEL 

901 Sherbrooke Street East, Montréal, Québec H2L 1L3

(800) 567–7217; (514) 522–6861

Rates: $18 Canadian (about $12 U.S.) per person; $75 ($53 U.S.) for a private room
Credit cards: AMEX, MC, VISA
Office hours: 24 hours
Beds: 61
Private/family rooms: Available at hotel
Single rooms: None
Private bathrooms: None
Affiliation: None
Extras: TV, laundry, restaurant, lockers

There are times when you mind staying in a small hostel, and then there are times when it really isn't so bad. The Hôtel de Paris

Hostel, set on a busy main thoroughfare of Montréal, is a good example of the latter.

The hostel quarters are divvied up between two buildings. One set of dormitories lies across busy Sherbrooke Street, and the other resides in the sleek and swanky Hotel de Paris on the other side. Both are in the basement. You may have as few as three other roommates, or you may get packed in with as many as fourteen others.

Best bet for a bite:
Marché St. Jacques

Insiders' tip:
Square St. Louis

What hostellers say:
"Take me to your bars."

Gestalt:
Les bon temps

Safety: A

Hospitality: B

Cleanliness: B

Party Index:

The newer digs in the hotel also have their own common room and kitchen; but, since there's a bistro on site, you might want to check out the discounted Backpacker's Special supper and the really cheap breakfasts.

Plans are also in the works to design a terrace for the annex, which could help loosen up shy hostellers. Nightlife abounds in the Latin Quarter of Rue-St.-Dénis, just a hop away, and Rue Ontario is nurturing its own bohemian scene down the hill. Book lovers can also amble a couple of blocks over to Montréal's main library.

Not all is perfect here. Renovations are taking time, they charge for parking and lockers, and the owner is legendary for his efforts to attract the backpacker set. (Rumor has it that he once hired a couple of people to patrol the bus and train station areas of the city, looking for telltale backpacks! Once they spotted one, it's said, they homed in like buzzards on fresh roadkill.)

KEY TO ICONS

 Attractive natural setting

 Romantic private rooms

 Good for business travelers

 Ecologically aware hostel

 Comfortable beds

 Especially well suited for families

 Superior kitchen facilities or cafe

 Among our very favorite hostels

 Good for active travelers

 Offbeat or eccentric place

 A particularly good value

 Visual arts at hostel or nearby

 Superior bathroom facilities

 Wheelchair-accessible

 Music at hostel or nearby

Still, this hostel is clean and comfortable—if somewhat cramped at times—and, as such, is a decent and inexpensive option.

How to get there:

By bus: Bus lines stop downtown. From bus station, take subway orange line to Sherbrooke station; walk east on Sherbrooke to corner of St.-André. Hostel is on left.

By car: Call hostel for directions.

By plane: From either airport, take shuttle bus to bus terminal; walk north up Beri or St.-Hubert to Sherbrooke; turn right, walk to corner of St.-André. Hostel is on left.

By train: VIA Rail stops downtown. From train station, take subway orange line to Sherbrooke station; walk east on Sherbrooke to corner of St.-André. Hostel is on left.

VACANCES DE QUARTRE SAISONS (FOUR SEASONS VACATION HOSTEL)

5155 Rue de Gaspé, Montréal, Québec H2T 2A1

(514) 270–4459

Rates: $11.50–$12.50 Canadian (about $8.00 U.S.) per person
Credit cards: MC, VISA
Office hours: 8:00 A.M.–midnight
Beds: 550 (summer); 250 (winter)
Private/family rooms: Yes; number varies; call for availability
Single rooms: None
Private bathrooms: Yes; number varies; call for availability
Affiliation: None
Extras: Basketball court, cafeteria, off-street parking

There are some good reasons to try out this quite basic hostel: location, parking, and breakfast, for starters.

You want location? You got it. What a neighborhood—dozens of different ethnic restaurants in the surrounding blocks, everything from bagels and natural-foods stores to Russian, Ethiopian, Slovakian, Hungarian, Portuguese . . . whew. You get the idea. This is an astonishing neighborhood in which to walk around and do what Montréalers do best: Eat. Parking's free, in a lot right at the door (no small matter in a big city). And the managers start off each day right by offering inexpensive, filling breakfasts.

As a bonus, most bunkrooms come with their own bathroom. That's a very nice surprise in a place where you'll often have three roommates. (The hostel maintains eighteen bigger bunkrooms holding seven travelers apiece, however, if you really like that sensation. Rooms that size would be great for groups.) There aren't, officially, any private rooms here—but if the hostel isn't too full, the managers will gladly section off a two- or four-bunk room for you and your *chéri*. Further amuse yourself by decoding the multilingual graffiti that the young ones etch onto the walls each school session.

An overflow annex of the hostel, up the street, offers more of a chance to sample the local color; here, the bathroom facilities and general condition of the place just aren't as nice. But it's still okay in a pinch.

Best bet for a bite: Latina on St. Viateur

Insiders' tip: Mile-End neighborhood

Gestalt: Kids in the hall

Safety: B

Hospitality: A

Cleanliness: B

Party index:

How to get there:

By bus: Bus lines stop downtown. From terminal, take Metro subway to Laurier stop; call hostel for directions.

By car: Call hostel for directions.

By plane: Two large airports in Montréal. Call hostel for transit route.

By train: VIA Rail and Amtrak stop downtown. From train station, take Metro subway to Laurier stop; call hostel for directions.

AUBERGE LES VAGUES NR (HOSTEL OF THE WAVES)

84 Rue Cloutier, Mont St.-Pierre, Québec G0E 1V0

(418) 797–2851

Rates: $14–$17 Canadian (about $11 U.S.) per person; semi-private rooms $25 (about $17 U.S.); private rooms $25–$38 ($18–$27 U.S.)
Credit cards: MC, VISA
Office hours: 6:30 A.M.–3:00 P.M. (summer); 8:00 A.M.–10:00 P.M. (winter)
Beds: 90
Private/family rooms: 9
Single rooms: Yes; number varies; call for availability
Private bathrooms: 9
Affiliation: None
Extras: Laundry, restaurant, bar, pool table

This old three-story motel—which partly functions as one during the summer—sits in little Mont St.-Pierre, a village on the St. Lawrence River. The village's major feature is a 400-meter-high (1,200-foot) sea cliff of the same name. What we're saying is this: You'll know when you've gotten there!

It's essential to reserve a bed in the summer at this place, because the motel business sucks up most of the beds, and you could get shut out if you just show up. But in the off-season, the hotel has lots of comfy double rooms for hostellers. Affable hostel owner Dénis Fortier is also working on a new annex called the "little house" *(la petite maison)*, which has eight rooms of its own, a living room, and a much-coveted kitchen—possibly the place of choice, if it's available and construction isn't going on.

Best bet for a bite: Marché Cloutier for groceries

What hostellers say: "To the beach!"

Gestalt: Roll your own

Hospitality: A

Party index:

That's important to note, because a kitchen isn't available for the main hostel in the summer (it's used by the management to cook meals for motel and hostel guests). On the up side, the place serves supper each and every night for $12.00 to $13.00 Canadian (about $9.00 U.S.), usually featuring the local catch. But if you're not up to shelling out those kind of bucks, it's off to the local supermarket for some prepared foods.

Fortier says there's plenty of activity happening in this sleepy area—and there must be, because, curiously enough, the hostel office stays open until 3:00 A.M. in summertime. We can't imagine what one does at that hour in Mont St.-Pierre. During the day, though, you might try anything from hiking to the top of that cliff to hang gliding off it. (Hey, lots of others have done it.) Or go roll a few frames at the little bowling alley in town. You can rent gear galore in the village, too, from bikes to canoes to kayaks, and two docks provide fishing possibilities as well.

KEY TO ICONS

 Attractive natural setting

 Romantic private rooms

 Good for business travelers

 Ecologically aware hostel

 Comfortable beds

 Especially well suited for families

 Superior kitchen facilities or cafe

 Among our very favorite hostels

 Good for active travelers

 Offbeat or eccentric place

 A particularly good value

 Visual arts at hostel or nearby

 Superior bathroom facilities

 Wheelchair-accessible

 Music at hostel or nearby

It's only 25 km (15 mi.) to spectacular Gaspésie Park, a great place to hike. Unfortunately, the park is closed in winter—it would be great snowshoeing and backcountry skiing territory, too. But fear not. Fortier is developing a small backcountry ski mountain in the area for next winter; plans call for seven slopes and 550-meter (1,650-foot) vertical drop, plus a twenty-five-passenger lift. Check with the hostel for updates.

Of course, some visitors don't want all this action. They just want to hang out on the hostel terrace or lie on the great little beach. And that's fine with us, too.

How to get there:

By bus: Call hostel for transit route.

By car: From Québec City, drive south *(sud)* across river and take Route 20 east *(est)* approximately 200 km (125 mi.) to end. Switch to Route 132 and continue east *(est)* another 340 km (210 mi.) to village of Mont.-St.-Pierre. Look for building with terrace downtown, on right.

By plane: Airport in Québec City. From Québec City, call hostel for transit route.

By train: VIA Rail stops in Québec City. From Québec City, call hostel for transit route.

AUBERGE INTERNATIONAL DU MONT-TREMBLANT

2213 chemin Principal, CP 1001, Mont-Tremblant, Québec JOT 1Z0

(819) 425-6008

Fax: (819) 425-3760

E-mail: tremblant@hostellingmontreal.com

Rates: $16.50 Canadian (about $11.00 U.S.) per Hostelling International member, private rooms $53.00 Canadian (about $35.00 U.S.)

Credit cards: AMEX, MC, VISA

Office hours: 8:00 A.M.–1:00 P.M.

Beds: 80

Private/ family rooms: Yes

Affiliation: Hostelling International-Canada

Extras: Kitchen, pub, pool tables, volleyball, lockers, laundry

One of Canada's newest hostels, but already one of its best, this place is way up in the Laurentian Mountains of Québec province—a place reserved, until now, for the super-rich, largely American tourists who came here to ski and whip out their platinum credit cards.

Auberge International du Mont-Tremblant
Mont-Tremblant
(photo courtesy HI-Canada)

Now hostellers can enjoy the views, too. This three-story place, resembling a barn, has got it all—everything from a kitchen and a laundry to great private rooms and an English-style pub. Plus it's mighty close to all the ski lifts and bike paths. Staff is decent and attuned to any outdoorsy needs you might have. Other extras include a game room with pool tables, lockers, and a volleyball net. Plus they run a shuttle daily from the Hostelling International hostel in downtown Montréal, making arrival a snap if you wake up early enough.

What hostellers say: "Ain't no mountain high enough . . ."

Gestalt: Mountain magic

Hospitality: A

Cleanliness: A

Party index:

Just remember that winter is even busier here than summer, which is itself quite busy. Try to book ahead if you can.

How to get there:

By bus: From Montréal, shuttle bus runs daily from Auberge de Montréal hostel at 9:00 P.M. Otherwise, call hostel for transit route.

By car: From Montréal, take Highway 145 north to Route 117, then take 117 north to junction with Route 327 north. Continue on 327 to village of Mont-Tremblant.

AUBERGE DE LA GRANDE FUGUE (GRAND FUGUE HOSTEL)

3165 Chemin du Parc, Orford, Québec J1X 3W3

(819) 843–8595

Fax: (819) 843–7274

E-mail: arts.orford@sympatico.ca

Web site: www3.sympatico.ca/arts.orford

Rates: $15.00 Canadian (about $12.00 U.S.) per Hostelling International member; single rooms $15.00–$22.50 Canadian ($10.00–$16.00 U.S.) per Hostelling International member; private rooms $30.00–$60.00 ($21.00–$42.00 U.S.)
Credit cards: MC, VISA
Office hours: 8:00–11:00 A.M., 4:00–11:00 P.M.; July–mid-August 8:00 A.M.–11:00 P.M.
Season: May 1–October 31
Beds: 240
Private/family rooms: Number varies; call for availability
Single rooms: 3
Private bathrooms: Number varies; call
Affiliation: Hostelling International-Canada
Extras: Cafeteria, laundry, free concerts, park passes, bicycle rentals, bar

This new hostel hit the ground running and already has generated a well-deserved buzz as one of Québec's very best. Its summertime pairing with a world-class music school from July to mid-August creates a harmonic duet, featuring soon-to-be famous performers working in a great natural setting.

Because it's ensconced in lovely woods beside a mountain and lakes—think Vermont with a French twist and much better food—you'll get the perfect summer-camp experience without grouchy counselors, mandatory naps, and homesickness. And you can catch free top-drawer classical music, too, if that happens to be your bag.

Staff coordinate bike rentals, hostellers, music-school arrivals, and concert-ticket sales and pull it all off with panache. Dorms are superb, the equivalent of hotel rooms—no room has more than three beds, so you won't get that sardine-can feeling, and some even have balconies and private bathrooms!

Let's not forget to mention the meals, either. Since this is first and foremost a school, the hostel gets the use of a professional chef during midsummer. However, budget-minders can also prepare their purchases from supermarkets in Magog in a serviceable kitchen. There's a classy, artfully designed bar, too, in summer: a nice place to strike up some conversations with the music folks.

If you come when the music school is in session (July to mid-August), you'll quite possibly get put in one of seventeen rustic cabins scattered in the woods. These are extremely private and romantic, excellent for nature-lovers—but they're also quite simple. There's no running water or heat, a minimum of furniture, and the camp-style group bathroom could seem like quite a hike at 4:00 A.M.

Best bet for a bite: In-house cafeteria

What hostellers say: "Yo-Yo Ma!"

Insiders' tip: Free classical music (in season)

Gestalt: Family fugue

Hospitality: A

Cleanliness: A

Party index:

Québecois families are most likely to use this hostel as a weekend getaway from the hard crank of Montréal, though we have a feeling that Americans will soon discover the place, too. Those Québeckers, by the way, must be just about the most active people on the planet. We watched, open-jawed, the buzz of physical activities here and at nearby Lac Memphremagog. Hundreds of bicyclists, rollerbladers, and walkers of all ages whizzed by, just happy to be alive on a sunny day.

Hike or bike Mount Orford—park passes are available at the desk for a $20 deposit, and you can almost always rent a bicycle. Too tired? Loll around the hostel pond, or swim in one of a fistful of local lakes. Too keyed-up? All right, then tap on one of the pianos scattered around the place. Hungry for culture? The bigger nearby town of Magog thrums in summer with tourists, arts, and restaurants.

This world-class hostel delivers superior eats, soothing music, comfy beds, and careful staff in a tranquil setting—for a fraction of the cost of pricey hotels in this pretty little corner of rural Québec. So what are you waiting for? Go!

Oh, it's full of musicians on a midsummer weekend? Then ring up nearby Auberge de la Grande Ligne (see Racine, Québec, p. 95)—a different experience, no less wonderful.

How to get there:

By bus: Sherbus lines stop in Magog; take Mount Orford Park shuttle bus ($2.00 Canadian/about $1.50 U.S.) and ask for drop-off at Center for the Arts. (This bus runs only in July and on weekends in August.) Or take a cab ($12.00 Canadian/about $8.00 U.S.) to hostel.

By car: From Montréal, drive Route 10 east *(est)* toward Sherbrooke for 118 km (70 mi.) and take exit 118. Follow route 141 north *(nord)* approximately 4 km (3 mi.) to Mount Orford Park. Bear right at hostel sign; at driveway, bear right and drive behind buildings. Hostel office is in large circular building. From Québec City, drive south across river and then take Route 20 west *(ouest)* approximately 150 km (90 mi.) toward Montréal. Take Route 55 (Drummondville) exit and drive south *(sud)* on Route 55 approximately 70 km (45 mi.) to junction of Route 10. Go west *(ouest)* on Route 10 toward Montréal for 25 km (15 mi.) and take exit 118. Follow route 141 north *(nord)* 4 km (3 mi.) to Mount Orford Park. Bear right at hostel sign; at driveway, bear right and drive behind buildings. Hostel office is in large concrete circular building.

By train: VIA Rail stops in Drummondville, approximately 100 km (60 mi.) away. Call hostel for directions.

AUBERGE DU CHATEAU BAHIA 

152 Boulevard Perron, Pointe-à-la-Garde, Québec G0C 2M0

(418) 788–2048

Rates: $19 Canadian (about $13 U.S.) per Hostelling International member; private rooms $28–$39 Canadian (about $20–$27 U.S.)
Credit cards: MC, VISA
Office hours: 7:00 A.M.–10:00 P.M.
Beds: 48
Private/family rooms: 14
Single rooms: None
Private bathrooms: 10
Affiliation: Hostelling International-Canada
Extras: Laundry, dinner, breakfast, turrets, jousting (just kidding)

Now this is really something to behold: a castle beside a river with three towers and seven turrets, and it's not somewhere in Bavaria but right in Québec. The owner, Jean Roussy, worked with his father for ten years building this castle overlooking the St. Lawrence River, a dream he held onto and saw through to its eventual completion. Hostellers now can share this fantasy made real by making the long traverse to the Gaspésie region in search of these mythical digs, which come complete with turrets—and meals in a real medieval dining hall!

Accommodations at "le chateau" are actually spread throughout three buildings. The castle towers, which are the most popular (and most expensive) lodgings, are open only from May until November. The other two buildings, more conventional-style homes, stay open throughout the winter and the early spring and cost a bit less. All are nice.

Either way, hostellers are always relieved to learn that a great hot breakfast is included in their bed rate. This being Québec, that usually means fluffy wild-berry pancakes topped with the ultimate Canadian sweetener: local maple syrup. Yummm! Dinners can also be taken in that grand dining hall for an additional cost of $10.00 Canadian (about $7.00 U.S.) per person. As yet another wonderful little touch, an afternoon tea is poured daily outside on a terrace, where you can take in the swiftly flowing St. Lawrence River.

They really play up the medieval theme around here, so much so that—get ready for this—if you want to, you can even approach the castle on horseback by request! (We didn't find out whether it's kosher to try the Lady Godiva method, but who knows? Maybe no one has asked yet. Now don't say we never told you anything useful.)

Budding paleontologists—we know you're out there—will be exhilarated to learn that one of the world's most important fossil sites is nearby, at Parc de Miguasha. Head for the park, and you might even encounter a dig in process. If you didn't bring your digging tools, you can still swim from the banks of the St. Lawrence (during summer) or hoof it on the foot trails that run alongside the river.

This is one dream castle that everyone can afford.

Best bet for a bite: Right here

What hostellers say: "Wherefore art thou, washroom?"

Insiders' tip: Horseback arrival

Gestalt: Camelot

Hospitality: B

Cleanliness: A

Party index:

How to get there:

By bus: Call hostel for transit route.
By car: Call hostel for directions.

L'AUBERGE GITE L'ANTIQUE-COSTI NR (ANTICOSTI HOSTEL)

CP 112, Port Menier, Québec J0J 2Y0

(418) 535–0111

Rates: $15 Canadian (about $10 U.S.) per person; private rooms $30 Canadian (about $21 U.S.)
Credit cards: VISA
Office hours: Vary; call for hours
Beds: 15
Private/family rooms: 2
Single rooms: None
Private bathrooms: None
Affiliation: None
Extras: Restaurant, bar

This hostel, way, way off the beaten path on huge but barely known Anticosti Island, occupies the site of Port Menier's former bakery.

This wooden house is located in the island's only town, and yet the grounds are still so wild that "deer eat from your hand," says oil painter-owner-manager Dénis McCormack.

There's one bunkroom and a new suite of private rooms. Breakfast is available for $2.50 Canadian (about $2.00 U.S.), and lobster dinners—for $12.00 Canadian (about $9.00 U.S.)—are a hostel specialty. McCormack even raises the lobsters himself in big saltwater tanks. Not feeling flush? You can order pizza, cooked fresh in the kitchen's wood stove, for less money. (Take note, however, that McCormack doesn't allow hostellers to use the kitchen.)

Best bet for a bite: Where else but here?

Gestalt: Anti-dote

Hospitality: B

Party index:

What to do? Roads aren't good on the island, and seas are too rough to get a full tour of Anticosti Island. But McCormack will gladly run you around the quiet bay where Port Menier sits. Canoeing a nearby lake and mountain biking everywhere are popular, and you sure won't have much company. (Since the ferryboat stopped running to this remote island from Havre-St.-Pierre, things have gotten extremely quiet. In fact, the only ways to get here now are either to fly in with an outfitter—recommended—or to risk the mail boat!)

Birdwatching is also superb here. Raining too hard for all that? Take heart: The hostel has its own little private fossil museum.

How to get there:

By ferry: Boat sometimes runs from dock at Sept-Îles to Port Menier (eight-hour trip, $42 Canadian/$29 U.S. one way).

By plane: Small airport in Havre St.-Pierre. Take flight on Canadian Air Satellit or Regionaire ($65–$100 Canadian/about $45–$70 U.S. one way). From airport, take bus or call hostel.

AUBERGE DE LA PAIX (PEACE HOSTEL)

31 Rue Coulliard, Québec City, Québec G1R 3T4

(418) 694–0735

Rates: $19 Canadian (about $13 U.S.) per person; private rooms $19 (about $13 U.S.) per person
Credit cards: None
Office hours: 8:00–2:00 A.M.
Beds: 59
Private/family rooms: 3
Single rooms: None
Private bathrooms: None
Affiliation: None
Extras: Bicycle rentals, breakfast

The giant peace sign on the house lets you know you're here. This independent hostel offers a looser alternative to the Hostelling International joint in Québec City. It's a smaller, more intimate place to stay in the province's walled capital city.

Surprisingly, this one doesn't take advance reservations for its much-sought-after private rooms, only for (oddly enough) bunks. That's right. You and your sweetie might have to slug it out with the dorm-rats for a few nights while you wait for your name to be drawn from the waiting list. At least the dorm rooms sleep no more than eight to a room; some rooms accommodate as few as three.

There are a number of *salles de bains* (washrooms). Other perks included with your bed are a continental breakfast of cold cereal, toast, and juice to get your day off to a kick-start; a backyard for warm-weather social gatherings; and the allowance of sleeping bags in the dorms in lieu of those dreaded sleep sheets.

Best bet for a bite:
La Joyeuse Carotte

Insiders' tip:
Picnicking on the city walls

What hostellers say:
"You gotta keep it separated. . . ."

Gestalt:
Peace pop

Safety: A

Hospitality: D

Cleanliness: B

Party index:

If you happen to be a Québecker, we hear there's a lot of discourse on separatism floating in the air around here; you might find someone prying your political alliance out of you or lecturing you about the evils of America.

This place tends to draw a young and wheel-less crowd, and most take in everything the city has to offer at night. Lots of the city's downtown bars even seem to cater to hostellers by enticing them with drink and cover-charge discounts. These bars are only a stumble away and provide insight into the sparkly, vapid nightclub lifestyle.

You'll be able to absorb most of the touristy stuff in compact Québec City in about two days, so make sure you get out and explore the surrounding area. Rue St.-Jacques will hold your interest if you like ethnic restaurants, cool used-record shops, and spiffy groceries that sell maple products in a variety of forms. One of our favorite spots outside the city is the famous Montmorency Falls.

This city gives you a lot of bang for your buck any time of year, but especially during the much-heralded Winter Carnival each February—a kind of mellower, cold-weather version of Mardi Gras. It's not quite as wild but just as fun, what with ice carving and parties and lots of other stuff to fend off the cold mid-winter temperatures. Book well ahead if you're going: The event is a massive draw in eastern Canada.

How to get there:

By bus: Bus lines stop in Québec City. Call hostel for transit route.

By car: Call hostel for directions.

By plane: Airport in Québec City. Shuttle available ($8.00–$9.00 Canadian/about $6.00–$7.00 U.S.); call hostel for transit route.

By train: VIA Rail stops in Québec City. Hostel is five-minute walk away, on Rue Coulliard.

CENTRE INTERNATIONAL DE SÉJOUR DE QUÉBEC (QUÉBEC CITY INTERNATIONAL HOSTEL)

19 Rue Sainte-Ursule, Québec City, Québec G1R 4E1

(418) 694–0755

Fax: (418) 694–2278

E-mail: cisq@mail.org

Rates: $15.40 Canadian (about $10.00 U.S.) per Hostelling International member
Credit cards: AMEX, MC, VISA
Office hours: 24 hours
Beds: 245 (summer), 200 (winter)
Private/family rooms: 9
Single rooms: None
Private bathrooms: None
Affiliation: Hostelling International-Canada
Extras: Laundry, cafeteria, vending machines, TV, lockers, pool table

Québec City's big, dormlike hostel draws a young crowd and, as a result, it can get noisy. The level of noise depends on your luck of the draw. With 200 or so beds, you might be in a quiet, family-oriented wing—or land straight in Beer-Breath Central.

Rooms come in a variety of dorm and private configurations, including—get ready—one, two, three, eight, ten, and twelve beds. Whew. They're all just fine, though the walls here are paper-thin and tend to let sounds in. The unisex bathrooms are reasonably clean, too, and there's a spacious cafeteria we didn't get to try.

The dining room and kitchen, while well equipped, are simply too small for such a huge hostel. It isn't odd to find a half-dozen or more solitary students hanging out, reading dog-eared classics while simultaneously flouting both the no-smoking and no-drinking rules. Meanwhile, families with children dance around and between in a desperate attempt to cook dinner.

In spite of the hostel's high activity level, you won't need to spend much time there, because its surroundings are without compare. At your feet is one of North America's oldest cities (and its only walled city). You can actually sit on top of the old ramparts, eating and looking out on the gorgeous Saint Lawrence. And the hostel is perfectly situated, just steps from grocery stores, crepe shops, churches, pubs, a riverwalk, and lots of obligatory tourist stops.

Best bet for a bite:
Crêpe houses

Insiders' tip:
Picnic on the ramparts

Gestalt:
Oui will rock you

Safety: B

Hospitality: B

Cleanliness: B

Party index:

Québec's nightlife is happy and lively—the food and drink are as good as any in North America, so who can blame 'em?—and travelers take advantage. Hostel doors are supposed to close at 2:00 A.M.; but, since you can still get in afterward, it's safe to assume that people will be coming and going for a good part of the evening. Most of the crowd will have come from elsewhere in Canada, but there might also be fussy English families grousing about the noise. Surprisingly, not many Americans find their way here.

You won't need to worry about crime, but parking can be tricky. Try to grab a street spot near the hostel as early in the day as possible (you won't need your car). Or park in one of the bizarre private parking lots that look like Roman stadiums. Once ensconced, remember that the hostel staff run tons of activities: everything from the usual pub crawls (which are really fun here) to skiing, snowshoeing, dogsledding, and ice-climbing outings. Plenty to do, plenty of views, one great romantic destination.

KEY TO ICONS

 Attractive natural setting

 Ecologically aware hostel

 Superior kitchen facilities or cafe

 Offbeat or eccentric place

 Superior bathroom facilities

 Romantic private rooms

 Comfortable beds

 Among our very favorite hostels

 A particularly good value

 Wheelchair-accessible

 Good for business travelers

 Especially well suited for families

 Good for active travelers

 Visual arts at hostel or nearby

 Music at hostel or nearby

How to get there:

By bus: Bus lines stop in Québec City. From bus station, take #3 bus to corner of Dauphine and Saint-Ursule.

By car: Take Autoroute 73 to exit 9. Go right on Chemin Saint-Louis (which becomes Rue Grande-Allée) through walls into old city, then take second left onto Sainte-Ursule. Hostel is less than 1 block, on right.

By plane: Airport in Québec City; call hostel for transit route.

By train: VIA Rail stops in Québec City. From train station, take taxi to hostel.

AUBERGE DE LA GRANDE LIGNE (LA GRANDE LIGNE HOSTEL)

318 Chemin de la Grande Ligne, Racine, Québec J0E 1Y0

(514) 532–3177

Fax: (514) 532–4082

Rates: $15–$16 Canadian (about $10–$11 U.S.) per Hostelling International member; private rooms $36 Canadian ($27 U.S.)
Credit cards: None
Office hours: Vary; call for hours
Beds: 23
Private/family rooms: Yes; number varies; call for availability
Single rooms: Vary
Private bathrooms: None
Affiliation: Hostelling International-Canada
Extras: Laundry, breakfast, dinner, bicycle rentals, UFOlogy workshops

10%

Gilles Veilleux must love this hostel a lot, because he's taken exactly one vacation in the last twelve years of running it.

Veilleux, a gentle and youthful sort who hostelled some in his own youth, bought the house from a friend who built it from scratch. After surveying the place he decided it was perfect hostel material. Hostelling International-Canada agreed, and in 1982 Veilleux opened the place. Today he continues to provide an extremely friendly and laid-back experience for those seeking a simple place to read, meditate, or amble about the trails he has laid out on his eighty acres.

Not only are you likely to land a private room with a double bed and assorted furnishings, but (a tremendous bonus) breakfast is included in the price—and it's good, featuring homemade sourdough French toast with locally tapped maple syrup, say, or some other of Gilles' creations. You might also catch one of the on-site workshops—they run the gamut from the urbane (entomology) to the, well, far out (UFOlogy, parapsychology, and so forth)—and, if a group is present, Gilles cooks great exotic lunches and dinners.

Best bet for a bite: Brandy Creek pub, Valcourt

What hostellers say: "Great place to find balance."

Insiders' tip: Snowmobile museum

Gestalt: Starry, starry night

Hospitality: A

Cleanliness: A

Party index:

As befits a home built more than twenty years ago, a few of the fixtures aren't in perfect shape, and the water pressure's low. But those quibbles will become minor when you take in a fine sunset over the mountains from the back deck, gaze at the myriad of stars, or strap on snowshoes beside your host Gilles.

There's no lockout here, but you won't necessarily need to hang around. Like anywhere in the frozen-in-time Cantons de l'Est (that's what they call these quaint little towns), there's actually a surprising amount of things to do in the area if you root around a little. A crystal quartz mine is right around the corner, so rockhounds and New Agers alike won't want to miss that tour. You could pass a fine afternoon exploring little towns and villages like Valcourt, where the snowmobile was invented by a fellow named Bombadier.

Or ask Gilles for directions to two nearby trailheads and hike a section of the Sentier d'Estrie (Eastern Townships Trail), a regional walking trail that winds tens of kilometers through some of the nicer woods and fields in eastern Canada.

A superb place to bliss out.

How to get there:

By bus: Bus lines stop in Magog, Richmond, and Sherbrooke. Call hostel for pickup ($5.00–$10.00 Canadian/about $4.00–$8.00 U.S.).

By car: Call hostel for directions.

By train: VIA Rail stops in Drummondville, approximately 60 km (35 mi.) away. Call hostel for transit route.

AUBERGE INTERNATIONALE DE RIVIÈRE-DU-LOUPE (WOLF RIVER HOSTEL)

46 Hotel de Ville, Rivière-du-Loupe, Québec G5R 1L5

(418) 862–7566

Fax: (418) 862–1843

Rates: $16.50 Canadian (about $12.00 U.S.) per Hostelling International member; private rooms $39.90 Canadian (about $28.00 U.S.)

Credit cards: MC, VISA
Office hours: 10:00–2:00 A.M. (summer); 3:00 –11:00 P.M. (winter)
Beds: 65 (summer); 35 (winter)
Private/family rooms: Yes; number varies; call for availability
Single rooms: None
Private bathrooms: 1
Affiliation: Hostelling International-Canada
Extras: Laundry, breakfast, bicycle rentals, TV, VCR

10%

This hostel makes its home high on a cliff above the mighty St. Lawrence River in a two-story woodframe home, and it boasts a surprising number of private rooms (between three and eight, depending on the season). One room even comes with its own bathroom and is wheelchair-accessible, although it is available only from May 1 until the end of November. At that point the hostel adjusts its bed count to 35 for the winter and shuts this part of the operation down.

This hostel is big on serving food. Continental breakfast is always included in the price of a bed, thanks to the large contingents of Europeans here who go for the croissants and juice and disdain heavier, North American-type morning meals.

Supper, although not all-you-can-eat, is still filling, we hear—and for $7.00 Canadian (about $5.00 U.S.), you get soup, a main course, and dessert. Try beating that, Mickey D's. These folks are so accommodating that they'll even cheerfully fill vegetarian requests. As an added bonus, during the summer the hostel puts on a tasty traditional maple celebration called *cabane à sucre,* whereby you get a traditional meal such as pancakes or tourtière (Québecois meat pie) as well as maple toffee for dessert. Then again, sometimes there are outdoor barbecues. Moral of the story: Bring your appetite.

Best bet for a bite:
Where else but here?

What hostellers say:
"Mmm, mmm, good."

Insiders' tip:
Local lighthouse tours

Gestalt:
Howlin' wolf

Hospitality: A

Cleanliness: A

Party index:

If you have any energy left after all those filling and delicious meals, there's lots to do in this area, so listen up. The region north of Québec City—known as the Bas St. Laurent, by the way—is an excellent stopover as you hostel-hop among a number of good hostels in the area. You can observe the stunning Rivière-du-Loupe waterfalls, take a trip to Île Verte, or gaze at billions and billions of stars at the local observatory. Commune with the whales that hang out here every summer. Just *do* something, for gosh sakes. Here we go again: this is a great base, and the Québecois hospitality is at its legendary best.

How to get there:

By bus: Bus lines stop in Rivière du Loupe. Call hostel for directions.

By car: Call hostel for directions.

AUBERGE LE P'TIT BONHEUR (HAPPY LITTLE HOSTEL)

183 Cote Lafleur, St.-Jean, Québec G0A 3W0

(418) 829–2588

Fax: (418) 829–0900

Rates: $16 Canadian (about $11 U.S.) per person; private rooms $50 Canadian (about $35 U.S.)
Credit cards: None
Office hours: 7:00 A.M.–midnight
Beds: 40
Private/family rooms: 5
Single rooms: None
Private bathrooms: None
Affiliation: Hostelling International-Canada
Extras: Bicycle rentals, breakfast, dinner, laundry, dogsledding

We'll try to be brief here, because we just want you to know that this place is great—then we'll shut up so that you can hightail it to Île d'Orleans, a surprisingly quiet little island near Québec City.

The property includes woods, a big river, vegetable gardens, a potato field, and an apple orchard. Two buildings house the facilities. One, a 350-year-old house was built with big picture windows facing the mighty St. Lawrence. It contains two of the five private rooms and the quarters of the owners. The second, much newer, house has one more family room plus two dormitories—each one has eight beds—plus two smaller dorms and three family rooms. Both houses have two bathrooms apiece, helping to alleviate that morning crush.

But wait: There's more. The property has three tepees, one sleeping six hostellers and two more sleeping four apiece. All are heated.

And get this: There is a wigwam, too—popular with lots of groups in winter—that you take a ten-minute dogsled ride to reach. The hostel thoughtfully provides a guide to ensure that everyone staying here is safe and has installed a fireplace to keep you toasty-warm. Dogsledding tours are offered as well.

Supper is a real treat: Québecois ragout, tourtiere, yummy stuff like that. Mom cooks, everything comes from the house garden, and it's only $8.00 Canadian (about $6.00 U.S.)! There's a kitchen, too, but why bother cooking yourself? Breakfast is an option, too: The hostel gives you both a freebie if you've got a private room, but lone hostellers can pay $4.00 Canadian (about $3.00 U.S.) and get the same vast choice of croissants, muffins, fruit, English muffins, eggs, cereal, French toast, bacon, eggs—whatever you want! Mom'll fix it up for ya.

If you have the energy after all this eating, you sure ought to make a tour around Île d'Orleans—particularly if you like pastoral small towns, quiet orchards, boat building, and stone churches. Go at the end of summer, when you'll be able to sample much of the local harvest. Some tips from our experience here: The strawberries are huge, said to be the most delicious in Québec, and maple syrup and cheese are sold at the farm stands that dot the oval island.

The hostel also offers an interesting educational program. Nathalie, a Montaignais (Native Canadian) on staff, demonstrates native crafts such as authentic cookery, song, dance, and storytelling.

In sum, this is everything a hostel should be—personal, educational, fun, delicious. Go and be amazed.

Best bet for a bite:
Local farm stands

What hostellers say:
"Beautiful island."

Insiders' tip:
Cross-island backroad

Gestalt:
Strawberry fields forever

Hospitality: A

Cleanliness: A

Party index:

How to get there:

By bus: Bus lines stop in Québec City. Call hostel for pickup ($5.00 Canadian/$4.00 U.S.).

By car: Call hostel for directions.

By plane: Airport in Québec City. Call hostel for transit route.

By train: VIA Rail stops in Québec City. Call hostel for pickup ($5.00 Canadian/$4.00 U.S.).

CIRRUS HOSTEL 

206 Ruisseau des Frenes, Sainte-Agnes, Québec GOT 1R0

(418) 439–2949

Rates: $12.00 Canadian (about $9.00 U.S.) per person; private rooms $24.00 (about $18.00 U.S.)
Credit cards: None
Office hours: Vary; call
Season: Varies; call
Beds: 12
Private/family rooms: Sometimes; call for availability
Single rooms: None

Private bathrooms: None
Affiliation: None
Extras: Laundry, bicycle rentals, canoe rentals, tours

This tiny hostel is homey, which makes sense, because it's a home. Literally. The manager lives here (it's her house), and her daughter comes to help out in the summer. Doors are never locked. This gives the place a cozy, familial feel that is absent from the big hostels. On the other hand, it's quite basic, and the small size means that you can't bring twenty of your former college classmates with you on a memory-dredging fishing trip.

Best bet for a bite: BYO Food

Insiders' tip: Biking Île aux Coudres

Gestalt: Sainte Elsewhere

Hospitality: A

Cleanliness: A

Party index:

Oh, well. This hostel is a very well-kept secret—they don't promote it much at all—so you're likely to find room, we think. Once there, enjoy the friendly management and take advantage of the laundry to soap up.

The real story here is the Charlevoix region of Québec Province—the wild northern shore of the St. Lawrence River that stretches east and slightly north from the provincial capital of Québec City. It's a place of tiny villages and natural treats. Hiking opportunities abound, of course. Other folks prefer to canoe the rivers sliding off the mountains or head east for whale-watching tours.

Skiing and dogsledding expeditions are additional possibilities in wintertime, and the hostel staff like arranging guided rock-climbing tours of the area through a local club. That's not to mention the good swimming at a local beach and the cycling.

Otherwise, though, this place is about as quiet as it gets at a hostel—the town consists of a church, post office, and convenience store, and that's it. Need a bit more culture? A larger town called Clermont is located a few kilometers away and actually has a few restaurants. It's approximately 30 km (20 mi.) to the artists' haven of Baie-St.-Paul and its galleries. And it's 40 km (25 mi.) or so of driving—plus a quick free ferry ride—over to Île aux Coudres, an old-world island of hamlets that's absolutely ideal for biking. All the while, you're seeing that gorgeous Charlevoix scenery.

How to get there:

By bus: Bus line runs from Québec City to Sainte-Agnes three times daily. Ask driver to stop at Rousseau des Frenes, then walk uphill. Hostel is house #206.

By car: From Québec, drive Route 138 east *(est)* along the north shore of the St. Lawrence River. Go approximately 135 km (85 mi.)

east to Sainte-Agnes. Turn off main road onto Ruisseau des Frenes. Hostel is third house, #206.

AUBERGE INTERNATIONALE L'ÉCHOUERIE

295, 1er Avenue Est Sainte-Anne-des-Monts, Québec
G0E 2G0
(418) 763–1555
Fax: (418) 763–9229
E-mail: aujesadm@globetrotteur.net
Rates: $15 Canadian per HI member (about $10 U.S.)
Credit cards: MC, VISA
Office hours: 7:00–2:00 A.M.
Beds: 85
Private/family rooms: Yes
Affiliation: Hostelling International-Canada
Extras: kitchen

Summer and winter can both get quite busy at this new hostel, located right on the St. Lawrence River near terrific Gaspésie Park. The sprawling buildings contain eighty-five beds, including some private rooms, although there are few extra touches. A kitchen is one of them.

Some of the many recommended activities here include watching moose and caribou; sailing; snowshoeing; fishing; and cross-country skiing. The real bonus is a shuttle running between the hostel and the park, which saves you the trouble of legging or hitching it in.

Gestalt: Park place

Hospitality: A

Party index:

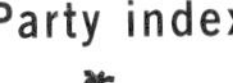

How to get there:

By bus: Call hostel for transit route.

By car: Take Route 132 north to intersection of Gaspésie Parc Road. At church, turn right on First (Premier/1er) Avenue. Continue 1.6 km (1 mi.) to hostel.

AUBERGE LE ROUPILLON DU CAPITAINE (CAPTAIN'S CATNAP HOSTEL)

147 Route du Fleuve, Sainte-Luce, Québec G0K 1P0
(418) 739–5152

Rates: $16.50 Canadian (about $12.00 U.S.) per Hostelling International member; private rooms $36.00 Canadian (about $27.00 U.S.) for Hostelling International members
Credit cards: None
Office hours: 7:00 A.M.–2:00 A.M.
Beds: 37
Private/family rooms: 3
Single rooms: None
Private bathrooms: None
Affiliation: Hostelling International-Canada
Extras: Laundry, breakfast, pickup, meals

This hostel opened in 1997, just in time to replace the hostel in nearby Rimouski that closed down operations the same year. Not much English is spoken here, but owners Marie-Claude Durette and Jean Landry and their staff do their level best to keep things rolling along. The building's a 125-year-old, three-story house; nearly all the beds are on the top two floors, and there are a laundry and cafeteria on the premises.

Best bet for a bite: Café du Moulin

Gestalt: Captain Crunch

Hospitality: A

Party index:

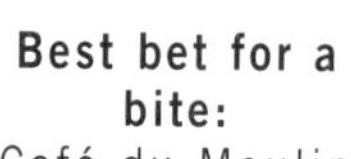

Sainte-Luce is a small village, old and beautiful, with a great beach and a little cafe. You might feel like you're in some undiscovered corner of the French Riviera, minus the beautiful people and the hot temperatures. OK, maybe that's going a bit far. But it's still a nice quiet place to pass the time.

Active sorts will want to get gear and kayak the river, or fish it. Culture vultures will make a beeline 20 km (12 mi.) east for Rimouski, which—though it certainly isn't Québec City—can offer more in the way of restaurants, nightlife, and the arts than little Sainte-Luce.

Oh, why the name? We couldn't find out. Just don't assume it means that this place is run by a briny sea captain or that the staff is usually asleep at the switch. Far from it.

How to get there:

By bus: Orleans bus line #64 runs from Montréal and Québec to Sainte-Luce. At bus stop, walk fifteen minutes west on main road to #147.

By car: From Québec, drive Route 20 north *(nord)* and east *(est)* until it ends and becomes Route 132, approximately 200 km (125 mi.). From that point, continue on Route 132 approximately 90 km (55 mi.) to Rimouski. Pass through town and drive 18 km (65 mi.) more until Route du Fleuve turnoff; make a left at sign for Sainte-Luce-sur-Mer. Hostel is on left, at #147.

By plane: Airports in Montréal and Québec City. From airports, Orleans bus line #64 runs from Montréal and Québec to Sainte-Luce. From bus stop, walk fifteen minutes west on main road to #147.

AUBERGE ÎLE-DU-REPOS DE PERIBONKA (RESTFUL ISLAND HOSTEL)

105 Route Île-du-Repos, Sainte-Monique-de-Honfleur, Québec G0W 2T0

(418) 347–5649

Fax: (418) 347–4810

Rates: $16 Canadian (about $12 U.S.) per Hostelling International member; private rooms $43–$52 Canadian (about $30–$36 U.S.)
Credit cards: VISA
Office hours: 10:00 A.M.–11:00 P.M.
Beds: 54
Private/family rooms: 12
Single rooms: None
Private bathrooms: 8
Affiliation: Hostelling International-Canada
Extras: Laundry, bar, lounge, meals, kitchen

If you took a brief glance at the map of Québec, you'd probably write off the area to the north of Québec City. From the look of it, the region doesn't have much going for it—remote, forested, desolate, lonely. Right?

Well, we'd have to correct you or tell you to go see for yourself. Life here is perhaps *more* interesting because of those factors; and, as such, the hostels compensate for the remoteness of the location by promoting a certain *joie de vivre.* This is demonstrated by their lively atmosphere, excellent food, and the peripheral programs that bring you into direct contact with local customs and traditions. Île-du-Repos is one such hostel—and the only one in Canada, so far as we know, that occupies a privately owned island.

Seven buildings make up the hostel on this lovely, forested island, which is accessible from the mainland by bridge. Six of those buildings contain the accommodations, just four rooms in each—a mix of shared and private rooms. The seventh building is where the magic happens. The self-catering kitchen is located here as well as the cafeteria and bar/performance space.

These folks really know how to put on a show. In the summertime professional Québecois and Francophones give outstanding

Best bet for a bite: Here, of course

What hostellers say: *"Trés bien!"*

Insiders' tip: All-day Sunday brunches

Gestalt: Miles from nowhere

Hospitality: A

Cleanliness: A

Party index:

musical, theatrical, and dance performances, mostly on weekend evenings. There's seating space for an audience of 140, and these performances are meant for everyone, not just the lucky-duck hostellers.

And that's not all. If you choose to *really* relax, you might not have to lift a finger at all for your meals: Three a day (breakfast, lunch, and dinner) are served during the summer. Again, the restaurant/bar is open to the public and has space for eighty gourmands. As befits the French eating experience, your meal will be embellished by the outdoor terrace. Jean François, the manager, claims that menus change so frequently that you can stay a week and never repeat the same meal twice. Dinner runs about $9.00 to $10.00 Canadian (about $7.00 U.S.) per person—but that includes soup, entrée, and dessert. Not bad, eh?

What is there to do up here in the North Woods? For starters, there's every manner of summertime outdoor activity—sea kayaking on vast Lac St.-Jean, which is a hop, skip, and jump from the hostel; hiking kilometers of trails; and, of course, swimming at a nearby beach. Winter opens a whole new set of possible pursuits, like sled-dog rides, cross-country skiing, and traversing the kilometers and kilometers of the snowy Trans-Québec snowmobile trail or *sentier de motoneige*.

This place, like all other hostels in this neck of the woods, is really, really popular (did we emphasize the word *really?)* in the summer with the French and other international types. Make sure you book way ahead, especially if you're in a group.

If you want to commune with nature, a campground has been set up. Even if you camp, you can still take advantage of all the other stuff the hostel has to offer. Just bring plenty of bug dope: The 'skeeters up here are legendary bloodsuckers.

All in all, a wonderful all-round experience in Québec's equivalent of the Outback.

How to get there:

By car: From Québec City, drive Route 73 (Autoroute Laurentienne) north *(nord)* until it becomes Route 175. Continue north approximately 120 km (75 mi.) and bear left onto Route 169. Continue north approximately 170 km (120 mi.) to Sainte-Monique-de-Honfleur. Cross over river; hostel is to left, on an island.

By train: VIA Rail stops in Jonquière. Call hostel for transit route.

AUBERGE INTERNATIONALE LE TANGON (TANGON INTERNATIONAL HOSTEL)

555 Cartier, Sept-Îles, Québec G4R 4L2

(418) 962–8180; (800) 461–8585

E-mail: TANGON@bbSI.net

Rates: $18 Canadian (about $13 U.S.) per Hostelling International member; single rooms $24 Canadian (about $17 U.S.); private rooms $36 Canadian (about $27 U.S.)
Credit cards: VISA
Office hours: 8:00–2:00 A.M. (summer); 8:00 A.M.–midnight (off-season)
Season: April 1–December 31
Beds: 46
Private/family rooms: 5
Single rooms: 1
Private bathrooms: None
Affiliation: Hostelling International-Canada
Extras: Laundry, meals, camping, storage

A former French trading post and a haven for Basque whalers in search of protection from the wild and wooly Atlantic, the town of Sept-Îles lies on the highly populated stretch of the northern shore of the St. Lawrence River, which winds east of Tadoussac and, eventually, widens into a bay. The town's name refers to seven nearby islands along the upper Saint Lawrence River. There's a hostel here, and it's some happening joint by the look of things.

Best bet for a bite: Theme nights

Gestalt: Seven Up

Party index:

Outdoors enthusiasts always seem to find their way to this hostel. Exploring the seven islands by kayak can be done via an outfitter in town who gives a 10 percent discount to hostellers. Or poke around the nearly circular bay that makes this area so ideal for shipping. Whales migrate here in the summertime, and visitors can watch for their large splashes via local boat tours. Binoculars would also enhance the great bird-watching at the National Fauna Reserve on Île-du-Corossol. And there's a good set of isolated beaches for those folks who want to do little more than while away several hours, basking in the sun.

Other land-bound activities include visiting a regional museum of the North Coast, buying native crafts at a local market, and attending the Native Canadian festival Innu Nikamu, which celebrates the culture of the local Innu people. The local boardwalk is the center of Sept-Îles' activity.

Like most of the other hostels north and east of Québec City, visitors here tend to be young French and Québecois on holiday. They especially enjoy the nights, when they can have a beer, play guitar, and indulge in weekly "theme night" meals. The hostel is famous for these nights, when a typical meal from a specified country is served. Usually the staff prepares the feast—it's $11.00 Canadian (about $8.00 U.S.) a pop—but on occasion a budding Pierre

Franey steps up to the plate (so to speak) and puts on a French spread.

Make reservations well in advance if you want the only private room that has a double bed, as it's in very high demand. Four other double rooms have two single bunks apiece but are also fine for privacy.

How to get there:

By bus: Voyageur bus line stops in Sept-Îles. From bus terminal, call hostel for walking directions, or take taxi ($5.00 Canadian, about $4.00 U.S.).

By car: From Québec City, drive Route 138 east *(est)* approximately 750 km (460 mi.) into downtown Sept-Îles. Go through intersection at Smith and take next right onto Regneault; then take eighth left onto Cartier. Hostel is on left, at #555.

AUBERGE DE JEUNE VOYAGEUR (YOUNG TRAVELER'S HOSTEL)

24 Montée des Cassandres, Stoneham, Québec GIA 4PI

(418) 848–7650

Fax: (418) 848–7650

Rates: $18–$35 Canadian (about $12–$24 U.S.) per person; doubles $50 Canadian (about $33 U.S.)
Credit cards: None
Office hours: 8:00 A.M.–11:00 P.M.
Beds: 11
Private/family rooms: Yes; number varies; call for availability
Single rooms: None
Private bathrooms: None
Affiliation: None
Extras: Laundry, fax, bicycles, meals (winter), dartboard, bike rentals

A newcomer to the hostel scene north of Québec City, this relatively small *auberge* promises to be as much fun as the others but without the commotion. Early reports are positive and business is on the increase.

A small, rustic home located right beside a provincial park—a sign of a giant trout marks its entrance—this hostel aims to please, with many amenities suited for its remote location. Meals are served in winter only with advance notice, and Brigitte, one of the managers, is happy to tailor meals according to hostellers' dietary preferences. Dinners with everything included set you back about $10.00 Canadian ($7.00 U.S.). Faxes can be sent and received at $1.00 to $2.00 Canadian (about $1.00 U.S.) per page here, depending on destination, an unusual (and nice) touch. Tea and coffee flow freely throughout the day *gratuit* (free).

The building's most unique feature is, perhaps, its mezzanine, from which you can look down onto the floor below. There is not one but two common rooms; each has a fireplace, and you can roll some dice while playing a board game, throw darts, or bury your nose in a book when you're not out taking in the scenery and fresh air. Two bicycles are for rent at $10.00 Canadian (about $7.00 U.S.) per day.

All three rooms are intimate, ideal for families or couples. One of the rooms, slightly less expensive, is considered the "dormitory." There is a bathroom within this room, and it also houses the laundry facilities, which are cheap, at $2.00 Canadian ($1.40 U.S.) per load. Also, linens require no initial deposit and are included in the fee for a night's stay.

There are two tiers of fees. *Avec service*—a few dollars extra—means that your bed is made up every day and you get a full breakfast of eggs and cereal. Basically, you're getting a bed-and-breakfast experience here, buckaroo. *Sans service* means that you'll stay in the dormitory and forage for your own breakfast.

Best bet for a bite: In-house or bust

What hostellers say: *"Donnez-moi des oeufs."*

Gestalt: Fished inn

Hospitality: A

Cleanliness: A

Party index:

There's scads of outdoorsy stuff to do. Trout fishing seems to be the major preoccupation, since this is (duh) Trout Park. Snowshoeing, sled-dog rides, skating, cross-country skiing, snowboarding, canoeing; yada yada yada. You get the picture.

The first summer season will be the true test of the success of this new hostel; the owners are already considering expansion if demand is high. Based on what we've heard and seen, it could be.

KEY TO ICONS

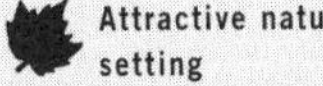

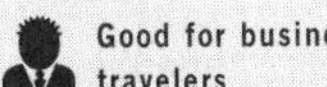

Ecologically aware hostel

Comfortable beds

Especially well suited for families

Superior kitchen facilities or cafe

Among our very favorite hostels

Good for active travelers

Offbeat or eccentric place

A particularly good value

Visual arts at hostel or nearby

Superior bathroom facilities

Wheelchair-accessible

Music at hostel or nearby

How to get there:

By bus: Bus lines stop in Québec City. Hostel offers free ride from bus station; call hostel for pickup.

By car: From Québec City, drive Route 73 (Autoroute Laurentienne) north *(nord)* approximately 15 km (10 mi.) until it becomes Route 175. Continue north approximately 25 km (15 mi.). Hostel is on left.

By plane: Small airport in Québec City. Hostel offers free ride from airport; call hostel for pickup.

By train: VIA Rail stops in Québec City. Hostel offers free ride from train station; call hostel for pickup.

MAISON ALEXIS

389 Des Pionniers, Tadoussac, Québec G0T 2A0

MAISON MAJORIQUE

158 Bateau Passeur, Tadoussac, Québec G0T 2A0

(418) 235–4372

Fax: (418) 235–4608

E-mail: ajt@fjord-best.com

Rates: $14 Canadian (about $10 U.S.) per person; private rooms $36 Canadian (about $27 U.S.)

Credit cards: MC, VISA

Office hours: 10:00 A.M.–11:00 P.M.

Beds: 97

Private/family rooms: 4

Single rooms: None

Private bathrooms: 2

Affiliation: Hostelling International-Canada

Extras: Laundry, breakfast, lunch, dinner, kayaks, canoes, Internet access

This hostel business stands as a testament to the enduring nature of man. See, the hostel owner once experienced a string of terrible misfortunes—love lost, an accident, you get the picture. Life was lookin' mighty gray. A lesser man might have crumbled, might have packed it in, but this guy took massive positive action instead and began letting out rooms in his home in the breathtakingly beautiful town of Tadoussac.

Since then he has built up an impressive little hostelling dynasty. You practically have to fight off the French with a stick in spring, summer, and fall. This is one rock-and-rollin' joint, legendary in France for its combination of bohemian partying and outstanding scenery.

It's two hostels, actually, if you count the quieter, summer-only Maison Alexis, which sits just a klick—that's a kilometer to a Canadian—away from the big house. But let's face the facts: The real draw here is the party-hearty ambience of the Maison Majorique. Tales of revelry here run the length and breadth of Canada (and France). So beware: If you're in need of sleep and reflection, the quieter Alexis will be a haven for your weary soul. If you want to party all night, go for Majorique in a flash.

Together the two hostels can accommodate around a hundred happy hostellers every night, not including the many tent sites in an adjacent, hostel-owned campground. Dorms vary in size—no more than ten and as few as four beds.

Best bet for a bite:
Right here, right now

What hostellers say:
"Oh, it's a scene, man."

Insiders' tip:
Old Catholic mission nearby

Gestalt:
Tadoushack

Hospitality: A *(Both)*

Cleanliness:
B *(Alexis);*
C *(Majorique)*

Party index:
(Alexis)

(Majorique)

As follows suit with other hostels of this region, sumptuous, filling meals are served that showcase the culinary skill of the rotating staff. Lunch for $5.00 Canadian (about $4.00 U.S.) is an outstanding deal—three courses, starting with soup and ending with dessert. After eating dozens of so-called breakfasts of weak coffee and stale doughnuts on the road, hostellers will go nuts here at the prospect of noshing on mounds of pancakes or eggs for $3.50 Canadian (about $3.00 U.S.). Sometimes a local Native Canadian hunter will even supply food like caribou, seal, and the ubiquitous beaver for a $7.00 Canadian (about $5.00 U.S.) native-style dinner.

As far as we're concerned, though, the real fun begins once you get outdoors. In case you haven't heard, Tadoussac is located right at the confluence of the mighty St. Lawrence River and its feeder river, the Saguenay. This confluence is internationally famous for the rare white beluga whales—as well as the more traditionally colored finback, blue—that congregate here in summertime to feed. The huge natural sand dunes along the riverbanks are popular for sunning as well; some folks like to ski down them in the summer, but that practice damages the dunes and might be outlawed soon.

Whatever you wanna do, the hostel staff is happy to accompany guests on these and other outdoor excursions. Did we mention kayaking along the Saguenay fjord or setting out on a boat in search of those whales? Like, call me Ishmael, dude. If it's possible, the list of outdoor activities grows in the winter—dogsledding, snowshoeing, and cross-country skiing lead the pack.

Bookworms and traveling spies will want to take note of a new Internet service in the hostel: You can cruise the Net for just pennies (actually, $4.00 Canadian; about $3.00 U.S.) per hour.

Finally, lest we've scared you off, we'd be remiss if we didn't point out that the Majorique hostel doesn't rage too too hard; after all, it sits next door to the police station. Of the men in blue, the hostel staff report that "They're cool, man."

That pretty much describes this place. Cool. Just remember that it gets super-tight on space in the summer, so the staff recommend at least a three-day notice in advance of your arrival. Go and be amazed.

How to get there:

By bus: Bus lines stop in Tadoussac. From station, walk about 1 km (0.6 mi.) to Maison Majorique for check-in at either hostel.

By car: Go to Maison Majorique for check-in at either hostel. From Québec City, drive Route 138 northeast *(nord-est)* approximately 210 km (130 mi.) to Baie-Ste.-Catherine. Take free ferry across river. Drive up hill into town; hostel is on first corner, next door to police station.

AUBERGE INTERNATIONALE LA FLOTTILLE (FLEET INTERNATIONAL HOSTEL)

497 Rue Radisson, Trois-Rivières, Québec G9A 2C7

(819) 378–8010

Fax: (819) 378–4334

E-mail: flottille.cagm@cgocable.ca

Rates: $16 Canadian (about $11 U.S.) per person; private rooms $30–$36 Canadian (about $21–$26 U.S.)
Credit cards: VISA
Office hours: 8:00 A.M.–11:00 P.M.
Beds: 45
Private/family rooms: 3
Single rooms: None
Private bathrooms: 1
Affiliation: Hostelling International-Canada
Extras: Laundry, breakfast, Internet access, bicycle rentals

10% $

Trois-Rivières' hostel is set right in the middle of the action. Literally. The town itself is conveniently positioned halfway between Montréal and Québec City, and the hostel follows suit with a position right in the center of town. This location certainly enhances a hosteller's social life, with tons of bars, restaurants, and other cultural diversions.

The hostel is housed in a two-story building of typical Québecois design—meaning it comes with at least two balconies and is graced with the flag of the province. Dormitories contain six to eight beds each. The three private rooms vary in size; one has just a double bed, while the other two can handle appropriate families or groups of four to eight. Both of those have a double bed, incidentally; one's got two sets of bunks, and one's got three sets.

In the morning don't even think of starting off your day without eating a good hot breakfast here for just an extra $3.00 Canadian (about $2.00 U.S.). It's all you can eat, and it's usually either crêpes bretonnes (thin pancakes filled with meat, cheese, or fruit) or a combination of eggs, bacon, and toast. *Merveilleux!*

If it's Québecois history you crave, this is a good, unassuming spot to learn about it. Trois-Rivières is more than 350 years old, which dates it back to about 1630 or so. There's a museum that features the Ursuline Order of nuns, who had a starring role in the development of the town. It's so good it might become a habit! Ba-dump ching. The Archaeological Museum has fossil facts and other nifty stuff that dates back even farther than the 1600s.

The hostel has quite a few other nifty features, too, like Web browsing access and a few bicycles for rent. Yep, it's yet another star hostel in lovely Québec Province; one more superb side trip on your way to or from Québec City or Montréal.

Best bet for a bite:
Super C

What hostellers say:
"Floats my boat."

Gestalt:
Happy fleet

Hospitality: A

Cleanliness: B

Party index:

KEY TO ICONS

 Attractive natural setting

 Romantic private rooms

 Good for business travelers

 Ecologically aware hostel

 Comfortable beds

 Especially well suited for families

 Superior kitchen facilities or cafe

10% Among our very favorite hostels

 Good for active travelers

 Offbeat or eccentric place

$ A particularly good value

 Visual arts at hostel or nearby

Superior bathroom facilities

 Wheelchair-accessible

 Music at hostel or nearby

How to get there:

By bus: Bus lines stop in Trois-Rivières. From depot, call hostel for transit route.

By car: From Montréal, drive Highway 40 northeast *(nord-est)* approximately 140 km (85 mi.). Take exit 199 and follow signs to Route 55; exit onto Highway 755 north *(nord),* then turn right onto St.-Roch. Make immediate left onto Bellefeuile, then go to Bonaventure and turn right. Turn right again onto Royale, then right again onto Radisson. Hostel is on right.

LE CHALET BEAUMONT (BEAUMONT HOSTEL)

1451 Beaumont, Val-David, Québec J0T 2N0

(819) 322–1972

Fax: (819) 322–3793

Rates: $16–$35 Canadian (about $11–$26 U.S.) per Hostelling International member; private rooms $46–$54 (about $32–$38 U.S.)
Credit cards: MC, VISA
Office hours: 8:00 A.M.–10:00 P.M.
Beds: 65
Private/family rooms: 18
Single rooms: None
Private bathrooms: 10
Affiliation: Hostelling International-Canada
Extras: Breakfast, ski rentals, canoe rentals, bicycle rentals

Sometimes a language barrier isn't such a bad thing. Here in the Laurentians, a well-loved ski-resort area less than an hour from Montréal, folks are unlikely to speak great English. After a week in Montréal trying out our rusty French and getting answered back in heavily accented *Anglais*, we were expecting outright stares of incomprehension as we muttered and stuttered our way through conversations.

Then we met the gracious receptionist at Chateau Beaumont in Val-David. Her English was minimal, so we all just continued along in a cobbled-together salad of our school-days French and her basic English; and we got our tour just fine, on a sparkling day up there in the beautiful hills.

Actually, this hostel pretty much speaks for itself. A traditional ski chalet that doubles as a part-hostel, it's cheery, comfortable, and clean. Summer flowers spilled out of window boxes. You can sketch *les montagnes* while seated in the bright sunroom. A super-equipped kitchen with lotsa toasters, lotsa elbow room, and lotsa burners opens up to a cute dining room with small tables and then an outdoor patio—perfect for an *aprés ski tête à tête* with your *p'tite amie*.

Rooms on the second floor vary in size quite a bit; there are two bunkrooms with eight standard-issue bunkbeds *(lits superposés)* apiece. All have access to bathroom facilities at the ends of the halls. As this is an inn, some of the private rooms are spectacular. One we saw was divided in two—half containing a single bed, half containing a double, and all framed with a spectacular view of the mountains. It came with a private bathroom, too; this was an inn room, but the *prix* was reasonable indeed for this pleasant and always popular area.

In an annex building next door are more large, private rooms. Three separate rooms here can all fit a family of five easily, and all have private bathrooms and extra cots.

As if this weren't enough, the hostel also has a ski-rental facility on the premises—winter is high season around here—a few places where you can eat your meal outdoors; and, after a day of hitting the slopes, your aches and pains could be relieved by a sauna or a massage. Arrange for both of these a day early; the sauna is just $4.00 Canadian (about $3.00 U.S.), the massage $30.00 Canadian (about $21.00 U.S.).

Don't miss the great bike trail that runs right through town, either. This being Canada, traffic stops for the cycles as they pass right through the town's main intersection on their way to the hinterlands.

Best bet for a bite:
Cafes galore

What hostellers say:
"Schuss!"

Insiders' tip:
Bike trails in town

Gestalt:
Valhalla

Hospitality: A

Cleanliness: A

Party index:

How to get there:

By bus: Regular bus lines run from Montréal to Val-David. Call hostel for transit route.

By car: From Montréal, take Route 15 north *(nord)* to exit 67; exit onto Route 117 north *(nord),* then turn right at stoplight toward Val-David. Continue straight through town; go up hill, and at top turn left onto Beaumont Street. Drive about 0.4 km (0.2 mi.); hostel is on right.

By plane: Two large airports in Montréal. Call hostel for transit route.

By train: VIA Rail stops in Montréal. Call hostel for transit route.

SENTIERS CARMAN (CARMAN TRAILS HOSTEL)

Chemin Carman Ouest, Wakefield, Québec J0X 3G0

(819) 459–3180

Fax: (819) 459–2113

E-mail: carman@magma.ca

Web site: www.magma.ca/~carman

Rates: about $16–$20 Canadian ($11–$14 U.S.) per person
Credit cards: VISA
Office hours: 10:30 A.M.–9:00 P.M.
Beds: 28
Private/family rooms: 1
Single rooms: None
Private bathrooms: None
Affiliation: Hostelling International-Canada
Extras: Laundry, meals, fireplaces, sauna, tours, shuttle, trails, massage therapist, grill, TV, VCR, slide shows, stereo

10% $

Farm Point, Québec, is a tiny dot on a map of the huge province, but it has the fortune of being located pretty close to Canada's national capital of Ottawa—about a twenty-five–minutes' drive or bus ride away. And this woodsy hostel, although a new entry in a lineup of already superb Québec hostels, delivers quality plus a wide range of services. Super-organized and ambitious manager Rob Grace has put together a hostel that's more an outdoors experience than just a cheap bed for the night.

This hostel takes itself very seriously. Rob plans on being here for a long time, and he's proud of his renovations to a once-abandoned property in a nice spot overlooking fields and hills. You begin in a main building sporting a classy reception area with smoothly planed floors, chalkboards, and a display case that holds natural insect repellent, maps, books, and other travel products.

Next to reception is the licensed restaurant Cafe Myxo: long wooden tables in a lodgelike setting. To the strains of your favorite folk music—you can pick from a lengthy chalked list on the wall—Rob cooks whatever's on his mind, using the hostel garden's produce. It's always good and always artfully presented. (Breakfast and dinner are included in the hostel price.)

The upstairs, which houses three decent rooms, includes a giant open common space with lots of windows, often used for yoga or tai ch'i classes. There's a little room for the visiting massage therapist, too, and several bathrooms (one of which has a jet-spray bathtub).

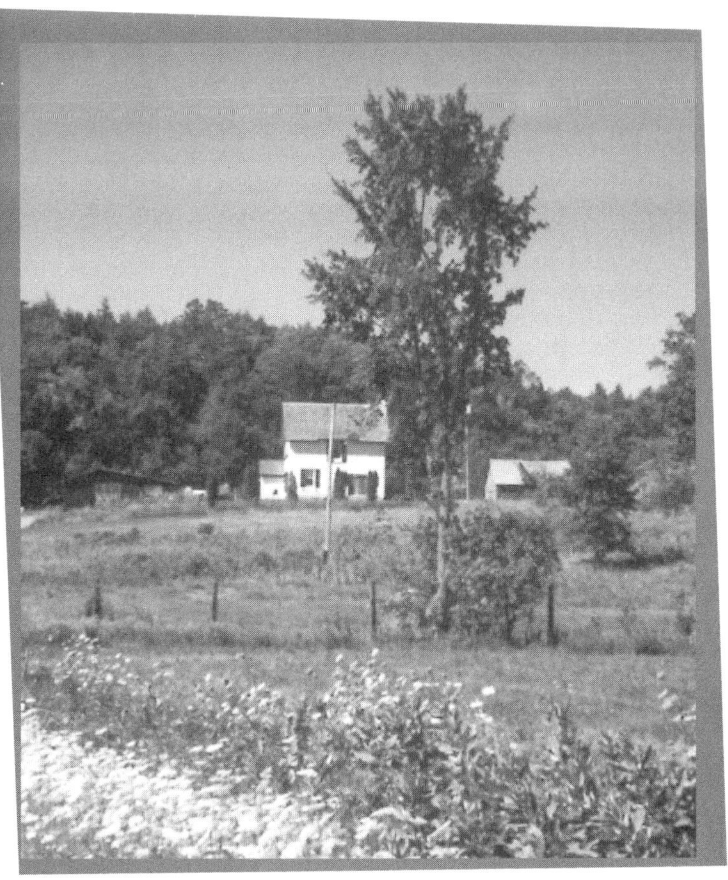

Sentiers Carman
Wakefield
(photo by Martha Coombs)

A second building houses the self-serve kitchen, a warming room for the local ski patrol in winter, and more overflow dorm rooms. Some of these rooms are great—close to the woods, well outfitted, lots of solitude. A few are kinda punky right now, though they're likely to improve as the hostel matures.

The eighty acres of surrounding grounds—the real star of the show here—include a swimmable pond, a Frisbee golf course, and plenty of hiking trails. Don't forget to check out the authentic Finnish sauna, either—it was built in Finland by a Finn who even shipped some of his local rocks across the Atlantic, so that users could fully capture the experience! It costs a few dollars to fire it up, but boy is it worth it. Lots more is planned for this property, such as the construction of an outdoor stage for backyard concerts.

This hostel is big on services, so an herbalist offers edible-plant walks on the hostel grounds, and that massage therapist is on call for straightening out the kinks. Rob's developing other tour packages all the time; call to get an update. It's nice to see such a cooperative spirit existing between the big hostel in nearby Ottawa and this one, too. Rob brings programs down to Ottawa all the time, and there's a shuttle between the two that whisks city mice to the country hostel and vice versa, for a small charge.

Best bet for a bite: Bakery near end of driveway

What hostellers say: "Got any Bruce Cockburn?"

Insiders' tip: Lakes in Gatineau Park

Gestalt: Amazing Grace

Hospitality: A

Cleanliness: A

Party index:

If you come in winter, this hostel supports many kilometers of both groomed and backcountry cross-country ski trails. The hostel's trails link up to the extensive trail network of adjacent Gatineau National Park for endless adventures. Summer and fall, which are actually the less crowded times here, are great times to hike, canoe, and mountain bike in that park, too. Whatever time of year you want to visit, though, make sure to call ahead—the place occasionally books full with a group or wedding.

After a night of listening to nothing but crickets chirping away, we knew that this was one backwoods hostel we'd be

KEY TO ICONS

 Attractive natural setting

 Ecologically aware hostel

 Superior kitchen facilities or cafe

 Offbeat or eccentric place

 Superior bathroom facilities

 Romantic private rooms

 Comfortable beds

 Among our very favorite hostels

$ A particularly good value

 Wheelchair-accessible

 Good for business travelers

 Especially well suited for families

 Good for active travelers

 Visual arts at hostel or nearby

 Music at hostel or nearby

returning to over and over again. Great hostelling in a beautiful setting.

How to get there:

By bus: From bus terminal, take Voyageur Wakefield bus line and ask driver to stop at corner of Highway 105 and Chemin Carman in Farm Point.

By car: From Ottawa, drive Highway 5 north *(nord)* to end; turn right at stop, then left at light onto Highway 105 north *(nord).* Drive 4.6 km (3 mi.) to Chelsea (Farm Point). From IGA in center of town, continue on Route 105 uphill 0.8 km (0.5 mi.); at top of hill, watch for yellow CAFE sign on left. Turn left at sign and follow driveway to end.

By plane: Airport in Ottawa. From airport, call hostel for transit route.

By shuttle: From downtown Ottawa, take shuttle from Nicholas Street hostel. Call hostel for details.

By train: VIA Rail stops in Ottawa. From station, take city bus to bus terminal. Take Voyageur Wakefield bus line and ask driver to stop at corner of Highway 105 and Chemin Carman in Farm Point.

ONTARIO

ONTARIO

Thunder Bay
Sault Ste. Marie
Temagami
Ottawa
Orillia
Peterborough
Barrie
Kingston
Toronto
Niagara Falls

Numbers on map refer to towns numbered at left.

ONTARIO

1. Barrie
2. Kingston
3. Niagara Falls
4. Orillia
5. Ottawa
6. Peterborough
7. Sault Ste. Marie
8. Temagami
9. Thunder Bay
10. Toronto

ONTARIO

Ontario is the literal and metaphorical crossroads of Canada. Hostels are scattered throughout the province—along the St. Lawrence River to Toronto, of course; but also in the wild, wild hinterlands of northern Ontario. Another concentration begins in Ottawa and runs up two river valleys.

To hit the best and most hostels, we'd begin in friendly and hip Toronto, where you can arrive by train from points east or west in Canada—even the United States—and fly in and out easily as well. There are a half-dozen or so choices here, few of them overwhelming, but most adequate for a stay. Then we'd make a day trip to thundering Niagara Falls. After that we would drive north to Ottawa (where Hostelling International-Canada is headquartered, by the way) and then on into the mountains for a couple of days to get a truly rustic hostel experience. Later we'd proceed along the St. Lawrence to Kingston, maybe, or go deep into the heart of wild Ontario by circling the Great Lakes and penetrating farther into the backcountry, to places with names like Thunder Bay and Temagami.

GEORGIAN GREEN SUMMER HOSTEL 

144 Bell Farm Road, Barrie, Ontario L4M 5K5

(705) 735–0772

Fax: (705) 739–8615

E-mail: georgiangreen@cois.on.ca

Rates: $18 Canadian per Hostelling-International member (about $12 U.S.)
Credit cards: VISA
Office hours: 4:00–10:00 P.M.
Season: May 1–August 15
Beds: 48
Private/family rooms: Yes
Private bathrooms: Yes
Affiliation: Hostelling International–Canada
Extras: TV

Located near the shores of Lake Simcoe north of Toronto, this summer-only hostel is a much better choice than the nearby place in Orillia, despite the apartment-block look to it. The forty-eight beds include a large number of single and double rooms, all with private bathrooms and some with kitchen access. There's a TV room, too.

Best bet for a bite: Weber's

Gestalt: Barrie good

Hospitality: A

Cleanliness: A

Party index:

Barrie itself is rather forgettable, though, notable only for its closeness to the decent lake. The casino here is a bore, the local museum slightly better. The beach in Centennial Park is actually the best reason to come, or take a drive or bike ride through the cuter Muskoka Lakes region.

How to get there:

By bus: From Greyhound station, take St. Vincent bus and get off at second stop on Bell Farm Road. Hostel is across the street (middle building on right side).

By car: Call hostel for directions.

LOUISE HOUSE SUMMER HOSTEL

329 Johnson Street, Kingston, Ontario K7L 1Y6

(613) 385–2033

Fax: (613) 385–1707

Rates: $18 Canadian (about $12 U.S.) per Hostelling International member
Credit cards: MC, VISA
Office hours: 4:00–8:30 P.M.
Season: April 1–August 31
Beds: 50
Private/ family rooms: Yes
Affiliation: Hostelling International-Canada
Extras: Kitchen, laundry

This new summer-only hostel replaces a former one in Kingston, and the city's hostels have shifted around so often we're not entirely sure how long this one will be here.

Best bet for a bite: Chez Piggy

Gestalt: Kingston for a day

Hospitality: A

Cleanliness: A

Party index:

This two-story stone building, constructed in 1847, is vaguely historic, and—as is usually the case with historic properties—rather simple inside. They've got fifty beds, a couple family rooms, a kitchen, a common room, and a laundry. All that you'd need.

What's to do in town? Well, fine architecture is all around you. And a short stroll around the neighborhood blocks reveals more old buildings. Downtown, city hall is an impressive limestone construction. Or check out the waterfront and several old forts before taking a cruise to one of the many islands nearby. Heck, they don't call 'em the Thousand Islands for nothing.

How to get there:

By bus: From bus station, take #2 bus to Princess Street, get off at Burger King, and walk 2 blocks south to Johnson Street.

By car: Call hostel for directions.

By train: From Kingston Station, take #1 bus to Princess Street, get off at Burger King, and walk 2 blocks south to Johnson Street.

HOSTELLING INTERNATIONAL NIAGARA FALLS HOSTEL

4549 Cataract Avenue, Niagara Falls, Ontario L2E 3M2

(905) 357–0770

Fax: (905) 357–7673

Rates: $16.00 Canadian (about $11.00 U.S.) per Hostelling International member
Credit cards: VISA, MC, JCB
Office hours: 11:00 A.M.–midnight
Private/family rooms: 5
Single rooms: None
Private bathrooms: None
Affiliation: Hostelling International-Canada
Extras: Laundry, lockers, small store, bike rentals, TV

The word among experienced hostellers used to be that in Niagara Falls, the Canada side was the place to stay. That was before the hostel moved out of its charming Tudor home and into a cement box 2 blocks away. Now it's a toss-up; overcrowding forced Hostelling International to abandon the popular old facility and take up residence in this (unintentionally) Bauhaus-style former apartment building.

But while this hostel's new home could easily be mistaken for a makeshift college dorm, it's still as full-service as they come—and it packs in a whole range of top-quality facilities. The staff are professional, knowledgeable, and friendly; rooms are spanking clean, and none has more than six beds. Many rooms carry only one bunk, so if you're travelling in a pair and are looking for some privacy at no extra cost, you've got a good shot at it if you call ahead. The bathrooms have super-strong showers and clean bathtubs.

Public transport that will zip you right down to the falls stops right across the street, though you might want to save the $2.00 Canadian (about $1.50 U.S.) bus fare in the daytime and opt to walk along the river instead. There's no charge for this bus service at night, by the way, when you'll want to go back downtown to view the illuminated falls.

Best bet for a bite:
Dad's Diner

Insiders' tip:
Barrel-jumping falls still illegal

Gestalt:
Honeymoon suite

Safety: B

Hospitality: A

Cleanliness: A

Party index:

There is no curfew here; only a coded door, unlike its sister hostel across the U.S. border. So you can roam forever amid the flashing neon of the tawdry Clifton Hill neighborhood adjoining the falls. Also, there's no all-day lockout—another big edge over the New York joint.

On the downside, the building and grounds are in serious need of some personality. The institutional common rooms and tiny kitchenettes also leave much to be desired. And, though this is a minor quibble, all five private rooms consist only of paired bunks; there's nary a double bed in sight.

Hostellers should take care not to overlook the variety of nearby attractions other than the falls. A scenic bike path runs parallel to the wild Niagara River for about 55 km (35 mi.), crossing nine bridges and passing through two historic forts. Touring the local wine region by bike is also popular. The hostel manager can tell you all about that stuff.

How to get there:

By bus: Stops in town. Walk 1½ blocks east (toward river) and turn right onto Cataract Avenue. Hostel is on right.

By car: From the U.S., take Rainbow Bridge straight to River Road and go right. Drive all the way to Bridge Street (where Whirlpool Bridge is) and take a left. Make another left onto Cataract; hostel is on right. From the Q.E.W., get off at Stanley Avenue exit and turn left onto Stanley. Several blocks down, go right on Bridge Street. Go right on Cataract; hostel is on right.

By train: Stops in town. Walk 1½ blocks east (toward river) and turn right onto Cataract Avenue. Hostel is on right.

NIAGARA FALLS BACKPACKERS INTERNATIONAL HOSTEL

4219 Huron Street, Niagara Falls, Ontario L2E 2G6

(800) 891–7022; (905) 357–4266

Rates: $18 Canadian (about $12 U.S.)
Credit cards: AMEX, MC, VISA

Office hours: 24 hours
Beds: 30
Private/family rooms: 3
Single rooms: None
Private bathrooms: None
Affiliation: None
Extras: Continental breakfast, dinner (sometimes), bicycle rentals, grill

Usually when we see the word *backpackers* on a hostel sign, we pause. Our experience with places carrying that appellation hasn't always been good, frankly—and we're not sure why that is. In places like New Zealand, the word *backpackers* is almost a sure sign of quality.

Fortunately, in Niagara Falls you've got a third decent alternative when Hostelling International's two hostels (one on each side of the U.S.–Canadian border) are full up. This joint seems to be trying hard to give a low-cost alternative to the kitschy honeymoon suites pasted up along both sides of the Niagara River, and it does justice to the *backpackers* label.

Occupying the first floor of the owner's three-story Victorian home, the place has thirty beds. Dorm rooms all have four beds apiece; and there are three private rooms here, each equipped with a double bed.

Food is well taken care of: A continental breakfast is included in the price of your stay; and at night the owner's mother sometimes actually cooks chili, spaghetti, or something else on request! Now that's home cookin'. There's a kitchen available, too, if you want to fix your own.

Best bet for a bite: Mom's cooking

Gestalt: True falls

Safety: A

Hospitality: A

Party index:

Activities here revolve almost solely around gaping at the famous falls. You can rent bicycles for $15 Canadian (about $11 U.S.) a day, allowing you to tool around—but not over—the falls. Or take a twenty-minute stroll along the walkway that edges the Niagara River. Or, finally, lounge around in the yard.

How to get there:

By bus: Greyhound stops in Niagara Falls. From bus depot, walk east on Bridge Street to Zimmerman; make a left on Zimmerman and continue to the corner of Huron Street. Hostel is on corner.

By car: Call hostel for directions.

By train: VIA Rail stops in Niagara Falls. From station, walk east on Bridge Street to Zimmerman; make a left on Zimmerman and continue to the corner of Huron Street. Hostel is on corner.

ORILLIA HOME HOSTEL

198 Borland Street East, Orillia, Ontario L3V 2C3
(705) 325–0970
Fax: (705) 325–9826

Rates: $13.00 Canadian (about $9.00 U.S.) per person
Credit cards: None
Office hours: 8:00–10:00 A.M.; 5:00–9:00 P.M.
Beds: 9
Private/family rooms: None
Single rooms: None
Private bathrooms: None
Affiliation: Hostelling International-Canada
Extras: Laundry, grill

There is little good to say about this odd and unfriendly "home" hostel—which didn't feel homey at all. Our visit got off on the wrong foot and went downhill from there; we can't recommend it to anyone we actually like.

Right from the start we were received with suspicion—outright hostility, even. The owners apparently demand that all folks doing business with them give them at least a two-day notice before arrival. But this information wasn't mentioned in the Hostelling International handbook; we simply called—as any hosteller would—during the listed office hours and arranged a visit.

Best bet for a bite: Plenty in town

What hostellers say: *"Neinnnnnn!"*

Insiders' tip: Keep on truckin'

Gestalt: Off the deep end

Hospitality: F

Cleanliness: D

Party index:

Upon our arrival the manager wasn't happy and refused to answer even basic questions. We were, however, subjected to a long screed about her problems running the hostel—even resorting, she said, to kicking snoring hostellers out of bed at 4:30 A.M.! Charming.

We eventually wangled a brief tour, and what we saw wasn't too impressive. Sleeping quarters are divided into three areas: the basement of the house, a little added-on room, and another room that we weren't allowed to see. The basement space consisted of a kitchen, washroom, and a small bedroom. The bedroom was furnished with three low-to-the-ground metal beds and not much else. These mattresses resembled upholstered cushions removed from the couch in a dentist's office; all were scratchy, woolly, and dull. Kitchen space was limited, although you could cook a full meal at the stovetop. There was no common area, either.

Two bedrooms and a washroom are located in the tiny upstairs apartment, with three similarly weird beds in each room. There's lots of tourist information on display, but it's a bit outdated.

Outside, in the yard, a small barbecue pit appeared to have been used mostly as an ashtray. Most people come to Orillia for Lake Simcoe, a large freshwater lake. And along the shore there is indeed a nice area for picnicking and bike riding. But next time through, we'll use the tourist information service in Orillia to find other accommodations. If you find yourself stuck in this lake town without a place to stay, we suppose this hostel would do in a pinch. A *real* pinch. Consider yourself warned.

How to get there:

By car: Call hostel for directions.

OTTAWA INTERNATIONAL HOSTEL

75 Nicholas Street, Ottawa, Ontario K1N 7B9

(613) 235–2595

Fax: (613) 234–7891

E-mail: hicoe@magi.com

Web site: www.magi.com/~hicoe/ottawa.htm

Rates: $17 Canadian (about $12 U.S.) per Hostelling International member; private rooms $37 Canadian (about $26 U.S.)
Credit cards: MC, VISA, JCB
Office hours: 24 hours (April–October); 7:00–2:00 A.M. (November–March)
Beds: 148
Private/family rooms: 5
Single rooms: None
Private bathrooms: None
Affiliation: Hostelling International-Canada
Extras: Bicycle and skate rentals, tours, laundry, TV, VCR, grill, travel store, grill, darts, lockers

10%

Located in an old jailhouse in central Ottawa, this hostel gets high marks for effort. Not only do you get the novelty of sleeping in former prisoners' cells (four to six beds per dorm room), but you can also—if you really want to—view the gallows where the last public hanging in Canada took place.

A fun attitude prevails among the staff, who often organize baseball outings, pub crawls, and the like. Fewer rules exist here than in the usual Hostelling International joint, too: There's no lockout, for instance, and drinking and smoking are even allowed in a second-floor common space and an outside courtyard.

Ottawa International Hostel

Ottawa

(photo by Paul Karr)

It's got a great location, too, close to Ottawa's lively downtown. Since this is Canada's capital, many of the best attractions around are free. The National Gallery, for one, houses great art, while the Museum of Civilization (across the river in Hull) is a popular and innovative walk through the history of humankind. Don't miss Parliament Hill, either—simply follow the other foot traffic west up Rideau Street—for an unforgettable look at some of Canada's most impressive buildings. There are enough restaurants and bars in the nearby By Ward Market, as well, to keep you occupied for days, and you can get good vantage points on the Ottawa River as it divides Ontario from Québec.

This might be the only hostel in North America situated directly across from a mall. A mall downtown? Yup; people actually come downtown at night here. Way too many opportunities to max out your credit card here, and the mall even comes with a park smack dab on top of it.

But we're getting way ahead of ourselves. The rambling old building, something like a maze, has been well converted. Dorms occupy three floors, and although things are a bit stuffy—not much air circulation in these cells—there's plenty of room. To lessen the trauma of sleeping in a cell, homey curtains have been draped across the barred doors. Bring your own padlock or shell out a buck for the handy lockers outside your cell. Showers and bathrooms are located at opposite ends of the dorm space. Don't worry about the myths about prison showers—these are all in separate stalls, with curtains to ensure privacy.

The coed dorm isn't located in a cellblock; it's just an ordinary hostel-type room with eight bunks in it. Family rooms, which are also quite nice—they're furnished with a combination of bunks and a double futon—also look surprisingly cheery, considering that this once was, well, a jail. The bathroom on this floor even features an original prison bathtub.

The enormous kitchen in the basement is a big hit, too. It features a giant walk-in fridge and enough seating space for dozens. You can munch on bagels and muffins sold at the desk, then gulp it all down with "designer" coffee from a coffee machine in the kitchen. A second (nonsmoking) lounge for quiet types is also located down here.

Besides an ironing board and some off-street parking for a few dollars, there's a good little travel store on the third floor, selling everything from maps and guidebooks to Eurail passes and those ubiquitous maple-leaf Canadian patches that non-Canadians love so much. Hostellers get a 15 percent discount here. A bike-rental company is located right on the premises and organizes tours as well as daily rentals.

Finally, despite rumors about the ghost of an innocent man pacing the hallways, the staff is working on installing a sauna right on (gulp) Death Row, where the hanged fellow spent his last days. Something to think about while you're sweatin' it out.

So to speak.

Best bet for a bite: By Ward Market

What hostellers say: "This jailhouse rocks!"

Insiders' tip: Avoid squeegee punks

Gestalt: Justice in Ontario

Safety: A

Hospitality: A

Cleanliness: C

Party index:

How to get there:

By bus: Bus lines stop in Ottawa. From terminal, take #4 bus to corner of Rideau and Nicholas Streets; walk 2 blocks up Nicholas. Hostel is on left, at #75.

By car: From Montréal, take Route 417 to Ottawa. Take exit 118 (Nicholas Street) and continue to Bessemer Street; make a left, then another left onto Nicholas. Hostel is less than 1 block, on left, at #75.

By plane: Airport in Ottawa. From airport, take #96 bus to Rideau Centre mall; walk through or beneath mall to opposite end, which is Nicholas Street. Hostel is across street.

By train: VIA Rail stops in Ottawa; from train station, take #95 bus to Rideau Centre mall. Walk through or beneath mall to opposite end, which is Nicholas Street. Hostel is across street.

REGINA GUEST HOUSE AND HOSTEL NR

205 Charlotte Street, Ottawa, Ontario K1N 8K7

(613) 241–0908

Fax: (613) 241–2141

Rates: $18 Canadian per Hostelling International member (about $12 U.S.)
Credit cards: MC, VISA
Office hours: 2:00–11:00 P.M.
Season: April 1–August 31
Beds: 56
Private/family rooms: Yes
Private bathrooms: Yes
Affiliation: Hostelling International-Canada
Extras: Kitchen, laundry, breakfast

The second "official" hostel to open in Canada's capital city, this one is a smaller and quieter version—and, interestingly, it is completely separate from the other place in town. Different management, different advertising, the whole deal. In theory it will be cooperating with the jail hostel, not just competing with it. But we'll see.

Best bet for a bite:
Zak's Diner

Gestalt:
Capital gang

Party index:

Housed in a bland, three-story brick affair, it's got more beds than you'd think: fifty-six in all, mostly in small double or quad configurations—lots of privacy here. There's a lounge, a storage area, a kitchen, and a laundry, all of which are important. A small breakfast is a possibility.

Ottawa, as we've said elsewhere, is not a 100 percent thrill but does contain more than enough culture to occupy you for a few days, especially if you're into things Canadian. There are also several hip districts to explore.

How to get there:

By bus: From bus station, take #4 bus to Rideau Centre, transfer to #7 or #2 bus going east on Rideau Street, and get off at the corner of Rideau and Charlotte Streets.

By car: Call hostel for directions.

By plane: From airport, take #96 bus (Carlingwood) to Rideau Centre, cross through the Centre, and transfer to bus #7 or #2 going east on Rideau Street. Get off at the corner of Rideau and Charlotte Streets.

By train: VIA Rail stops in Ottawa. From train station, take #95 bus to Rideau Centre, cross through the Centre, transfer to #7 or #2 bus going east on Rideau Street and get off at the corner of Rideau and Charlotte Streets.

SEVERN COURT SUMMER HOSTEL 

555 Wilfred Drive, Peterborough, Ontario K9K 1W1
(705) 740–1150
Fax: (705) 740–0944

Rates: $18 Canadian per Hostelling International member (about $12 U.S.)
Credit cards: MC, VISA
Office hours: 4:00–10:00 P.M.
Season: April 1–August 31
Beds: 48
Private/family rooms: Yes
Affiliation: Hostelling International-Canada
Extras: Courtyard, laundry, kitchen

It's unlikely that you'll end up in Peterborough on purpose, but the small university city does stand partway between Ottawa and Toronto—so it's possible you'll pass through needing a bed en route to somewhere else. If so, this summer-only joint fills the bill.

It's a modern, converted dorm, with some private rooms available. There's the usual common area, plus a kitchen and laundry. The place is wheelchair-accessible, and there's a nice patio.

Peterborough is slow moving enough that its chief attraction is a unique hydraulic canal lock; this thing lifts boats a full 60 feet in the air to higher water. There are also a couple of museums in town.

How to get there:

By bus: From Greyhound and Trentway-Wager bus stations, take local #6 bus (Sir Sandford Fleming College/Kawartha) and get off at the gates to Sir Sanford Fleming College. Hostel is across the street.

By car: From Highway 115, exit onto Airport Road (Highway 11), and drive north for four minutes. Hostel is on right side, across from college.

KEY TO ICONS

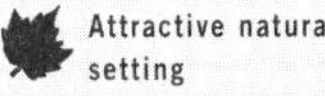

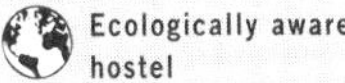

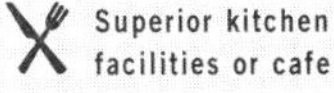

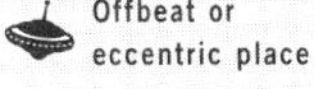

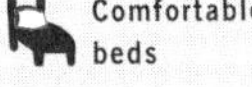

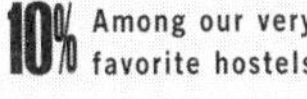

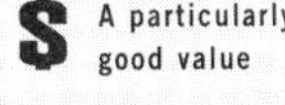

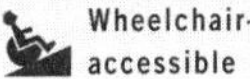

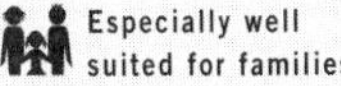

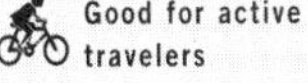

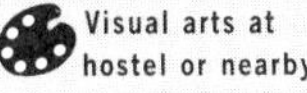

ALGONQUIN HOTEL HOSTEL 

864 Queen Street East, Sault Ste. Marie, Ontario P6A 2B4
(705) 253–2311

Rates: $19–$21 Canadian (about $13–$15 U.S.) per Hostelling International member; private rooms $30 Canadian (about $21 U.S.)
Credit cards: None
Office hours: 24 hours
Beds: 45
Private/family rooms: Yes; number varies; call for availability
Single rooms: 5
Private bathrooms: None
Affiliation: Hostelling International-Canada
Extras: Restaurant, bar, pool table, TV, darts

This place really isn't so much a hostel as it is a hotel; rooms here, when available, are rented to hostellers at a reduced rate. (The place is here only because two other hostels in the area closed a few years back; when Hostelling International-Canada rang up hotel owner David Stenghetta and asked him to help out, he didn't bat an eye.)

There are pluses and minuses to this arrangement—you get the privacy and furnishings of a hotel room, but there's no kitchen, and the bathroom facilities are minimal.

Stenghetta, a local fellow with a real sense of humor, is the best thing about this place. His local knowledge and ability to get along with folks really helps welcome a traveler. Rooms are standard single or double hotel lodgings—linens, water glasses, soap, and such are included, nice touches for the bunk-weary hosteller.

However, with no kitchen in sight, you must either eat in the humdrum cafe in the basement or brave the city's uninspiring restaurant scene. Rooms don't have televisions. And the halls seemed filled with cigarette smoke; allergic types wouldn't want to stay here.

At least the location is good. Most of Sault Ste. Marie's downtown attractions are within a few kilometers of walking. For starters, check out one of Canada's oldest breweries (free tastings, too), a neat airplane museum housed in a hangar, and the locally famous Stone House.

Best bet for a bite: Head for the A&P

What hostellers say: "Which way to the beer tour?"

Insiders' tip: Bushplane Museum

Gestalt: Soo-Soo

Safety: B

Hospitality: A

Cleanliness: C

Party index:

To spend even less on your day excursion, walk down to the canal and lock system, checking out the waterfowl or just gazing over to the U.S. side of the water.

How to get there:

By bus: Greyhound Canada stops in Sault Ste. Marie, Ontario. Walk 3 blocks up Queen Street, away from bridge to U.S. Hostel is on left.

By car: From the U.S., take Interstate 75 across toll bridge into Sault Ste. Marie. Off bridge, turn onto Bay Street. Get in left lane and continue almost to the exit for Route 17; turn left just before exit, go 1 block, and bear right onto Queen Street. Make immediate left into hostel parking lot.

By plane: Small airport near Sault Ste. Marie. Take taxi or shuttle ($15–$30 Canadian/about $10–$21 U.S.) to hostel.

SMOOTHWATER WILDERNESS LODGE HOSTEL

Box 40, Temagami, Ontario P0H 2H0

(705) 569–3539

E-mail: temagami@onlink.net

Web site: www.smoothwater.com

Rates: $20–$25 Canadian (about $14–$18 U.S.) per person; private rooms $62–$90 Canadian (about $43–$63 U.S.)
Credit cards: MC, VISA
Office hours: 8:00 A.M.–9:00 P.M.
Beds: 25
Private/family rooms: 5
Single rooms: None
Private bathrooms: 5
Affiliation: None
Extras: Canoe rentals, mountain bicycle rentals, meals, tours, sauna, woodstove, store

This is more an outfitting operation and a lodge than a hostel, but it is situated near beautiful Temagami Lake—a strangely shaped body of water whose long, deep fingers are more like fjords.

Owners Caryn Colman and Francis Boyes focus heavily on canoe trips, so you can easily rent a canoe—or a mountain bike—at the office. Lots of tours, classes, and courses are offered as well, usually (but not always) geared toward the twin recreational pillars of canoeing and cross-country skiing.

Best bet for a bite: On site

Gestalt: Smooth ride

Hospitality: A

Cleanliness: A

Party index:

As for the hostel facilities, two bunkrooms here sleep ten hostellers apiece; each has its own washroom and showers. Lots of wood and windows, high cathedral ceilings, and a woodstove furnish the rustic atmosphere. Rates are higher in high summer season than the rest of the year, you should note. There are also five private rooms in the lodge, each with private washroom, but these are essentially rustic hotel rooms—nice ones, though they cost somewhat more than the hosteller's normal daily budgetary allowance. Oh, well. This still appears to be a fine place to get away from it all and see western Ontario's wild side.

How to get there:

By bus: Bus lines stop in Temagami. Call hostel for details.
By car: Call hostel for directions.
By train: VIA Rail stops in area. Call hostel for details.

CONFEDERATION COLLEGE HOSTEL

960 William Street, Thunder Bay, Ontario P7C 4W1

(807) 475–6381

E-mail: lalonde@confederationc.on.ca

Web site: www.confederationc.on.ca

Rates: $15–$25 Canadian (about $10–$18 U.S.) per Hostelling International member; private rooms $30–$50 Canadian (about $21–$35 U.S.)
Credit cards: None
Office hours: 9:00 A.M.–11:00 P.M.
Season: May 17–August 14 *Sometimes closed without advance warning*
Beds: 20
Private/family rooms: Yes (number varies; call for availability)
Single rooms: Yes (number varies; call for availability)
Private bathrooms: Yes (number varies; call for availability)
Affiliation: Hostelling International-Canada
Extras: Laundry, cafeteria, e-mail, game room

All ten rooms in this college-dorm-turned-summer-hostel are doubles, a great deal at just $15 per person. They getcha on linens, though: it's five bucks—per person!—plus taxes for sheets, and towels aren't supplied.

Some of the rooms in Sibley Hall have their own washrooms, though you'll pay an extra five bucks per person for that privilege, too. At least there's a small fridge and microwave in every room, somewhat making up for the hostel's lack of kitchen, but there are no toasters, ovens, or hotplates allowed for cooking purposes. It's cheaper to stay in the West Wing, where bathrooms and showers are all shared; East Wing rooms with full bathrooms right in the rooms go for more.

Other features of this place include common rooms on each floor—with game rooms and movie nights, no less—a small convenience store in the front office, and a computer lab that hostel guests are welcome to use for Web noodling, e-mailing, or whatever else fancies them.

There's one more big if here: The hostel sometimes closes without advance warning if some sort of academic or other conference is booking up the rooms in town. So call ahead before you make that long, long haul up to Thunder Bay; it might be full.

Food choice is good here. A cafeteria serves three meals each day, the on-site convenience store stocks a full line of microwaveable meals (yuck), and it's just a twenty-minute walk to a local grocery store. Of course you can't spend all day focused on food. The surrounding scenery is so wild and beautiful, you'll want to hike as much as possible.

Best bet for a bite: Cafeteria

Gestalt: Boom town

Hospitality: A

Cleanliness: A

Party index:

How to get there:

By bus: Bus stops in Thunder Bay. From depot, call hostel for transit route.

By car: Take Harbour Expressway (Route 17/11) downtown to Balmoral Street; turn south on Balmoral, then make a right onto William Street. Enter college grounds from William.

THUNDER BAY INTERNATIONAL HOSTEL

1594 Lakeshore Drive, Thunder Bay, Ontario P7B 5E4

(807) 983–2042

Rates: $15 Canadian (about $10 U.S.) per person
Credit cards: None
Office hours: Vary; call
Beds: 30
Private/family rooms: Yes; number varies; call for availability
Single rooms: Yes
Private bathrooms: None
Affiliation: None
Extras: Meals (sometimes)

Lloyd Jones has done a lot of traveling in his lifetime, and now he has put together one of the most unusual hostels we've ever seen. If you find yourself wandering around the beautiful Thunder Bay area, it's worth seeing for the kitsch factor if nothing else.

Named after a typical building found in villages in Borneo, this is a long house—literally. It's an ex-motel, tube-style building, the type that is usually found on secondary roadsides near interstate highways.

You also have the choice of sleeping in a converted school bus or a trailer . . . or tenting on the property. And that's not all. There's also a mobile-home park in back of the hostel called the Longhouse Village with, um, street names that seem plucked from *South Pacific*. Getting our drift? This is one iconoclastic cat.

Best bet for a bite: In town

What hostellers say: "Let's climb the Giant!"

Insiders' tip: Better hostelling in Minnesota (See *Hostels U.S.A.*)

Gestalt: Hodge-podge lodge

Hospitality: A

Cleanliness: B

Party index:

When he first came up with the hostel idea, in fact, his neighbors' perception of a hostel was so skewed that some supposedly kept their daughters behind closed doors for their own protection. Typical reaction, that, and Jones has worked to correct the impression. Perhaps he's gone a bit too far, however; this fellow envisions himself as the prime mover and shaker in educating the general Canadian public about independent hostelling.

His resulting Backpackers Canada network is a motley crew of a few certifiable hostels and lots of places that might have a few bunks but whose primary mission could well be something entirely different; often they're Christian organizations, back-to-the-land communal retreats, Native Canadian relocation programs, or even (in one case) tree farms without bunks. Go figure.

Anyway, back to Thunder Bay International. Hosteller reaction is divided; lots of folks seem to find Lloyd's hostel agreeable enough, though it's a real hike from the center of town. Others object to the oddity of the place. All agree that it's unusually decked out, sporting a collection of blowpipes, carvings, and tapestry brought back from Borneo.

A communal kitchen serves as a kind of focal point for social lubrication. Sometimes Lloyd's wife, Willa, whips up a traditional Southeast Asian dish she claims as a specialty, and food is also sold here in case you forgot to bring some.

Take it or leave it: This is the only year-round hostel in this corner of Canada. And, since the location is fairly rustic, lots of local fauna—like moose, bears, even caribou—might be roaming around. It's not far to the famous Sleeping Giant rock formation, with its gorgeous lake views, either, nor from the community of Thunder Bay—unusual itself, in that it has two city centers. How come? Because, until about thirty years ago, it was actually two separate municipalities that decided to join at the hip.

In sum: If you don't mind a hodge-podgey campus of varied accommodations and flaky management, this place would be okay. Joseph Conrad would probably love this place.

How to get there:

By bus: Greyhound stops in Thunder Bay and also near hostel. From downtown bus station, buy ticket to outskirts (about $5.00 Canadian/about $4.00 U.S.); driver will drop you at hostel.

By car: Call hostel for directions.

TORONTO-AREA HOSTELS: A Summary

	RATING	PROS	CONS	COST	PAGE
Neill-Wycik Hostel		great rooms	summer only	$16.00	p. 144
HI-Toronto		helpful staff	neighborhood	$17.95	p. 140
Havinn B & B		friendly	not cheap	$25.00–$40.00	p. 138
Global Village Backpackers		fun, central	so-so kitchen	$21.00	p. 137
Marigold Hostel		hoppin'	crowded	$23.00	p. 143
Leslieville Hostels		quiet	not friendly	$15.00	p. 141
Mimico Hospitality House		laid-back	odd	$20.00–$30.00	p. 136

MIMICO HOSPITALITY HOUSE 

150 Queens Avenue, Etobicoke (Toronto area), Ontario M8V 2N6
(800) 364–4410; (416) 255–9984

E-mail: derekb@ican.net
Web site: home.ican.net/~derekb
Rates: \$20–\$30 Canadian (about \$14–\$23 U.S.) per person; private rooms \$30–\$45 Canadian (about \$23–\$34 U.S.)
Credit cards: AMEX, JCB, MC, VISA
Office hours: 8:00 A.M.–11:00 P.M.
Beds: Number varies; call
Private/family rooms: None
Single rooms: None
Private bathrooms: None
Affiliation: None
Extras: E-mail, bicycle rentals, motorcycle

This quite small hostel sits inside a three-story, turn-of-the-century house in a quiet suburb southwest of Toronto. The manager proudly boasts that "one Scottish guest stayed over thirty years!" We're not so sure that this is a true accomplishment, but there you have it. He can be genuinely proud, though, of his no-smoking policy.

Some nice extras are included here. You get to use e-mail and can rent either a bicycle or (if you pass the test) a motorcycle. However, you can use the hostel laundry only if you stay more than five nights; in fact, long-term stays here are encouraged and rewarded with discounts. Hmmmmm.

For fun, you could go swimming in Lake Ontario or a local public swimming pool. There's a repertory theater nearby as well, but most folks will be heading into Toronto. Figure on up to an hour to get there by public transit—less by car, though traffic snarls at rush hour could put a crimp in your day.

Best bet for a bite: Plenty

What hostellers say: "Odd."

Gestalt: Etobicoke is it

Safety: A

Hospitality: B

Party index:

How to get there:

By bus: Greyhound stops in Toronto. From terminal, take Bay Bus to Queen Street; switch to #501 streetcar (Queen Street) and travel west to Mimico Avenue and Lakeshore Boulevard; walk 1 block west to Queens Avenue. Hostel is on right.

By car: From downtown Toronto, take Gardiner Expressway (Highway 2). It becomes the Q.E.W. expressway; stay on highway to Islington Avenue, then take exit 142 and drive south on Islington through four lights to Lakeshore Boulevard West. Turn left on Lakeshore, drive 3 km (about 2 mi.) to Mimico Avenue; turn left, then make a right onto Queens Avenue. Hostel is at #150.

By plane: Large airport in Toronto. From airport, take Express bus to Islington subway station, then take subway east to Royal York subway station. Take #76 (Lakeshore) bus south to Mimico Avenue and Lakeshore Boulevard. Walk 1 block west to Queens Avenue. Hostel is on right.

By train: VIA Rail stops in Toronto. From station, take Bay Bus or subway to Queen Street; switch to #501 streetcar (Queen Street) and travel west to Mimico Avenue and Lakeshore Boulevard; walk 1 block west to Queens Avenue. Hostel is on right.

GLOBAL VILLAGE BACKPACKERS TORONTO

460 King Street West, Toronto, Ontario M5V 1L7

(888) 844–7875; (416) 703–8540

Rates: $21 Canadian (about $14 U.S.) per person; private rooms $50 Canadian (about $33 U.S.)
Credit cards: MC, VISA
Office hours: 24 hours
Beds: 145
Private rooms: 4
Single rooms: None
Private bathrooms: None
Affiliation: None
Extras: Laundry, pool table, video games

The owners of this place have gussied up the old Spadina Hotel in downtown Toronto and converted it to bunkrooms. We came with high hopes, but hosteller complaints have led us to the conclusion that they haven't put enough time into the aging building yet. Cleanliness and facilities are still suffering; at least it's a good time.

Rooms have no more than four bunks to a room, remarkable considering it's a big hostel in a big urban destination, and the couples' rooms consist of a double futon on a classy frame, painted walls, and new lighting fixtures. The bathrooms are still hurting here, though, a major sticking point with our visitors. Showers continue to sometimes blast shots of scalding and freezing water and are not kept nearly clean enough. The dorms could have been cleaner, too, a number of hostellers complained.

The former hotel kitchen is now an enormous hostel kitchen, with nighttime views of

Best bet for a bite:
Hot-dog stands

Gestalt:
Global warming

Safety: B

Hospitality: B

Cleanliness: C

Party index:

the skyscrapers. There's also a really big laundry on the premises. Front desk staff—working out of a space that used to be part of a bar featured in the Jack Nicholson flick *Barfly*—is multilingual, helpful, and courteous. For fun, there's a game room including pool table, video games, and numerous other modern distractions. Free coffee's offered in the morning, although the coffeemaker seemed to work properly only about half the time. What to do here? Most hostellers hung out in the streetside patio, guzzling beer—as opposed to hitting one of Toronto's zillions of bars, we guess. Go figure.

This joint is a five-minute walk to everything: theaters, stores, bars, the needle-like CN Tower (with its rocket elevator and revolving-dish restaurants), the retractable SkyDome (with Blue Jays baseball), and so on. Queen Street is full of cheap eats when there's no time or desire to cook. And the hostel's situated right smack in the heart of Toronto's fashion district; you could pick up yards of discount fabric or that half-price coat or something else of that ilk practically right outside the doors.

Just don't come expecting perfect beds or cleanliness.

How to get there:

By bus: Bus lines stop in Toronto. From bus station, walk south to Dundas and take Dundas streetcar westbound to Spadina; at Spadina, change to southbound Spadina streetcar (get transfer on Dundas car) and get off at King Street. Hostel is at corner of Spadina Avenue and King Street.

By car: From Route 401, take Don Valley Parkway exit (375) southbound to the Gardiner Expressway at the lake; go west on Gardiner to Spadina Avenue exit. Go through three lights to King Street. Hostel is at corner of King and Spadina. To park, turn left on King. Parking meters, though not right in front of building, are a short distance up right side of King Street. From Niagara, take Q.E.W. until it becomes the Gardiner Expressway. Take Spadina Avenue exit, go through three lights to King Street. Hostel is at corner of King and Spadina.

By subway: Take subway to St. Andrew stop. Then walk 4 blocks west on King Street. Cross Spadina Avenue; hostel is at corner of King Street and Spadina Avenue

By train: VIA Rail stops in Toronto. From train station, take TTC light rail ($2.00) to King Street stop. Hostel is at corner of King Street and Spadina Avenue.

HAVINN B&B HOSTEL

118 Spadina Road, Toronto, Ontario M5R 2T8

(888) 922–5220; (416) 922–5220

E-mail: havinn@lglobal.com

Web site: www.lglobal.com/~havinn

Rates: $25–$40 Canadian (about $19–$30 U.S.) per person; private rooms $50–$60 Canadian (about $38–$45 U.S.)
Credit cards: None
Office hours: 4:00 A.M.–midnight
Beds: 12
Private/family rooms: Yes; number varies; call for availability
Single rooms: 3
Private bathrooms: None
Affiliation: None
Extras: Parking, breakfast, TV, ironing board, lockers

Gary Moodie and Donna Johnson call their place a "bed-and-breakfast hostel," something we'd never really heard of before, but it seems to work well here in Toronto's hip Spadina-Bloor neighborhood.

The Victorian house is outfitted with wide twin beds and one double bed in various combinations; the configurations change depending on hostellers' needs. What's that? Yes, you heard right—there are no bunkbeds here at all, folks, a welcome change from the usual sardinelike arrangements. A front common space serves for socializing. The owners have even thoughtfully provided an ironing board; use it after doing your laundry at a place around the corner.

In the morning you get whatever's for breakfast for free: bagels, muffins, fruit, even eggs and waffles if it's a Sunday. The kitchen isn't fully equipped, however, consisting of only a small refrigerator and a microwave oven. Nice for light meals, but not much use for lunch or dinner. Fortunately, you're falling all over restaurants on Dupont and Bloor Streets.

While we're on the subject of the neighborhood, this is a great location for young travelers. For one thing, it's only a couple of blocks from the world-renowned University of Toronto; walking tours of the grounds are available from the student union, or just stroll around on your own. Also try to check out the crazy Casa Loma, which is close by—a financier's castle that became so expensive to keep up that it bankrupted the owner.

Best bet for a bite:
Bloor Street west

What hostellers say:
"Pass the toast, please."

Gestalt:
New Havinn

Safety: A

Hospitality: A

Cleanliness: B

Party index:

Numerous other hip shops, cafes, and quirks are sprinkled about this neighborhood, too, but we're going to let you find them on your own. That's half the fun of a visit to Canada's nerve center, after all: just following your nose. And this is a good base to do it from, in a relatively quiet but fairly central location.

How to get there:

By bus: From bus station in Toronto, take TTC subway (University

Line) north to Dupont stop. From Dupont, walk 1 block south to hostel on Spadina.

By car: From Route 401, take Allen Road exit (exit 365). Drive south down Allen Road until it ends at Eglinton; make a left and continue to Spadina. Turn right onto Spadina. Hostel is at #118.

By plane: Airport in Toronto. From airport, call hostel for transit route.

By train: VIA Rail stops in Toronto. From station, take TTC subway (University Line) north to Dupont stop. From Dupont, walk 1 block south to hostel on Spadina.

HOSTELLING INTERNATIONAL TORONTO HOSTEL

76 Church Street, Toronto, Ontario M5C 2G1

(416) 971–4440

Fax: (416) 971–4088

E-mail: thostel@hostellingint-gl.on.ca

Web site: www.hostellingint-gl.on.ca

Rates: $17.95 Canadian per Hostelling International member (about $12.00 U.S.)

Credit cards: JCB, MC, VISA

Office hours: 24 hours

Beds: 170

Private/family rooms: 5

Affiliation: Hostelling International-Canada

Extras: Kitchen, laundry, Internet access, lockers, travel store, tours

Toronto's official hostel has moved more times in the last three or four years than *you* have—but they've finally got it right, purchasing a big building right smack downtown in 1998. No more getting turned away late at night, or wandering around an iffy part of town. This place is just much better than the hostel's previous incarnations: It's closer to transit points and food, more comfortable, and it draws a crowd that's actually more interested in travel than in getting wasted.

Architect/hostel manager Robert Bisson has done a great job here, completely renovating a former high-rise hotel to uncover some of its former splendor and adding new touches like a colorful common area in the basement decorated in purple, yellow, and terra-cotta paint.

Dorms are mostly four- to six-bedded, with one larger ten-bedded room too—all with en-suite bathrooms. High ceilings aid circulation, and they've added three Internet terminals recently. There's also a second, annex facility in summertime with 300 beds in nearby Ryerson University; these are bland and not in as inviting an area, but they will definitely do in a pinch.

There's plenty to do in the area of the hostel, including a huge public market and downtown's churches, shops, and sights.

How to get there:

By bus: Walk south on Bay Street to Adelaide Street; turn left and walk east on Adelaide to Church Street, then turn right on Church and continue to hostel on right.

By car: Call hostel for directions.

By plane: From Pearson Airport, take airport express from all terminals to downtown. Call hostel for subsequent directions.

By train: VIA Rail stops at Toronto's Union Station. From train station, take subway to King Station. Walk east on King Street to Church Steet, turn left, and walk north on Church to hostel on left.

Best bet for a bite:
St. Lawrence Market

What hostellers say:
"Good effort."

Gestalt:
Blue Jay way

Safety: B

Hospitality: A

Cleanliness: B

Party index:

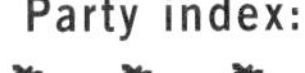

LESLIEVILLE HOME HOSTELS

185 Leslie Street, Toronto, Ontario M4M 3C6

(800) 280–3965; (416) 461–7258

E-mail: leslieville@sympatico.ca

Rates: $15 Canadian (about $10 U.S.) per person; single rooms $35 Canadian (about $25 U.S.); double rooms $45 Canadian (about $32 U.S.)

Credit cards: None

Office hours: 7:00 A.M.–11:00 P.M.

Beds: 65

Private/family rooms: 8

Single rooms: None

Private bathrooms: None

Affiliation: None

Extras: Laundry

This hostel is kind of unusual and kind of hard to figure out. People either really like it or don't like it at all.

For starters, it's located in a total of three unconnected townhouses scattered around a quiet residential neighborhood in the southeast of Canada's biggest city. That's great, if you want to observe the everyday goings-on in the lives of actual residents. Not so great, though, if you want a view of the SkyDome. Still, that's no big stumbling block, thanks to Toronto's innovative streetcar transportation system, which runs very close to the hostel. It's just a twenty-minute ride to the daily adrenaline rush of Yonge Street.

Best bet for a bite: St. Lawrence Market

What hostellers say: "Work in progress."

Insiders' tip: Third-floor bathroom

Gestalt: Church chat

Safety: B

Hospitality: A

Cleanliness: B

Party index:

And, thankfully, a good, nourishing breakfast is included in the rates. However, there is no kitchen here for guest use—a definite point to consider when picking your bunk for the night. The city's closest thing to an Indian neighborhood is very close by if you've got a craving for authentic bhaji or vindaloo. It's just that eating out twice every day can get expensive in a hurry.

At least the place is close to a nice set of lakeside beaches, set in a quaint and moneyed neighborhood called (imagine this) The Beaches. Jolly good place for a stroll, we say, old chap. Can you guess what ethnic group settled and still prevails around here? Bloody good.

The hostel also gets points for being accessible twenty-four hours a day and for maintaining dormitory rooms that don't try to squeeze in too many hostellers.

On the other hand, we've heard a number of complaints about the management being somewhat difficult to deal with. If you've come to Toronto to have fun, this could be a problem. They seem to take pride in running a tight ship here, and sometimes that's the right attitude. But how tight is too tight?

Tell you what: You make up your own mind on this one. We're going back to our room to flip a coin over it.

KEY TO ICONS

 Attractive natural setting	 Romantic private rooms	Good for business travelers
 Ecologically aware hostel	 Comfortable beds	 Especially well suited for families
 Superior kitchen facilities or cafe	 Among our very favorite hostels	 Good for active travelers
 Offbeat or eccentric place	 A particularly good value	 Visual arts at hostel or nearby
 Superior bathroom facilities	 Wheelchair-accessible	 Music at hostel or nearby

How to get there:

By bus: Bus lines stop in Toronto. From bus station, call hostel for transit route.

By car: Call hostel for directions.

By plane: Airport in Toronto. From airport, call hostel for transit route.

By train: VIA Rail stops in Toronto. From train station, call hostel for transit route.

MARIGOLD INTERNATIONAL TRAVELERS' HOSTEL

2011 Dundas Street, Toronto, Ontario M6R 1W7

(416) 536–8824

Web site: www.hostels.com/marigold

Rates: $23 Canadian (about $15 U.S.) per person
Credit cards: None
Office hours: 24 hours
Beds: 54
Private/family rooms: None
Single rooms: None
Private bathrooms: None
Affiliation: None
Extras: Coffee, doughnuts, laundry, lockers, TV

At first glance, the location seems unattractive—but it's near the High Park neighborhood, with a huge park of the same name and Roncevalles Avenue brimming over with Polish bakeries, Polish restaurants, fruit stands, and so forth. A real neighborhood, the kind you thought went extinct in the 1970s.

However, some hostellers grumble about the lack of a stovetop or even a refrigerator in the minimal kitchen. Good thing they keep the coffee and doughnuts—and muffins and green tea and black tea—going nonstop.

This hostel is often full in summer, maybe because of the super-ubiquitous flyers we saw all over Toronto. When you arrive at the hostel, you'll be welcomed in a warm and gracious manner by the owner John, manager Laire, or the humorous comanager Mike. You'll get freshly laundered sheets and towels at no charge at check-in. They might be full, but they will magically be able to conjure up a space for you (even if it is a bunk within millimeters of the reception area).

Some rooms (mostly single-sex) are packed with bunks; you have to really like people. A lot. There is a cozy family room with comfortable mattresses that can fit only three people, but the room leads to the popular outdoor deck, so you might have to deal with folks traipsing in and out of your room at all hours. Oh, well.

Thankfully, smoking is allowed outside—but not within the hostel.

On the downside, the building is rather threadbare. Most hostellers didn't seem to notice much, though, as they congregated in the tiny kitchen trading travel tips and exchanging addresses. We also had a problem with the bathrooms: The only full female bathroom is located on the third floor and is inside one of the dorm rooms. The line gets rather long in the morning, so don't drink anything just before bedtime. The bathroom sink and toilet could have used a good scrubbing, too.

On the upside, though, hostel managers can get no more helpful or friendly than these three guys, and they manage to make the limited space work and to pay attention to guests' needs—more than at most other hostels we've seen in North America. Not the prettiest facility, not the greatest neighborhood, but it's definitely an option.

Best bet for a bite: Up and down Roncevalles

What hostellers say: "Spare a buck?"

Insiders' tip: Streetcars run all night

Gestalt: Flower power

Safety: B

Hospitality: A

Cleanliness: C

Party index:

How to get there:

By bus: Bus lines in Toronto. From depot, call hostel for transit route.

By car: Call hostel for directions.

By plane: Airport in Toronto. From airport, call hostel for transit route.

By train: VIA Rail stops in Toronto. From station, call hostel for transit route.

NEILL-WYCIK COLLEGE HOTEL HOSTEL

96 Gerrard Street East, Toronto, Ontario M5B 1G7

(800) 268–4358; (416) 977–2320

E-mail: wycik@inforamp.net

Rates: $16 Canadian (about $11 U.S.) per person; private rooms $40 Canadian (about $28 U.S.); vary with season

Credit cards: MC, VISA

Office hours: 24 hours

Season: May 4–August 26

Beds: 500

Private/family rooms: 250

Single rooms: None

Private bathrooms: None

Affiliation: None

Extras: Laundry, breakfast, TV, sauna, telephones

10%

The seasonal Neill-Wycik Hostel (it's pronounced *kneel-WY-zek)* provides incredible downtown Toronto accommodations with a staff made up entirely of college students. It's a residence hall during the school year, then it morphs into Super-hostel for a surprisingly long summer season. They've made the place more like a hostel than before, too; you'll pay much less now to share a dorm, rather than pay lots for a whole lonely room if you're just one person.

Best bet for a bite: All over the place

What hostellers say: "I get what??"

Gestalt: Neill diamond

Safety: A

Hospitality: A

Cleanliness: C

Party index:

You'll nearly fall over backwards when you hear that you get a private bedroom with a key—they've all got two single beds, not doubles—and that you'll be sharing your washroom, kitchen, and common room with just a few other hostellers. Each unit is a four- or five-bedroom student apartment, basically; sheets, towels, and basic furnishings come with it. So do phones in the rooms! However, bring your own pots—none are supplied by the hostel. Or dine out at one of dozens of restaurants in the area; this is downtown Toronto at its multicultural best, ya know, so go out and see it.

We've heard that the cleaning isn't always well attended to, but maybe you can overlook a few lapses when the range of guest services is so vast. For example, you can buy a hot, filling breakfast in a cafe spelled with a "k" (boyyyy do we hate that); get discounts on package tours to Niagara Falls; pick up lots of helpful tourist information; and get picked up or dropped off at the airport. Nice sauna here, too.

Prices vary according to the part of the summer. The managers have divided the rates into "shoulder season" and "high season." This slightly confusing situation is made worse when the weighty provincial and government sales taxes are added in. Also, all reservations—essential in July and August—must be confirmed with a credit card. Cancel less than twenty-four hours before your scheduled arrival, bucko, and you're out some money.

Overall, this place should be commended for opening its doors to budget travelers during the summer months and offering such spacious digs in a city strapped for hostel-like accommodations.

How to get there:

By bus: Bus lines in Toronto. From depot, call hostel for transit route.

By car: Call hostel for directions.

By plane: Airport in Toronto. From airport, call hostel for transit route.

By train: VIA Rail stops in Toronto. From station, call hostel for transit route.

ALBERTA AND THE PLAINS

Numbers on map refer to towns numbered below.

ALBERTA
5 Edmonton
9 Nordegg
6 Jasper
Lake Louise 8
1 3 Canmore
4 Drumheller
Banff 7
Kananaskis
2 Calgary
Waterton Lakes
10 International Park

ALBERTA

1. Banff
2. Calgary
3. Canmore
4. Drumheller
5. Edmonton
6. Jasper
7. Kananaskis
8. Lake Louise
9. Nordegg
10. Waterton Lakes International Park

MANITOBA

11. Powerview
12. Winnipeg

SASKATCHEWAN

13. Regina
14. Saskatoon

Alberta is an odd place. It contains some of Canada's flattest prairie—and some of its most spectacular mountain ranges. It's home to the Calgary Stampede, a boot-stompin' cowboy extravaganza, but also home to a Banff scene of tourists falling all over one another to buy the longest camera lens.

It's also got the most interesting set of hostels in the country. A string of mostly rustic hostels runs up and down the spine of the incredible Icefields Parkway; in a couple of days, you could conceivably see more than a dozen of these places. (We did.) They range from extremely basic but invigorating huts—with boards for bunks, outhouses, and no running water—to lodgelike accommodations with all the modern blessings of hot showers, private rooms, and even a restaurant or two.

To hit the most hostels here, simply drive that parkway; you'll never want to leave it. Shuttle operators sometimes run up and down this corridor, stopping at the hostels along the way. Other hostels exist just east of the Rockies, on the Plains, in the cultural outposts of Edmonton and Calgary; bus and plane connections are much cheaper and easier in those cities. Finally, VIA Rail will drop you in Edmonton during the afternoon if you're going that route.

BANFF INTERNATIONAL HOSTEL

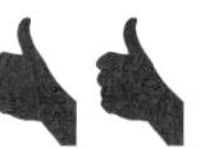

Tunnel Mountain Road, Banff, Alberta TOL OCO

(403) 762–4122

Fax: (403) 762–3441

E-mail: banff@HostellingIntl.ca

Web site: www.HostellingIntl.ca/Alberta/Hostels/Banff.html

Rates: $19 Canadian (about $14 U.S.) per Hostelling International member; private rooms $44–$52 Canadian (about $31–$36 U.S.)
Credit cards: MC, VISA
Office hours: 24 hours
Beds: 216
Private/family rooms: 7
Single rooms: None
Private bathrooms: None
Affiliation: Hostelling International-Canada
Extras: Laundry, lockers, cafe, conference rooms, game rooms, playground, meals

If we had to choose just one "luxury" hostel to visit in western Canada, it might well be this one, set on a rise above downtown

Banff International Hostel
Banff
(photo courtesy HI-Canada)

Banff. Other upscale hostels in the area offer similar amenities—cafe, laundry, game room, and such—but this hostel just seems more homey and less self-conscious than the others.

The building itself looks like many of the other condominiums surrounding it: mostly wood and windows. Inside, a high-ceilinged sitting room with fireplace sets the tone. You'll find a foyer with pay phones and a reception desk staffed by seasoned, cheery professionals. Doors lead to a patio with a nice view of the surrounding mountains.

The popular Cafe Alpenglow is adjacent and serves up moderately priced eats: Breakfast runs from as little as $1.25 Canadian (about $1.00 U.S.) for toast and jam to about $6.00 Canadian ($4.50 U.S.) for a rib-stickin' meal like pancakes or an omelet. You can get breakfast until 2:00 P.M. Lunch and dinner offerings cost from $3.00 Canadian (about $2.50 U.S.) for a salad to about $8.25 Canadian (about $6.00 U.S.) for a real meal like pasta. Can't afford those prices? Neither can we. Fortunately, there's a grocery store across the street.

Work off the calories by walking down to town and then—of course—walking steeply back uphill to get here. Can't face it? The town runs a nice Banff Transit service that, for a mere loonie (that's $1.00 Canadian, or about $0.70 U.S.), will spirit you downtown.

Back to the hostel. Dorm rooms here are a real departure from the rustic places around the province; you'll be sleeping with no more than five other people per room, and often fewer, in comfortable bunks. Family rooms are a pleasure, with actual double beds (not double bunks) and sets of twin bunk beds. These come with reading lights as well as clothes hangers. Be sure to book well in advance for these, though, because they fill up fast.

Other pluses include the game room (which also serves as overflow dorm space)—fun, fun, fun here, in the form of a stereo, pool table, dartboard, and more, and it stays open late. There's a laundry room with three washers and dryers, plus a sink for hand-washables and an ironing board. Across the street, the hostel's handsome office building is used for groups needing separate space for meetings and such.

This hostel is big on information, providing separate bulletin boards for daily weather reports (important in these high mountains), local tour operators, items for sale, and rides offered or needed. The government of Canada has also installed a computerized job bank in the hostel for recently posted jobs, mostly in the travel/tourism industry. Other amenities include a meeting room, which often hosts skiing or cycling workshops, and on-site parking, which includes—this is a first—plug-ins! (For the uninitiated, those are electrical outlets that you plug your car into so that the engine won't freeze solid overnight.)

Best bet for a bite: St. James' Gate pub

What hostellers say: "No worries, mate."

Insiders' tip: Good binocular prices

Gestalt: Banff-tastic

Hospitality: B

Cleanliness: A

Party index:

The townsite of Banff itself is more touristy than a town in a national park should be, offering a few too many tacky gift shops. However, many businesses cater to hostellers by offering discounts on meals or photo processing and such, so take advantage. Also, if you're in town in early October, hit the Taste of Banff/Lake Louise, a fun event where, for very little money, you can try small portions of meals served at the most expensive restaurants in town and grab glasses of beer or berry pancakes for dessert.

This is one of the better hostels in the West, and that's amazing. This kind of popularity would run a lesser hostel right into the ground.

How to get there:

By bus: Greyhound stops in Banff. Bus station is walking distance to hostel. From depot, call hostel for directions.

By car: Call hostel for directions.

By plane: Airport in Calgary. Call hostel for transit route.

CASTLE MOUNTAIN HOSTEL

Bow Valley Parkway, Banff, Alberta TOL 0C0

(403) 762–2367

E-mail: banff@HostellingIntl.ca

Web site: www.HostellingIntl.ca/Alberta/Hostels/Castle

Rates: $12.00 Canadian (about $8.00 U.S.) per Hostelling International member
Credit cards: None
Office hours: 8:00–10:00 A.M.; 5:00–10:00 P.M.
Beds: 36
Private/family rooms: Yes; number varies; call for availability
Single rooms: None
Private bathrooms: None
Affiliation: Hostelling International-Canada
Extras: Fireplace, grill, store, laundry, bicycle rentals, campfires, volleyball court, library, games, fireplace

Mountains and other natural geological features seem to inspire whimsical and mythic names, and Castle Mountain is no exception. This hostel plays the part of fairy-tale cottage in the woods beneath the grandiose turreted solid mass of rock towering just above, and the combination works.

Best bet for a bite: PowerBars at grocery store

What hostellers say: "Goo."

Insiders' tip: Take Bow Valley Parkway

Gestalt: Magic kingdom

Hospitality: A

Cleanliness: A

Party index:

Located between the towns of Banff and Lake Louise—quite close to Banff, actually—the diminutive building consists of two coed dorms, a kitchen, and a living room. That's it, but the common room is attractive: a soothing, semicircular space with good heating, and its windows are perfect for gazing out into a spruce-and-pine forest teeming with wildlife. And, unlike almost all the other Parkway hostels, this one has indoor plumbing and *hot showers.* Yippee! One more bonus: New manager's quarters have freed up one to two new family rooms in the manager's old living space.

Basic food is sold by the honor system; you can buy a single egg by dropping a quarter into a can, for instance, or shell out $2.50 Canadian (about $2.00 U.S.) for a full breakfast that you'll fix yourself. The small kitchen is homey and well loved, by the look of things. And there's a combination gas station/general store right across the road—unusual on the Parkway, and handy for stocking up on things you just didn't remember to bring.

Of all the hostels we visited in Canada, this one seemed among the most suitable for families with children: Lots of kid-oriented activities, games, and other distractions are scattered about, enough to make the most hardened hostelling parent break down and weep with sheer gratitude for a moment of silence. (Someone has even painted a vividly colored mural at the entrance.) Don't forget to hit Johnston Canyon, Rockbound Lake, or any of numerous other wilderness areas around here, either.

This is definitely one hostel to consider when you need more peace than frenzy yet can't sacrifice a hot shower and quick access to the store.

How to get there:

By car: From Lake Louise, drive Trans-Canada Highway (Highway 1) or Highway 1A (Bow Valley Parkway) approximately 30 km (19 mi.) north to junction with Highway 93. Turn onto Highway 93; hostel is 1.5 km (1 mi.) east of junction with Highway 1 and less than 100 meters (300 feet) from junction with Highway 1A. From Banff, drive Trans-Canada Highway (Highway 1) or Highway 1A (Bow Valley Parkway) approximately 30 km (19 mi.) south to junction with Highway 93. Turn onto Highway 93; hostel is 1.5 km (1 mi.) east of junction with Highway 1 and less than 100 meters (300 feet) from junction with Highway 1A.

HILDA CREEK HOSTEL 

Highway 93, Banff, Alberta TOL OCO

(403) 762–4122

E-mail: banff@HostellingIntl.ca

Web site: www.HostellingIntl.ca/Alberta/Hostels/Hilda

Rates: $10.00 Canadian (about $7.00 U.S.) per Hostelling International member
Credit cards: MC, VISA
Office hours: 8:00–10:00 A.M.; 5:00–11:00 P.M.
Season: Closed Sunday–Wednesday, February 1–May 14
Beds: 28
Private/family rooms: None
Private bathrooms: None
Single rooms: None
Affiliation: Hostelling International-Canada
Extras: Bicycle rentals, store, campfire, sauna

Another Banff hostel with an impeccable location, practically sitting on top of the famed and popular Columbia Icefields and right at the foot of big and beautiful Mount Athabasca.

We can tell you that it's super-basic. The hostel's work crew recently added a new seven-bunk, pine-paneled cabin, including a double bunk with a single on top—perfect for families—to ratchet up the comfort factor a bit.

Best bet for a bite: Icefields Centre snack bar

What hostellers say: "Don't fall in!"

Insiders' tip: Mountain goats on highway

Gestalt: Ice, ice, baby

Hospitality: A

Cleanliness: A

Party index:

But toilets are still outdoors. There's no indoor plumbing whatsoever; to cook or clean, you're going to have to collect some water from the creek. A wood-burning sauna does enhance the experience, however.

Since this is a high-elevation hostel, occasionally (even in fall or late summer) you might find snow blocking the hostel driveway. But you're in the wild, so get an excellent view of the nearby Saskatchewan Glacier by taking the Parker Ridge trail that runs behind the hostel: Hike it in summer or—for more challenge—ski it in winter. (Just remember that the hostel is open weekends only from February through May 14.)

To get a closer view of the glacier, lots of tourists elect to take snowcoaches—special tractor-type vehicles that go right up onto it. Don't bother, we say. Save the hefty ticket price and walk this great alpine trail instead.

How to get there:

By car: From Lake Louise, drive 120 km (75 mi.) north on Icefields Parkway (Highway 93). Hostel is 8 km (5 mi.) south of Columbia Icefield Centre, on left.

MOSQUITO CREEK HOSTEL

Highway 93, Banff, Alberta TOL OCO

E-mail: banff@HostellingIntl.ca

Web site: www.HostellingIntl.ca/Alberta/Hostels/Mosquito

Rates: $12.00 Canadian (about $8.00 U.S.) per Hostelling International member; private rooms $30.00–$38.00 Canadian (about $21.00–$27.00 U.S.)
Credit cards: None
Office hours: 8:00–10:00 A.M.; 5:00–11:00 P.M.
Beds: 38
Private/family rooms: 2
Single rooms: None
Private bathrooms: None
Affiliation: Hostelling International-Canada

Extras: Sauna, store, bicycle rentals, campfire, fireplace

This hostel another in the chain of rustic huts located along Alberta's brilliant Icefields Parkway—takes the sting out of paying for high-priced resort hotels by providing oodles of scenery at a fraction of the cost.

It's located next to the rushing creek (you'll soon figure out where the hostel got the name) and a campground. You get the same smallish buildings and outdoor no-flush bathroom facilities as at most of the other hostels in this area—but also the bonus of a cheery sauna and an inviting, semicircular living room with a fireplace and bay windows. The place maintains a small honor-system store selling typical quick-to-fix eats and snacks. And the kitchen is homey, with lots of cooking equipment, including a refrigerator and a gas stove, so you're not exactly roughing it. You do have to boil your creek water, however.

Best bet for a bite: Hostel store

Insiders' tip: Wear bear bells

Gestalt: Good buzz

Hospitality: A

Cleanliness: A

Party index:

Dorms are divvied up among four cabins, featuring quite basic triple-decker bunk beds; sometimes the dorms are coed, depending on the mix of visitors. There are also two family rooms, located in a great little cabin that has its own small kitchen—excellent if you're packing the young'uns. If you bring the little ones in tow, though, remember that this is bear country: Keep them (the kids, not the bears) in sight at all times.

How to get there:

By car: From Lake Louise, drive 26 km (15 mi.) north on Highway 93. Hostel is on left.

KEY TO ICONS

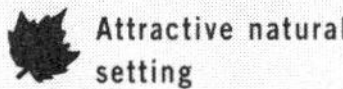

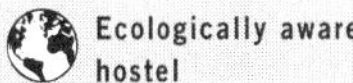

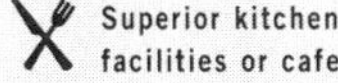

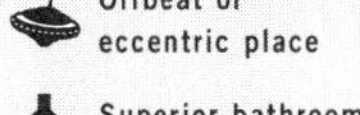

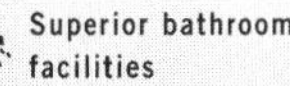

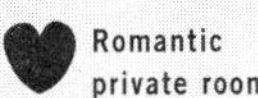

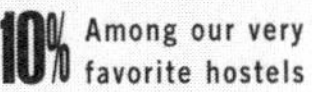

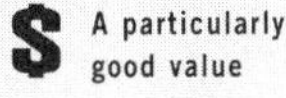

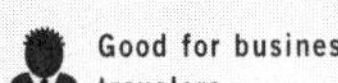

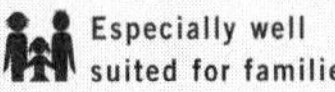

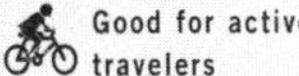

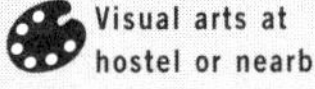

RAMPART CREEK HOSTEL

Highway 93, Banff, Alberta TOL OCO

(403) 762–4122

E-mail: banff@HostellingIntl.ca

Web site: HostellingIntl.ca/Alberta/Hostels/Rampart

Rates: $11.00 Canadian (about $9.00 U.S.) per Hostelling International member
Credit cards: None
Office hours: 8:00–10:00 A.M.; 5:00–11:00 P.M.
Season: Closed some days, November–May; call hostel for updates
Beds: 30
Private/family rooms: None
Single rooms: None
Private bathrooms: None
Affiliation: Hostelling International-Canada
Extras: Sauna, food, wood-burning stoves, campfires, bicycle rentals, volleyball court

Sometimes simpler is better. In the case of the Rampart Creek Hostel, this rings especially true. How can you fault a place that only has pit toilets when the scenery here is so pristine? Glaciers, fiercely running streams, towering cliffs, pungent spruce—this hostel has it all in spades, making the lack of creature comforts unimportant by contrast.

Best bet for a bite: Foraging

What hostellers say: "Nirvana."

Insiders' tip: Sauna-tub combo

Gestalt: Stoked

Hospitality: A

Cleanliness: A

Party index:

This hostel is part of the chain of Hostelling International hostels located along Alberta's gorgeous (and we mean that literally) Icefields Parkway. It's a small operation, just thirty simple beds in two small cabins—and, get this, the bunks are triple-deckers! We'd hate to have that middle bunk, that's for sure.

Anyhow, the main building houses a well-lit and cozy common room; a newly constructed, self-catering kitchen; and loads of recreational information, including detailed descriptions of hiking and biking trails in the vast surrounding parklands. What else do you get? The "best sauna in the Rockies," claim some; it's a little log cabin fired by wood, with space for about five folks. Wash off afterward beneath startling snow-covered peaks in the (also wood-fired) outdoor bathtub.

What more can you do here? Lots. Cook in the firepit, scramble up some interesting cliffs, swim a beautiful little rushing river that sits flush up against the mountain, listen for bears, watch for goats,

Rampart Creek Hostel

Banff National Park

(photo by Paul Karr)

and just generally bask in the solitude if you've come anytime other than during the high summer season. Rugged day hikes to places like Glacier Lake, Sunset Lookout, and Mistaya Canyon are nice possibilities. The truly hardy might ice climb at Murchison Falls, Ice Nine, or the aptly named Transparent Fool.

Truly Spartan, truly enlightening, truly wonderful.

How to get there:

By car: From Lake Louise, drive 95 km (about 60 mi.) north on Icefields Parkway (Highway 93). Hostel is on right.

CALGARY INTERNATIONAL HOSTEL

520 Seventh Avenue Southeast, Calgary, Alberta T2G 0J6

(403) 269–8239

Fax: (403) 266–6227

E-mail: chostel@HostellingIntl.ca

Web site: www.HostellingIntl.ca/Alberta/Hostels/Calgary

Rates: $15 Canadian (about $10 U.S.) per Hostelling International member

Credit cards: MC, VISA

Office hours: 24 hours
Beds: 122
Private/family rooms: 4
Single rooms: None
Private bathrooms: 2
Affiliation: Hostelling International-Canada
Extras: Laundry, lockers, snack bar, game room, barbecue, tours, movies, massage therapist, bicycle shed, tours, kitchen TV, pool table

10%

The city that hosted the 1988 Winter Olympic Games has already fallen out of the world spotlight, but Canadians know how interesting Calgary is. It is tucked up almost against the huge Rockies, yet it is full of interesting cultural things to do.

The city's hostel is a very good one, too. It's set in a two-story, wooden, lodge-style building right in the heart of big, brawny Calgary, yet it's hardly noticeable because of its relatively sedate residential location. That's right. This unassuming little house sits close by skyscrapers, parks, city hall, and department stores, only 2 blocks east of Olympic Plaza. But you can still have a nice, quiet stay.

Best bet for a bite: Local beef

What hostellers say: "Giddyup!"

Insiders' tip: Devonian Gardens

Gestalt: Stampede

Safety: A

Hospitality: A

Cleanliness: A

Party index:

Most dorm rooms hold either six or eight beds apiece. Two family rooms are also added during the winter, when demand for the bunkrooms is lower. But the main focus of social life here is a convivial, Western-themed lounge dominated by two overstuffed couches that face each other across a coffee table. Walls are decorate with paintings of horses, horseshoes, cowboy implements—you get the picture.

This is a very active hostel. Among the activities here are movie nights, city tours, road trips, barbecues, and discounts on entrance fees to such local attractions as the Calgary Tower (ho-hum) and the Calgary Zoo (hmmm). We didn't get to try the advertised massage therapist, but maybe you'll have better luck.

As we've said, the city itself is full of other fun stuff to do, too. The annual Calgary Stampede is one of North America's biggest rodeos—cowboy hats and boots are absolutely necessary during the thing—and a good restaurant and club scene has also sprung up in recent years. It's unlikely you'll be bored, and it's mighty easy to get to public transportation from this spunky little place: It sits right on a transit mall, so buses race past the hostel doors all day long.

How to get there:

By bus: Greyhound stops in Calgary. From bus station, take free shuttle bus to Seventh Avenue; transfer to C Train and take to city hall, then walk 2 blocks east on Seventh Avenue to hostel.

By car: Call hostel for directions.

By plane: Airport in Calgary. From airport, take Airporter shuttle to hostel. Delta Bow Valley Hotel; walk to hostel on Seventh Avenue South.

CANMORE CLUBHOUSE 

P.O. Box 8040, Canmore, Alberta T1W 2T8

(403) 678–3200

E-mail: alpclub@telusplanet.net OR acc@mail.culturenet.ca

Web site: www.culturenet.ca/acc/facility/clubhous.htm

Rates: $20 Canadian (about $14 U.S.) per person; $5.00 Canadian (about $4.00 U.S.) discount for club members
Credit cards: MC, VISA
Office hours: 9:00 A.M.–8:00 P.M.
Beds: 28
Private/family rooms: None
Single rooms: None
Private bathrooms: None
Affiliation: None
Extras: Laundry, lockers, climbing gear rental, local phone, travel store, fax, library, snack bar, sauna, fireplace

10%

Tucked onto a bench of land above the quiet and pretty Bow Valley Highway, the Canmore Clubhouse serves a number of functions. It's the place where the Alpine Club of Canada runs its national operations; and it's home to a twenty-eight–bed hostel, a good alternative for athletes and families that's located close to all the real-world amenities of Banff and Canmore.

The main building contains all the bunks—they're housed in six upstairs rooms of four to six beds each, away from ground-floor bustle—plus the usual kitchen and common living room. The living room features a fireplace and a great little library of outdoor reading; you can buy a beer or snacks here, too, though not any sort of substantial groceries. (Luckily, there are two grocery stores in the area and a number of restaurants.) One set of bathrooms is located near the dorms, and another set is also hidden away in the basement to accommodate a full house.

On the surface, this building is a place of business—but scratch beneath the surface and you'll realize it was really built for gear-

Best bet for a bite: Sherwood House

What hostellers say: "Bum a crampon?"

Insiders' tip: Fax Mom that you're alive

Gestalt: Fire and ice

Hospitality: A

Cleanliness: A

Party index:

heads. Climbing gear can be rented at the front desk, good guidebooks and maps are sold right here, and there are lockers and a laundry. Slide shows occasionally take place, too. No wonder the hostel becomes a magnet for ice climbers each winter! People come to test themselves on one of more than 150 local routes—everything from Grade 2 climbs that you can do right from the roadside, to white-knuckle, Grade 6 climbs in the Ghost River area.

Other stuff? The staff here will let you send or receive faxes for a small charge. And there's a special room, called the Guides Room, that's usually reserved for meetings, climbing courses, and that sort of thing. You might get the chance to sign up for something if it's happening and not full up yet.

Also, while it's not part of the hostel, Bell Cabin, on the same property, is a great place to bring large groups of up to fifteen people. This building comes with a kitchen, two bathrooms, and a set of showers, a large living room with fireplace, and an incredible view.

How to get there:

By car: Call hostel for directions.

ALEXANDRA INTERNATIONAL HOSTEL 

30 Railway Avenue North, Drumheller, Alberta T0J 0Y0

(403) 823–6337

Rates: $17.50 Canadian (about $12.50 U.S.) per person
Credit cards: MC, VISA
Office hours: 10:00 A.M.–11:00 P.M.
Beds: 55
Private/family rooms: 4
Single rooms: None
Private bathrooms: Yes; number varies; call for availability
Affiliation: None
Extras: Laundry, meals, snack bar, bicycle rentals, lockers, meeting room, game room

This handsome, three-story former hotel has been running for eight years now as a hostel. Most of the dorm rooms here have eight beds, although there are a few other configurations; some have fewer beds, some feature private bathrooms, and private rooms for couples and families are also available.

We haven't heard many reports about this place since the recent handover, but it's still got lots of travel-friendly amenities: a laundry, cafe, and storage and locker space, for example.

Why would someone come to this spot? Because this is dinosaur country, baby! Giant Barneys (not purple ones, either) used to roam the earth around here chomping on whatever Jurassic salad they could scrounge up, and some of them have been preserved here in the muck of ages. For the interested, the surrounding area's 50-km (30-mi.) Dinosaur Trail hits all the major paleontological plot points. The highlight in town is the Tyrell Museum, full of those old bones. You might also try your own hand at fossil hunting out in the hills if you're hankering for a piece of ol' T. Rex.

Insiders' tip: Fossil Shop

Gestalt: Land of the lost

Hospitality: C

Cleanliness: B

Party index:

How to get there:

By bus: Bus lines stop in Drumheller. From bus depot, walk north on Highway 9 across train tracks; make a left onto Railway Avenue and walk approximately 0.3 km (0.2 mi.) to hostel.

By car: Call hostel for directions.

EDMONTON INTERNATIONAL HOSTEL

10647 Eighty-first Avenue, Edmonton, Alberta T6E 1Y1

(877) 467–8336; (780) 988–6836

Fax: (780) 988-8698

E-mail: eihostel@hostellingintl.ca

Rates: $15 Canadian per Hostelling International member (about $10 U.S.)

Credit cards: None

Beds: 104

Private/family rooms: No

Affiliation: Hostelling International-Canada

Extras: Kitchen, laundry, game room, courtyard, grill, bike rentals

A much-needed replacement for the former hostel here—located in a dodgy area—this one's been placed much better, in the city's most interesting district, Old Strathcona in south Edmonton.

A modernish complex with nice trees in a courtyard outside, the place includes two kitchens, a laundry, game room, barbecue area, and mountain bikes for hire. Good job. And it's really close to the historic Strathcona area, with all the shops, restaurants, and old buildings you could expect to see in an oil town.

Best bet for a bite: Smokey Joe's

What hostellers say: "Strap on the feed bag."

Insiders' tip: Underground walkways in winter

Gestalt: Oil's well

Safety: A

Hospitality: A

Cleanliness: A

Party index:

For other entertainment, if you must, head for the gargantuan West Edmonton Mall—yeah, the world's largest shopping center, featuring 800 shops, 110 restaurants, a wave tank, indoor bungee jumping, and a whole lot more. Hostel staff can tell you how to get there. Much better, the Edmonton Folk Festival in summer is one of North America's better ones. Or check out the Oilers hockey team in winter.

How to get there:

By bus: From bus station, walk east to 101st Street and catch #9 Southgate bus or #7 Belgravia bus south. (Bring exact change of $1.60). Get off at Whyte Avenue and 109th Street. Walk 2 blocks east and 1 block south to hostel.

By car: Call hostel for directions.

By train: VIA Rail stops in Edmonton. Call hostel for transit route.

ATHABASCA FALLS HOSTEL

Highway 93, Jasper, Alberta T0E 1E0

(780) 852–5959

E-mail: jihostel@HostellingIntl.ca

Web site: www.HostellingIntl.ca/Alberta/Hostels/Athabasca

Rates: $9.00–$10.00 Canadian (about $7.00–$8.00 U.S.) per Hostelling International member

Credit cards: MC, VISA

Office hours: 8:00–10:00 A.M.; 5:00–11:00 P.M.

Season: Closed Tuesdays, October–April

Beds: 40

Private/family rooms: None

Single rooms: None

Private bathrooms: None

Affiliation: Hostelling International-Canada

Extras: Volleyball, horseshoes, Ping-Pong table, basketball hoop, kitchen

When you've got stunning scenery and spectacular natural features like Athabasca Falls, the hostel plays second fiddle. Here,

Athabasca Falls Hostel
Jasper
(photo courtesy HI-Canada)

the place does what it has to do—provide decent accommodations—and keeps in total harmony with its environment.

The complex of three cabins plus a main building resembles a fishing camp. Thirteen beds are nicely arranged in each well-heated and insulated cabin, plus there's a double bed in one of the cabins—no privacy for honeymooners at all, but still a chance to sleep side by side instead of bunk-over-bunk.

The main building works well as combination mess hall, rec room, and sock dryer. Huh? Well, the cozy central fireplace area with the comfy couches is ideal for lazing, warming up, and sock drying. There's a public pay phone, too, a necessity out here in the backcountry.

There's no question of what to do once you're here: Hit the trails. Hiking till your toes hurt is the reason for being here; there are trails encompassing Geraldine Lake and Leach Lake. Improve your nosedive off the cliffs at Horseshoe Lake. Or cross-country ski during winter, which might be as early as the beginning of October in these parts. There are also, of course, the famous waterfalls very close by—a treat.

This hostel even has its own built-in entertainment. Sort of. A basketball hoop was being tested when we arrived, and a volleyball court has been set up along the driveway. You can discuss the merits of NAFTA around the campfire pit while toasting that big,

Best bet for a bite: Buy food in Jasper

What hostellers say: "I fall down."

Insiders' tip: Bring a flashlight

Gestalt: Over the waterfalls

Hospitality: A

Cleanliness: A

Party index:

soft, gooey marshmallow; or you can play that old-fashioned game of aim, horseshoes.

Of course, this wouldn't be the wilderness without the presence of certain predators who've got a hankerin' for garbage, chocolate—and, very occasionally, nosy humans. Remember that bears just might be lurking around the corner as you're stumbling to the loo at midnight, so bring your "bear bells" and a flashlight just in case you unexpectedly come nose-to-snout with one of 'em.

How to get there:

By car: From Jasper, drive south on Icefields Parkway (Highway 93) for 32 km (about 20 mi.). Turn left at signs for hostel, near other signs for Athabasca Falls.

BEAUTY CREEK HOSTEL

Highway 93, Jasper, Alberta T0E 1E0

(780) 852–3215

E-mail: jihostel@HostellingIntl.ca

Web site: www.HostellingIntl.ca/Alberta/Hostels/Beauty

Rates: $9.00 Canadian (about $7.00 U.S.) per Hostelling International member

Credit cards: MC, VISA

Office hours: 8:00–10:00 A.M.; 5:00–11:00 P.M.

Season: May 1–September 30

Beds: 24

Private/family rooms: None

Single rooms: None

Private bathrooms: None

Affiliation: Hostelling International-Canada

Extras: Wood-burning stoves, food, campfires

Of all the hostels on the Icefields Parkway, this one ties with Rampart Creek for our very favorite location. It's perched literally inches from the blue, blue rushing Sunwapta River, a sublimely beautiful spot that reminds one of, say, Alaska.

This place is pretty small, but, as they say, it has to be. The facilities consist of a simple row of three cabins—two of which are sleeping cabins, and a third that contains the common area and kitchen. Things are really basic; there is no refrigerator in the kitchen, for instance, so don't pack in a side of beef or some ice cream for dessert. Wood-burning stoves heat the hostel, and plumbing is strictly of the point-and-shoot variety.

For some reason—possibly the flat stretch it's located on, and the fact that it lies about a day's biking from Jasper or maybe Banff—this hostel is a popular resting point for people biking up or down the Parkway.

Still, Beauty Creek itself is the true highlight here. It flows into the Sunwapta and then descends almost 1,700 meters (5,000 feet) through a limestone gorge into the Parkway Valley feeding eight (count 'em, eight) spectacular waterfalls. Find your way to the last one, Stanley Falls, and you've reached nirvana, say some. The popular Columbia Icefield Centre is also quite close by, with its tourist information, snacks, weather updates, and glacier tours.

Best bet for a bite: Miles away

What hostellers say: "   " (speechless)

Insiders' tip: Point and shoot

Gestalt: Real beauty, eh?

Hospitality: A

Cleanliness: A

Party index:

How to get there:

By car: From Jasper, drive 87 km (about 50 mi.) south on the Icefields Parkway (Highway 93). Hostel is on left.

JASPER INTERNATIONAL HOSTEL

Skytram Road, Jasper, Alberta T0E 1E0

(780) 852–3215

Fax: (780) 852–5560

E-mail: jihostel@telusplanet.net OR jihostel@HostellingIntl.ca

Web site: www.HostellingIntl.ca/Alberta/Hostels/Jasper

Rates: $15 Canadian (about $10 U.S.) per Hostelling International member
Credit cards: MC, VISA
Office hours: 8:00 A.M.–midnight
Beds: 80
Private/family rooms: 3
Single rooms: None
Private bathrooms: None
Affiliation: Hostelling International-Canada
Extras: Lockers, meals (sometimes), events, bicycle rentals, grill

As you pull into the town of Jasper—by train, plane, automobile, or bus, it doesn't matter—you'll be awestruck by the place. It charms even as it makes you draw a breath. Gigantic mountains loom on all sides; audacious elk plunk themselves down on the lawn of the local tourist office and play their annual fall mating game. Throngs of camera-toting tourists clamor to take in the Canadian Rockies in all their splendor, choosing the town as a quaint and manageable base—this sure isn't Banff!—for forays into the wild.

Select the Jasper International Hostel as your base and you'll be in awe again. This relatively small hostel accommodates lots of happy hostellers with apparent ease and even adds to the mind-blowing experience of the area.

Best bet for a bite: Tasty Meats, downtown

What hostellers say: *"Ohaiyo gozaimasu."*

Insiders' tip: Hiking Whistler Mountain

Gestalt: Jasper the friendly host

Hospitality: A

Cleanliness: A

Party index:

The hostel is situated a bit of a jaunt up a mountain road, so be prepared to either hitchhike from the bus/train station or call a cab. Once there, though, the view is spectacular—especially of Whistler's Mountain, which rises to a height of 2,300 meters (about 7,000 feet) right out the backyard of the hostel.

The building itself is a barnlike structure. With the cool mountain air cascading down into it, it can occasionally feel as drafty as a barn. But the friendly and hospitable staff really go the distance to do right by hostellers, so if you're a bit chilly, head for the kitchen and make some new friends. You'll probably notice signs announcing a special dinner, slide show, or other event run by staff members—one seems to occur every day during the slow season. Since this hostel lacks the space and other amenities of similar-sized hostels around Canada, it goes the extra distance to keep hostellers well looked after.

Keep this in mind when you descend the stairs to the frigid coed dorm—a room with more than forty (yes, forty) beds packed together in one big open room—and a men's bathroom that holds just three showers and three toilets for the whole bunch. The women's dorm upstairs is slightly more spacious (only about thirty bunks here) with a nice sitting area and a better bathroom. The three private rooms are the real stars here, though, each containing one family-style double plus either a "hide-a-bed" for smaller children or an extra mattress to fit in a family of four comfortably.

The no-shoes policy really helps cut down on excess noise, especially since many hostellers are sleeping right below the kitchen/common area. Just bring thick wool socks to help cushion those tender feet, especially when you're in the kitchen or bathroom. The staff thoughtfully provides slippers if you forgot yours.

Jasper International Hostel

Jasper

(photo by Paul Karr)

The kitchen gets crowded but is well maintained. Extra points for the sharp knives (usually absent from a hostel) and microwave. The dining room and common room offer lots of opportunities to strike up conversations with dozens of the Japanese, English, and Australians who love this area, and you'll find lots of great reading material and games as well. But you might be most content just to stare out the large plate-glass windows at the mountains.

For fun, the SkyTram, a gondola near the hostel that rides to the top of 2,300-meter-high (about 7,000 feet) Whistler's Mountain, is extremely popular with some hostellers; others choose to make a day hike to the top, watching for bears all the way.

Yes, you heard right. If you do choose to hoof it up, do so with caution: This is bear territory, and we don't mean the Winnie-the-

Pooh type. Grizzlies and black bears are everywhere, and this mountain is no exception. Try to hook up with another hosteller; even if you're alone, keep the noise level up by talking, singing, shouting, or jingling your keys. (In fact, follow these precautions for any of the woodsy hostels located in Banff, Jasper, or Yoho parks.)

"*Beaucoup* mountains." That's how one three-year-old French hosteller put it for us, and we couldn't agree more.

How to get there:

By bus: Greyhound stops in Jasper. From depot, take shuttle or taxi ($10.00 Canadian/about $7.00 U.S.) to hostel.

By car: From Jasper, drive south on Highway 93 about 5 km (3 mi.) to Whistler's Mountain Road (Skytram Road); turn right and continue uphill approximately 2 km (1 mi.). Hostel is on left.

By train: VIA Rail stops in Jasper. From station, take shuttle or taxi ($10.00 Canadian/about $7.00 U.S.) to hostel.

MT. EDITH CAVELL HOSTEL

Edith Cavell Road, Jasper, Alberta TOE 1EO

(780) 852–3215

E-mail: jihostel@HostellingIntl.ca

Web site: www.HostellingIntl.ca/Alberta/Hostels/EdithCavell

Rates: $9.00–$10.00 Canadian (about $7.00 U.S.) per Hostelling International member
Credit cards: MC, VISA
Office hours: 8:00–10:00 A.M.; 5:00–11:00 P.M.
Beds: 32
Season: Mid-June–September 30
Private/family rooms: None
Single rooms: None
Private bathrooms: None
Affiliation: Hostelling International-Canada
Extras: Food, wood-burning stoves, scenery

This is one of the most remote hostels in Canada, located 13 km (8 mi.) down a road that's so cold and snowy it gets closed in wintertime and so rough that campers can't negotiate. But if you can make it, it's a beautiful and very quiet spot to take in some of the grandest scenery in Jasper National Park.

The soaring 3,363-meter (about 11,000-feet) peak of Mount Edith Cavell—biggest in Jasper Park, don'cha know—towers over the place. In a cirque valley on the northeast slope shines the famous Angel Glacier, so named because its stretched-out sides remind one (we guess) of an angel. The mountain, by the way, was named for a British wartime nurse who stayed in Brussels to help Allied prisoners of war escape the Germans. She was executed for her heroism, and in remembrance she will always be associated with the other angel of the glacier.

Best bet for a bite: Nutter's, in Jasper

What hostellers say: "Wow!"

Insiders' tip: Wildflower meadows

Gestalt: Touched by an Angel

Hospitality: A

Party index:

On to the hostel. It consists of two basic sleeping cabins with a total of thirty-two bunk beds. You know the drill. Wood-burning stoves supply the heat; there's no fridge in the quite simple kitchen area; and, as with many of the rustic hostels in Alberta, toilets are outdoors. No running water, either.

The main attraction, of course, is the jaw-dropping wilderness scenery. You can actually hike to the foot of the Angel Glacier and explore its moraines; the hostel staff further recommend the colorful wildflowers of the Cavell Meadows—accessible via a three- to four-hour hiking loop that begins at the Mount Edith Cavell parking lot—and the turquoise waters of Cavell Lake just below. Sometimes you'll hear a distant sliding sound, and that will be the sound of enormous rockslides slipping down the faces of these young mountains.

Remember that the access road is so rough that trailers and camper vans won't be able to make it in; as an alternative, some operators in Jasper might try, but it'll likely cost \$20–\$30 Canadian (\$15–\$22 U.S.).

How to get there:

By car: From Jasper, drive Highway 93 south approximately 7 km (5 mi.); turn right onto Highway 93A (Mount Edith Cavell Road) and

KEY TO ICONS

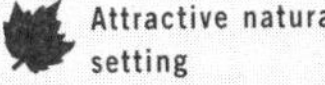

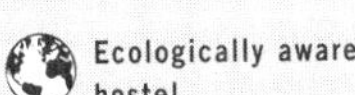

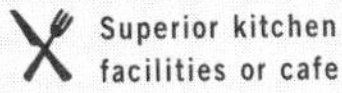

Offbeat or eccentric place

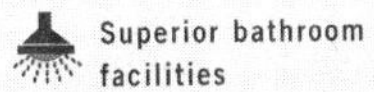

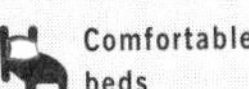

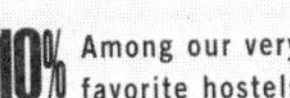

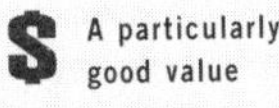

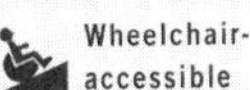

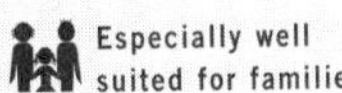

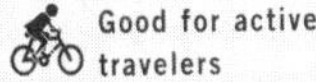

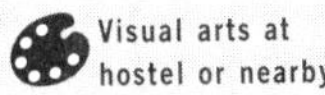

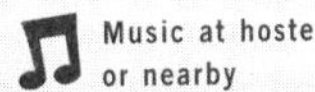

continue 13 more km (8 mi.). Hostel is on left, just before Angel Glacier parking area.

MALIGNE CANYON HOSTEL 

Maligne Lake Road, Jasper, Alberta T0E 1E0
(780) 852–3584
E-mail: jihostel@HostellingIntl.ca
Web site: www.HostellingIntl.ca/Alberta/Hostels/Maligne
Rates: $9.00–$10.00 Canadian (about $7.00–$8.00 U.S.) per Hostelling International member
Credit cards: MC, VISA
Office hours: 8:00–10:00 A.M.; 5:00–11:00 P.M.
Season: Closed Wednesdays, October–April
Beds: 24
Private/family rooms: None
Single rooms: None
Private bathrooms: None
Affiliation: Hostelling International-Canada
Extras: Heat, fireplace

Talk about rustic: This really small hostel sits practically on top of big and deep Maligne Canyon. If you seek to commune with Mother Nature, this is definitely the place. If you're lookin' for the Hilton, though, keep movin'.

The place isn't unlike the other small, rustic hostels dotted up and down the Icefields Parkway between Banff and Jasper National Parks. It consists of three buildings—two cabins and a cookhouse. These cabins are neat as a pin, each containing two rooms of six exceedingly simple bunks. Heat is included via a propane heater. Each cabin has a tiny porch, too, excellent for relaxing while listening to the nearby creek rush by.

The cookhouse–common area is also very basic; there's no running water, so all water used for cooking and drinking must be boiled. Still, it's outfitted with all the equipment you need to prepare a good meal—propane stove and refrigerator being the key items here. Stock up on food at the grocery stores in Jasper before you arrive, though. And be prepared to brave the elements when you need to use the toilet: It's outside. 'Nuff said on that subject.

Best bet for a bite: Teahouse at Maligne Canyon

What hostellers say: "Bear aware!"

Insiders' tip: Hot springs

Gestalt: Lean and Maligne

Hospitality: A

Cleanliness: A

Party index:

Maligne Canyon Hostel
Jasper
(photo courtesy HI-Canada)

It isn't immediately clear why this hostel—like the other rustic hostels in the area—separates cooking areas from the sleeping areas. But take a gander at the bear-observation board and you'll get the picture in a hurry. Just a few days before our arrival, a bear had in fact meandered onto the hostel grounds in search of a good meal. We don't think he was leafing through copies of *Vegetarian Times,* either, if you know what we mean. And we think you do.

This hostel is a great escape if you want a change from the crowds at the big Jasper hostel a short distance away. The best reason to stay here is to gawk at the magnificent canyon about a five-minute walk from your front door. There's quite an extensive trail surrounding it, with six bridges crossing the narrow, deep defile at different points.

If you've got your own wheels, motor north (toward Edmonton) a little ways to Miette Hot Springs, where you can soak in a mineral bath for $4.00 Canadian (about $3.00 U.S.) while inhaling the majestic mountains surrounding you. That's living! Then return to the hostel for sleepytime among the stars, the quiet, and—eek!—the crunching of bears through the forest.

How to get there:

By bus: Greyhound stops in Jasper. From depot, take cab to hostel.

By car: From Jasper, drive 11 km (7 mi.) east on the Yellowhead Highway (Highway 16) to Maligne Lake Road. Turn right, cross bridge over Athabasca River, and bear left; cross a second bridge. Hostel is on right, across from Maligne Canyon access road.

By train: VIA Rail stops in Jasper. From station, take cab to hostel.

RIBBON CREEK HOSTEL

Box 1358, Banff (Kananaskis), Alberta TOL OCO

(403) 591–7333

E-mail: banff@HostellingIntl.ca

Web site: www.HostellingIntl.ca/Alberta/Hostels/Ribbon

Rates: $12.00 Canadian (about $9.00 U.S.) per Hostelling International member; private rooms $32.00–$40.00 Canadian (about $24.00–$30.00 U.S.)

Credit cards: None

Office hours: 8:00–10:00 A.M.; 5:00–11:00 P.M.

Beds: 47

Private/family rooms: 5

Single rooms: None

Private bathrooms: None

Affiliation: Hostelling International-Canada

Extras: Laundry, store, fireplace, volleyball, kitchen

This squat little one-story lodge with a stone chimney is way off the beaten path, and it surprises some folks with its amenities. It's got indoor plumbing, hot showers, and electricity something you don't normally get when you're staying at Alberta's rustic hostels. The common space here includes a cozy fireplace to read by, and the staff at the front desk will sell you a few basic food supplies if you haven't brought enough from Calgary.

Best bet for a bite: Distant Calgary

What hostellers say: "Ski you later!"

Gestalt: Blue Ribbon

Hospitality: A

Party index:

Another surprise here is the large number of beds and, especially, the bonus of five couples'/family rooms. Five! This is the kind of place that could recharge a marriage (or just a long-term thang) in a hurry, we'd bet. We're not guaranteeing this, of course. Just hopin'. Actually, though, there's a good reason for all these beds: This place is popular. So much so that, even though it's way out of the way, you could get shut out in high summer season. Book ahead if you're really hankering to see this hostel. There is a pair of dorms, lest we forget to mention 'em, with fourteen beds apiece; three family rooms with bunks for kiddies plus beds for adults; and two couples' rooms with double beds.

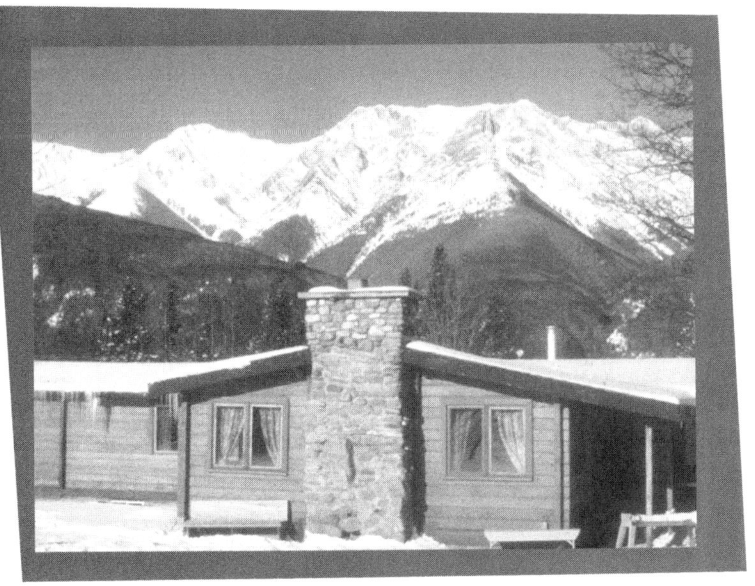

Ribbon Creek Hostel
Kananaskis
(photo courtesy HI-Canada)

Among other perks and activities here, you can buy discounted ski packages at the nearby Fortress and Nakiska resorts and get special hosteller rates on stuff like horseback rides and whitewater rafting. The hostel even helps coordinate educational programs such as eagle tours.

Wilderness plus comfort: Now that's our idea of a great destination.

How to get there:

By car: From Calgary, drive 70 km (45 mi.) west on Trans-Canada Highway (Highway 1) to Highway 40. Turn right and drive 25 km (15 mi.) south to Nakiska Ski Hill access road. Turn right again, cross river, and turn left. Continue approximately 1.5 km (1 mi.) to hostel.

CANADIAN ALPINE CENTRE HOSTEL

Village Road, Lake Louise, Alberta T0L 1E0

(403) 522–2200

E-mail: llouise@HostellingIntl.ca

Web site: www.HostellingIntl.ca/Alberta/Hostels/LakeLouise

Rates: $20.25 Canadian (about $14.00 U.S.) per Hostelling International member; private rooms $51.10 Canadian (about $38.00 U.S.)

Credit cards: MC, VISA
Office hours: 24 hours
Beds: 150
Private/family rooms: 25
Single rooms: None
Private bathrooms: None
Affiliation: Hostelling International-Canada
Extras: Restaurant, library, laundry, tours, sauna, lockers, game room, fireplace, meeting room

10%

We heard a lot of buzz on the road about this hostel: It had come, at some point, to attain near-legendary status as a super-plush oasis in a sea of flimsy wooden bunks. Thus, we had big expectations when we rolled into this little alpine village on a bright blue day when the surrounding peaks were shining with a dusting of new snow.

Best bet for a bite: Bill Peyto's Cafe

What hostellers say: "Pass the Cabernet."

Insiders' tip: All-day tours for $10.00 Canadian (about $7.00 U.S.)

Gestalt: Geez Louise

Hospitality: C

Cleanliness: A

Party index:

Well, we're here to tell you that the building sure didn't disappoint us one bit; it's a beauty. So are the bunks and the amenities. However, there's more to hostelling than just a soft bed. And so, we must confess, we came off a bit disappointed by the staff—who were hip to the point of being downright aloof—and the jet-set character of some of the guests.

Come to think of it, the whole dang town feels a little like a movie set: more cardboard than substance.

But let's back up a bit. This hostel is located in the postage-stamp town of Lake Louise, tucked among fancy ski condos and the grossly grandiose Château Lake Louise. Contrary to what you'd expect, the town isn't right next to the spectacularly aquamarine glacial tarn that gives the town its name and lifeblood.

Facilities here are deluxe; you couldn't ask for a more comfortable stay. You get a choice between a private room or bunks. Private rooms usually come with two twin beds and crude lockers. You can control the heat, and you share your en-suite washroom with just one other couple. (There are locks on both bathrooms and showers, if you can believe it.) Linens are included in the price, although you pay extra for towels.

Bunkroom occupants get nice bunks in rooms that aren't too big; there are about four shower rooms on each floor and plenty of bathrooms, so waiting to wash up isn't a problem, thank goodness.

The hostel basement houses a great little sauna with another washroom and a coin-operated laundry, both of which close

Canadian Alpine Centre Hostel
Lake Louise
(photo courtesy HI-Canada)

promptly at 10:00 P.M. There's also a kitchen, which isn't nearly as terrific as the fairly pricey cafe. They charge nearly $8.00 Canandian (about $6.00 U.S.) for a hamburger, though some claim this food's worth the extra buckolas. There wasn't nearly enough preparation space in the kitchen to handle the heavy flow of thrifty hostellers packed into the place, and the equipment was mismatched or missing. The hot water in the taps was scalding, too.

We'd guess the idea is to getcha to eat at the cafe, which really is nice—and the only place you can consume beer on premises. How convenient that it's sold there.

Other highlights include a spacious common room with an open-beamed ceiling and wonderful stone fireplace. The room also contains a good mountaineering resource library—which is appropriate, as this place is comanaged by the Alpine Club of Canada—although you must plunk down a deposit if you want to take books back to your room for perusal. The Canadian government has also set up a job computer for those who want to make some legal extra dough during the lucrative winter months.

Still, in spite of all these pretty touches, something's lacking. Reception is a bit on the frosty side, contrasting with the crackling warmth emanating from the fireplace and that convivial in-house cafe. Folks working here just don't project those fuzzy feelings we usually get from Hostelling International-Canada joints in western

Canada. And there are too many yuppies trying to save a few bucks by slumming it at the hostel while off on a ski weekend.

As an escape, though, there's no denying this area's great. The town mostly consists of upscale accommodations and condos, plus an expensive general store and a so-so shopping mall; that's about it. The real draws here are the lovely lake—you can't believe how blue it is (because of the ground-up rock in it) until you stand there and see for yourself—a ski facility, and numerous hikes into the surrounding hills.

This hostel is an unlikely place to make friends and influence people, but it's still a beautiful place for a solitary stay.

How to get there:

By car: Take Highway 1 to Lake Louise exit, then turn right onto Village Road and continue 750 meters (0.5 mile) to hostel.

SHUNDA CREEK HOSTEL

General Delivery, Nordegg, Alberta TOM 2HO

(403) 721–2140

Web site: www.HostellingIntl.ca/Alberta/Hostels/Shunda

Rates: $14 Canadian (about $10 U.S.) per Hostelling International member

Credit cards: MC, VISA

Office hours: 8:00 A.M.–11:00 P.M.

Beds: 48

Private/family rooms: Yes; number varies; call for availability

Single rooms: None

Private bathrooms: None

Single rooms: None

Affiliation: Hostelling International-Canada

Extras: Laundry, food, hot tub, grill, meeting room, climbing wall

A very handsome two-story lodge set among acres of unpopulated wilderness, this hostel achieves a superior outdoors experience without sacrificing comfort. That means a big dining area, hot showers, indoor plumbing—perfect if you've been roughing it in the hills a little too long.

You sleep in one of ten rooms, nearly all the same size, each containing four to five bunk beds; some of these quad rooms are specially outfitted to be sectioned off as family rooms. The common area has a fireplace, and outdoor facilities include a grill for barbecuing whatever you've brought along to barbecue. One of the really big draws here, though, is the hostel's outdoor hot tub—maybe the best hostel hot tub in western Canada, from what we've been hearing.

Shunda Creek Hostel
Nordegg
(photo courtesy HI-Canada)

You can't possibly run out of athletic things to do here. This is the so-called David Thompson Country—off the beaten path of the Icefields Parkway, yet still packed with the same array of long valleys, clear lakes, frothing streams, and huge mountains. Among the recreational opportunities are more than 700 km (430 mi.) of trails in the Bighorn area, great fishing, windsurfing on dammed-up Lake Abraham, and oodles of canoeing and rock-climbing spots.

The hostel stays open in winter, and there's usually tons of dry, powdery snow, ideal for snowshoeing and cross-country skiing. The staff even maintains an outdoor ice-climbing wall in wintertime for practicing those death-defying moves only a meter or two (as opposed to a few hundred or thousand meters) above Earth sweet Earth.

Best bet for a bite: Beats us

What hostellers say: "Last one in's a rotten egg!"

Gestalt: Nordegg track

Hospitality: A

Cleanliness: A

Party index:

How to get there:

By car: From Icefields Parkways (Highway

93), turn east onto Route 11 at village of Saskatchewan River Crossing and drive approximately 90 km (about 55 mi.) to Nordegg. At Nordegg, turn north onto Shunda Creek Recreation Area Road. Go 3 km (2 mi.), bearing left at fork in road and following signs to hostel.

WATERTON LAKES INTERNATIONAL HOSTEL

P.O. Box 4, Waterton Lakes International Park, Alberta T0K 2M0

(403) 859–2150; (403) 859–2151

Fax: (403) 859–2229

E-mail: info@watertonresort.com

Web site: www.hostellingintl.ca/Alberta/

Rates: $19.55 Canadian (about $14.00 U.S.) per Hostelling International member
Credit cards: MC, VISA
Office hours: 8:00–10:00 A.M.; 3:00–10:00 P.M.
Beds: 22
Private/family rooms: None
Affiliation: Hostelling International-Canada
Extras: Kitchen, laundry, bike rentals, shuttle, meals ($), health food bar, spa ($), playground, gym

Gestalt: Tap Waterton

Hospitality: A

Cleanliness: A

Party index:

This nice new hostel is situated on some of the most amazing territory you could ask for—the giant park that straddles the U.S.–Canada border, called Glacier Park in the States and Waterton Lakes up here in Canada.

With lots of private rooms—most containing private bathrooms—this is more a hotel than a hostel. They've got a health food bar, a day spa, tennis courts, a gym, and more. The facilities are terrific, you're paying a fraction of what you should be, and the gorgeous surrounding mountains make for hours of good hiking and sight-seeing.

How to get there:

By bus: Call hostel for transit route.

By car: Drive into Waterton Lakes National Park using Highways 5 and 6; continue into town and take Wildflower Avenue to corner of Cameron Falls Drive.

By train: Call hostel for transit route.

Unrelentingly flat in places, Manitoba becomes more interesting as the traveler moves north into a land of lakes and mountains. It's also got more than meets the eye in terms of culture, with a heritage that's rich in Native Canadian, French, Icelandic (yes, that's right), Mennonite, and Ukrainian history.

Hostels are few and far between here, however. To hit 'em, simply head for Winnipeg—you're probably going there anyway, as it's on the Trans-Canada and the only site of diverse culture out here. There's another hostel up in the forested Canadian Shield portion of the province, a pleasant day trip from the plains and the city streets.

MASKWA PROJECT HOSTEL 

Maskwa Road, Powerview, Manitoba ROE 1PO

(204) 367–4390

E-mail: maskwa@hotmail.com

Web site: www.kencom.net/~tfs/maskwa.htm

Rates: $11.00 Canadian (about $8.00 U.S.) per person
Credit cards: None
Office hours: Vary; call
Season: Varies; call
Beds: 35 (summer); 25 (winter)
Private/family rooms: Yes; number varies; call for availability
Single rooms: None
Private bathrooms: None
Affiliation: Hostelling International-Canada
Extras: Sauna, canoes, deck

This rustic hostel set on a hundred acres of wilderness in eastern Manitoba should be up and running by summertime. And the owners have plans. Soon to come, for instance, could be a set of insulated and heated yurts—some single-occupancy and some doubles—that might go for around $6.00 Canadian (about $4.00 U.S.) a night.

As it stands now, the lodge sleeps roughly thirty-five in summertime. It's really a place geared to groups, although single and double hostellers are certainly welcome, too. Get food at the Northern grocery store in Powerview, or hit the nearby eatery for local grub.

There seems to be plenty to do out here in the hills, a refreshing break from the prairies. You can swim or canoe the Maskwa River,

Best bet for a bite: Pedden's Place

Gestalt: Powerview play

Hospitality: A

Cleanliness: A

Party index:

shoot the rapids and waterfalls, take hikes, and relax afterward in the hostel sauna. Wildlife? Sure. After all, *maskwa* means "bear" in Cree, and there are indeed black bears in the area. Deer and otter, too. In fact, the nearest neighbor is a few kilometers away. Peace and quiet is all you'll get here.

How to get there:

By bus: Grey Goose stops in Powerview. From bus stop at Esso station, call hostel for pickup (small charge).

By car: Call hostel for directions.

GUEST HOUSE INTERNATIONAL

168 Maryland Street, Winnipeg, Manitoba R3G 1L3
(800) 743–4423; (204) 772–1272
E-mail: BMacdonald@msn.com
Web site: www.ourworld.compuserve.com/homepages/BACKPACKERS
Rates: $14–$16 Canadian (about $10–$12 U.S.) per person; single rooms $35 Canadian (about $26 U.S.); private rooms $35 Canadian (about $26 U.S.)
Credit cards: None
Office hours: Vary; call
Season: Varies; call
Beds: 35
Private/family rooms: Yes; number varies; call for availability
Single rooms: 1
Private bathrooms: None
Affiliation: None
Extras: Laundry, grill, game room, bike rentals, TV

Former teacher Bill MacDonald's rambling house sits right down the street from Winnipeg's official Hostelling International joint, and it's not a bad second option if that one's full.

Things get started in a homey living room complete with a good television, to which the manager can pipe in movies on request. Walls are decorated with working snowshoes and colorful pieces of art created by native children from northwestern Manitoba—a nicely authentic local touch and one you rarely find in a hostel.

Upstairs, rooms appear and disappear with startling suddenness. Here's a family room with a sink in it; there's another family-type space with a little refrigerator and a sink; there's a single bare bed in a room; and so on. Sort of like Alice in Wonderland, you just never know what you're going to find behind the next door. Furnishings range from adequate to garage-sale quality. However, "everything's air-conditioned," says MacDonald proudly—a useful boast, we'd guess, during

Manitoba's short but theoretically stifling summer.

The basement game room is a bit cramped and damp, but it does manage to pack in lots of distractions, in the form of Ping-Pong, foosball, and pinball. You can always escape, however, by clambering up some dodgy stairs and out the bulkhead into a small back lawn replete with grill. The neighborhood's a good one for walking, too, and you're quite close to the thrumming center of Winnipeg (which closes down too early for our taste, but that's another story). There is a grocery store nearby for eats, and Broadway is your street if you're looking to dine out.

The owner's got the right idea here; now he just needs to fix up the house some. A little more elbow grease and he'll have a serious contender.

Best bet for a bite: Alycia's for Ukrainian

What hostellers say: "Bill MacDonald had a hostel..."

Insiders' tip: Parking cops downtown are ruthless

Gestalt: A few small repairs

Safety: A

Hospitality: A

Cleanliness: B

Party index:

How to get there:

By bus: Greyhound stops in Winnipeg. From depot, walk east on Portage Avenue 1 block to The Bay department store on Vaughn Street. Catch #17 bus to Broadway and Maryland Streets. Walk 1½ blocks south on Maryland; hostel is on right, at corner of Alloway.

By car: Call hostel for directions.

By plane: Airport in Winnipeg. From airport, take #15 bus to Sargent and Maryland; change to #29 bus and take it to Broadway. Walk south 4 blocks to #168. Hostel is on right, at corner of Alloway.

By train: VIA Rail stops in Winnipeg. From train station, take #29 bus to Sherbrook; walk 1 block south to Sara, then walk 1 block west to corner of Maryland and Alloway. Hostel is at corner.

IVEY HOUSE INTERNATIONAL HOSTEL

210 Maryland Street, Winnipeg, Manitoba R3G 1L6

(204) 772–3022

Fax: (204) 784–1133

E-mail: iveyhouse@hotmail.com

Web site: www.ilos.net/~mslicky

Rates: $14 Canadian (about $10 U.S.) per Hostelling International member
Credit cards: JCB, MC, VISA
Office hours: 8:00–10:00 A.M.; 4:00 P.M.–midnight
Beds: 38 (summer); 36 (winter)

Ivey House International Hostel
Winnipeg
(photo courtesy HI-Canada)

Private/family rooms: Yes; number varies; call for availability
Single rooms: None
Private bathrooms: None
Affiliation: Hostelling International-Canada
Extras: Laundry, bike rentals, TV

This heartland hostel strives to uphold the hostelling spirit of one of the founders of Canadian hostelling, Grace Ivey, for whom it is named. And it succeeds, mostly because of a staff that is—as one guest said—"obsessively cheerful."

Though small for such a good-sized city—it has just thirty-six beds (thirty-eight in the summer)—Ivey House packs a big punch. There are well-laid-out rooms, some coming with the bonus of desks; a spacious basement, with laundry, bathroom, and shower facilities; and a roomy, sparkling kitchen-and-common room. A television room rife with jigsaw puzzles, quick-read novels, and board games rounds out the offerings. Staff will also sell you a number of items, including Canadian pins and patches.

Weary travelers will appreciate the staff, who really go the extra distance for them. Suzanne and her staff welcome all with big smiles and good tips on where to eat, what to see, and how to get there in this underappreciated prairie city. If you arrive on Christmas, you might even be served a holiday dinner complete with all the trimmings, no matter what your religion or food orientation may be.

What to do while you're staying here? Winnipeg is flat, offering endless and effortless bike-riding opportunities. Thankfully, the hostel will rent you a two-wheeler for a song. Speaking of songs, there's also a guitar floating about that might need a tuning but works well enough for prolonged noodling. Summertime, when the livin' is easy, brings occasional barbecues to the well-loved deck outside, as well.

The city of Winnipeg is considerably safer than most cities south of the (U.S.) border, but if you leave anything obviously valuable in your car here, you'll still likely lose it and your windows. (For more incentive to keep your stuff with you, see the amusing hostel poster here depicting a Mercedes and a satchel filled to the gills with money.) There are two parking spots behind the hostel for those who wish to avoid such a fate, just one more nice touch in an already good hostel experience. If only it weren't a three-floor walk from the top-floor dorms to the basement bathrooms, this would be heaven!

Best bet for a bite: Osborne Village

What hostellers say: "Just like home."

Gestalt: Ivey league

Safety: B

Hospitality: A

Cleanliness: A

Party index:

All things considered, though, Ivey House more than meets our test and comes off as a comfortable, homey, and friendly place to bunk up.

How to get there:

By bus: Greyhound stops in Winnipeg. From depot, walk east on Portage Avenue 1 block to The Bay department store on Vaughn Street. Catch #17 bus to Broadway and Maryland Streets. Walk 1 block south on Maryland; hostel is on right.

By plane: Airport in Winnipeg. From airport, take #15 bus to Sargent Avenue and Maryland Street; change to #29 bus and take it to Broadway and Maryland. Walk 1 block south on Maryland. Hostel is on right.

By train: VIA Rail stops in Winnipeg. From station, take taxi to hostel or take #29 bus to Broadway and Sherbrook, then walk 1 block west to Maryland Street and walk south on Maryland to hostel on right.

SASKATCHEWAN

Saskatchewan, like Manitoba, is more interesting than it might seem from a quick drive-through. But it requires some time to get to know, and cross-country travelers can't always take that time.

Nevertheless, the province's two hostels are in the big cities—along popular Trans-Canadian driving routes—and thus offer decent bases from which to venture out into the endless countryside. One of the hostels is not so great. But the other—well, it's simply one of the very best-run small hostels in North America, we say, blessed with terrific location and wonderful management. Who says there's no reason to head for Regina?

TURGEON INTERNATIONAL HOSTEL 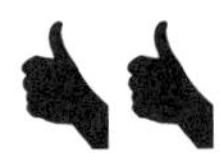

2310 McIntyre Street, Regina, Saskatchewan S4P 2S2

(306) 791–8165

Fax: (306) 721–2667

Rates: $13.00 Canadian (about $9.00 U.S.) per Hostelling International member; private rooms $25.00 Canadian (about $19.00 U.S.)
Credit cards: MC, VISA
Office hours: 7:00–10:00 A.M.; 5:00–11:00 P.M.
Season: February 1–December 24
Beds: 40
Private/family rooms: 1
Single rooms: None
Private bathrooms: None
Affiliation: Hostelling International-Canada
Extras: Library, laundry, TV, grill, picnic tables, piano

10%

Driving across the North American continent can be a tedious chore at times. Both the United States and Canada present endless stretches of highway—and often the stretch comes just as you're beginning to look forward to the end of the journey.

If you're booking it across the Trans-Canada, however, we can happily report two stellar hostels spaced about a half-day's drive apart that are each good for a few days of hanging out apiece—Winnipeg (the capital of Manitoba), described above, and this wonderful house in Saskatchewan's regal capital city of Regina.

The hostel owes its existence almost single-handedly to the hard work of Liane Gusway, who has since retired from directing the Saskatchewan Council. She purchased the historic building and had it moved on a flatbed truck to its current location—much to the chagrin of the locals, but its serene presence has changed their minds and proven that a hostel doesn't need to mean a refuge for panhandlers. The house, which she saved from the wrecking ball, was then beautifully restored.

Its location is impeccable. The house sits on a quiet and lovely residential street, right between the Wascana Centre (the largest urban park in North America) and the downtown Market Square district. It's also positioned within 2 blocks of the only vegetarian restaurant in the province. Public transportation, including city buses and Greyhound buses, is within easy reach.

Inside, the first things you see are a sparkling foyer, a stunning and complete travel library, a common room with television, and a piano room. A well-equipped kitchen, large dining room, laundry room, and showers are all located in the basement, but it never feels crowded. Guest rooms are upstairs on the second floor; a large room reserved for groups when they're in town sits on the third floor.

Sheets here are rented for half a buck. The lone family room comes already made up with fluffy comforters and a balcony—a steal at the price and wonderful for traveling families. Laundry is also a steal here at 75 cents per wash and 50 cents per dry, possibly the cheapest laundry in Canada! You can buy items like laundry powder, ramen noodles, and soda (except they call it pop here) from the helpful front-desk staff. More often than not, that will mean Edna, the cheerful Filipina manager who has been here for years and has somehow retained her good cheer throughout.

Best bet for a bite: Heliotrope

What hostellers say: "One of the best!!"

Insiders' tip: Wascana Centre parks

Gestalt: Regal beagle

Safety: A

Hospitality: A

Cleanliness: A

Party index:

KEY TO ICONS

 Attractive natural setting

 Ecologically aware hostel

 Superior kitchen facilities or cafe

 Offbeat or eccentric place

 Superior bathroom facilities

 Romantic private rooms

 Comfortable beds

 Among our very favorite hostels

 A particularly good value

 Wheelchair-accessible

 Good for business travelers

 Especially well suited for families

 Good for active travelers

 Visual arts at hostel or nearby

 Music at hostel or nearby

She's just one of many reasons this hostel ranks among the best in Canada.

How to get there:

By bus: Greyhound Canada stops in Regina. From bus station, walk 6 blocks west and 4 blocks south; or take taxi to hostel.

By car: Call hostel for directions.

By train: VIA Rail stops in Saskatoon. From Saskatoon, take Greyhound bus. From depot, walk 6 blocks west and 4 blocks south; or take taxi to hostel

MOHYLA INSTITUTE HOSTEL

1240 Temperance Street, Saskatoon, Saskatchewan S7N 0P1

(306) 653–1944

Fax: (306) 653–1902

E-mail: mohyla@sk.sympatico.ca

Rates: $18 Canadian (about $12 U.S.) per person
Credit cards: MC, VISA
Office hours: 8:00 A.M.–4:30 P.M.
Beds: 15
Private/family rooms: None
Private bathrooms: None
Affiliatiation: Hostelling International–Canada
Extras: Laundry, TV, cafeteria ($)

A strange hostel, this one, consisting of fifteen single rooms and such amenities as—well—a sewing room. Hmmmmm . . .

Best bet for a bite: Second Avenue South

What hostellers say: "Got any thread?"

Insiders' tip: Free Sunday admission to some museums

Gestalt: Sew-sew

Party index:

To put it in perspective, this summer-only joint replaces a former seedy hotel that was serving as the city of Saskatoon's only hostel. So it's an improvement over what existed, anyway. The TV room, breakfast, and optional meals service are also nice.

Frankly, we were a bit disappointed by Saskatoon the city—which had been hyped to us as a cool and happenin' place. But, like other cities of the prairies, this one's downtown just lacks oomph. Still, there is an interesting art museum nearby, a hip 'hood called Nutana to prowl around in briefly, and a little riverside Ukrainian museum that's a must-see. If you have wheels or can take the city bus, hit the Wanuskewin Center on the prairies outside town; the complex pays tribute to those native cultures that still reside in Saskatchewan in moving fashion—and they serve a mean buffalo stew, too.

How to get there:

By bus: Take #4 bus to Clarence Avenue and walk east on Temperance to Wiggins.

By car: From Highway 16, drive west on Circle Drive, then turn east on College and south on Wiggins. From Highway 11, go north on Circle Drive, then east on College and south on Wiggins.

By train: VIA Rail stops in Saskatoon. Call hostel for transit route from station.

BRITISH COLUMBIA AND THE YUKON TERRITORY

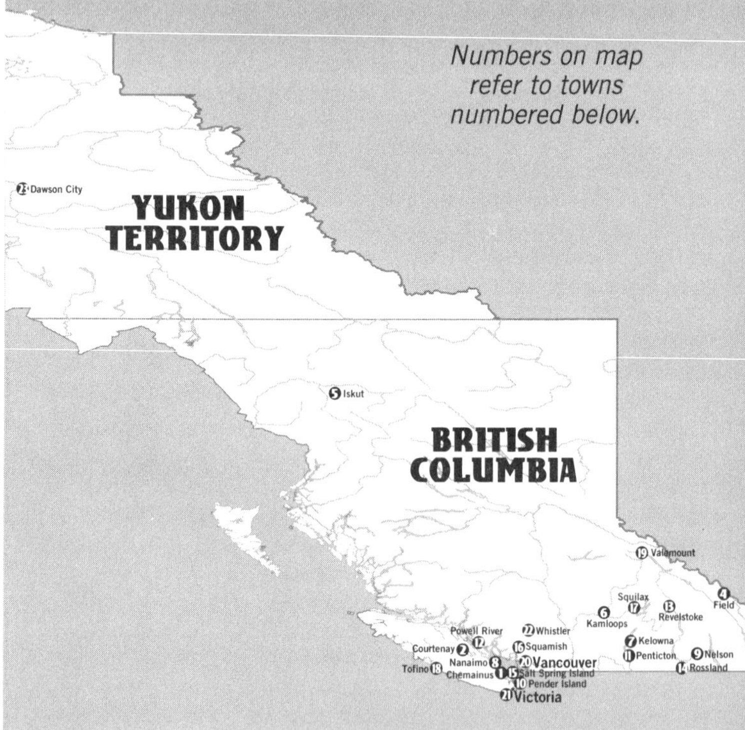

BRITISH COLUMBIA

1. Chemainus
2. Courtenay
3. Fernie
4. Field
5. Iskut
6. Kamloops
7. Kelowna
8. Nanaimo
9. Nelson
10. Pender Island
11. Penticton
12. Powell River
13. Revelstoke
14. Rossland
15. Salt Spring Island
16. Squamish
17. Squilax
18. Tofino
19. Valemount
20. Vancouver
21. Victoria
22. Whistler

YUKON TERRITORY

23. Dawson City

BRITISH COLUMBIA

It's no wonder British Columbia calls itself "super-natural": The province has got a little bit of everything, from ocean cliffs and beaches, to towering mountains, to salmon-rich rivers.

Not surprisingly, this is also the place to go to find the most hostels in Canada. Vancouver and Victoria are stuffed, of course, but even remote mountain ranges like the Kootenays and the Okanagan Valley offer lots more hostel beds than you'd expect them to.

To hit the most and best hostels, we'd begin in Vancouver and ferry across to southern Vancouver Island for friendly experiences in Victoria, Salt Spring Island, and Nanaimo. Back on the mainland, the Rocky Mountains are especially rich in really good outdoors-oriented, lodge-style hostelling; you get there by driving zigzag fashion.

CHEMAINUS HOSTEL 

9694 Chemainus Road, Chemainus,

British Columbia V0R 1K0

(250) 246–2809

Rates: $15 Canadian (about $11 U.S.) per person
Credit cards: None
Office hours: Vary; call
Season: March 16–October 31
Beds: 20
Private/family rooms: 1
Single rooms: None
Private bathrooms: 1
Affiliation: None
Extras: Laundry, bicycle rentals

This little hostel is an unlikely outpost in a tiny town near some great Vancouver Island scenery, but it's a good one to tuck in your back pocket—definitely a great place to stay when you need peace and quiet and don't feel like dealing with the bustling crowds in Victoria. Manager Tom Schmuck, the carpenter who started the hostel a few years ago, is especially pleasant and accommodating—and hostellers keep coming back as a result.

Unfortunately, the hostel was up for sale at press time. Perhaps its new owners, if any materialize, will continue the tradition.

The place is small but furnishes clean, standard-issue dorm rooms. Beds are built into the walls, eliminating that shaky feeling you get when the top bunkmate suddenly has to go wee-wee. Schmuck's hostel has a small lounge area built around one great big table, plus a surprisingly well-equipped kitchen. And there's a camper out back for families—a nice, semirustic experience. As an added bonus you can hang out all day here, since there's no lockout: Tom simply leaves the door open, and the last person in for the evening gets lockup duties.

There isn't a whole lot to do right in town, although a number of nice islands are nearby and easily reached by ferries. The town of Chemainus itself is really only known for one thing: its murals. They're everywhere and have somehow managed to transform a fading logging town into a growing tourist destination. A local dinner theater takes the murals' stories and brings them to life. If you've taken to totem poles, on the other hand, then Duncan—the self-anointed "Town of Totems"—lies just south of Chemainus.

In sum, this is a nice, quiet place to stop on Vancouver Island when you want to get away from the cheery bustle of Victoria. Let's hope it stays a hostel when the owner sells the building.

Best bet for a bite: Thrifty Foods in Mill Bay

What hostellers say: "I'll be back."

Insiders' tip: Brewpub on Thetis Island

Gestalt: Mural majority

Hospitality: A

Cleanliness: A

Party index:

How to get there:

By bus: Bus stops on Chemainus Road. Walk north into town; hostel is on left.

By car: From Victoria, drive Highway 1 north approximately 80 km (about 50 mi.) to downtown Chemainus exit; exit right. Turn left at stop sign onto Chemainus Road. Hostel is on left.

By train: VIA Rail stops in Chemainus. Cross tracks (after train is gone, of course) to Chemainus Road; walk to #9694. Hostel is on right.

VANCOUVER ISLAND HOSTELS: A Summary

	RATING	PROS	CONS	COST	PAGE
Salt Spring Island Hostel	👍👍	staff, location	gets busy	$15.50	p. 211
Nicol Street Hostel	👍	fun place	busy street	$15.00	p. 199
Chemainus	👍	homey, clean	small	$15.00	p. 187
North Comox Lake Hostel	👍👎	great views	odd guests	$17.00	p. 189

NORTH COMOX LAKE HOSTEL 

Box 3453, Courtenay, British Columbia V9N 5M5

(250) 338–1914

E-mail: comoxlakehostel@bc.sympatico.ca

Rates: $17 Canadian (about $12 U.S.) per person
Credit cards: None
Office hours: 8:00 A.M.–10:00 P.M.
Beds: 30
Private/family rooms: Yes; number varies; call for availability
Single rooms: None
Private bathrooms: None
Affiliation: None
Extras: TV, laundry, barbecues, campfires, camping, pickup

In the woods on the way out of the town of Courtenay, this hostel perches on the very edge of civilization. We were greeted by three amiable but suspicious canines who watched the grounds warily for cougars, wolves, and bears. Intrepid hostellers venture here for myriad outdoor pursuits, including glimpses of the glaciers and the formidable-sounding Forbidden Plateau that provide the backdrop for this hostel.

It's very basic here. Populated by transient travelers and a few seemingly long-term residents, the sleeping quarters (split between two buildings) feature stark rooms augmented by a common room stocked with a collection of old *National Geographics*. Although private rooms feature double beds, the mattresses are a little soft, making it hard for some of us to get up and at 'em in the morning. In the basement, you cook up meals in the kitchen while avoiding agenda-loaded hostellers.

The manager, whose father started this hostel awhile back, is really nice—always eager to start up a nightly fire in the well-used outdoor fireplace, making it easier for hostellers to feel warm even as the winds begin blowing down from the icy peaks of Strathcona Provincial Park, which are so close you feel you can touch them. And she maintains a cheap washer and dryer in the basement; if you forget your washing powder, she'll gladly sell you a scoop for half a buck.

If you're into group activity, nighttime gives you a chance to organize a hike or swim for the next day with your bunkmates. The hos-

Best bet for a bite:
Edible Island Natural Foods

What hostellers say:
"Will you shut up?"

Insiders' tip:
Hike Mt. Washington

Gestalt:
Super-natural

Hospitality: A

Cleanliness: B

Party index:

tel certainly provides solitude. Now if only the hippies-with-attitude would stay away, we'd really have something here.

How to get there:

By bus: Bus lines stop in Courtenay. From bus stop, call hostel for directions.

By car: From Route 1 in Courtenay, turn left onto Eighth Street. Continue to Willemar Road, make a left, and then a right onto Lake Trail Road. Follow Lake Trail Road through four-way at Comox Logging Road to hostel on right.

By train: VIA Rail stops in Courtenay. From station, call hostel for directions.

RAGING ELK HOSTEL 

892 Sixth Avenue, Fernie, British Columbia V0B 1M0

(250) 423–6811

E-mail: raginelk@elkvalley.net

Rates: $16–$25 Canadian (about $11–$19 U.S.) per Hostelling International member

Credit cards: MC, VISA

Office hours: 8:00–11:00 A.M.; 5:00–10:00 P.M.

Beds: 80

Private/family rooms: 8

Single rooms: Yes; number varies; call for availability

Private bathrooms: Yes; number varies; call for availability

Affiliation: Hostelling International-Canada

Extras: Sauna, game room, breakfast, laundry

This hostel took over what used to be the Sundown Motel and has retrofitted its image to appeal to a gnarly, snowboarding crowd.

The town of Fernie boasts the longest ski season in British Columbia, which means you can coast down the side of a mountain in May wearing nothing but your BVDs and shades. It wasn't always a ski town, though. Formerly a mining community, the downtown was nearly destroyed by fires in 1908; it was then rebuilt in stone, along wide streets, to avoid a repeat performance. When the mining industry eventually fizzled, the mountains were swiftly put to a different use.

In response to the new tourist boom, cheap motels have sprung up. Raging Elk Hostel was saved from that fate, though, when it was converted into this combination of dorm rooms and family rooms. Each space has its own washroom—certainly a bonus. You can also cook in the kitchen, which is fully equipped to handle hostellers' monumental culinary achievements in Kraft macaroni and cheese, canned spaghetti, and cold cereal.

You don't need to worry about breakfast, though, because the staff provides a free pancake-and-coffee breakfast to kick off mornings. (This must mean you're in the heart of the "U-fix belt" stretching from hostels in Washington and Idaho through to B.C. This nifty little scheme allows "U" to whip up a delicious dozen of doughy discs made fresh from some Bisquick-type substance.) Wash 'em all down with the coffee, and *voilà,* breakfast is done.

Other delights here include cattle-drive observation and mine-tour packages arranged through the hostel. When it's not snowing, mountain biking, kayaking, canoeing, and fishing occupy hostellers with too much on their hands.

Bring your own two wheels, and you can store them in the lockers provided. Same with skis.

Best bet for a bite:
U-git-'em

What hostellers say:
"Shred, dude."

Gestalt:
Fernie feeling

Hospitality: A

Cleanliness: B

Party index:

How to get there:

By bus: Bus lines stop in Fernie. From bus station, walk 1 block east along Sixth Avenue to corner of Ninth Street. Hostel is at corner.

By car: Call hostel for directions.

WHISKEY JACK HOSTEL

Field, British Columbia, Box 1358, Banff, Alberta TOL 0C0

(403) 762–4122

E-mail: banff@HostellingIntl.ca

Web site: www.HostellingIntl.ca/Alberta/Hostels/Whiskey

Rates: $13 Canadian (about $10 U.S.) per Hostelling International member
Credit cards: MC, VISA
Office hours: 7:00–10:00 A.M.; 5:00–11:00 P.M.
Season: Mid-June–September 30
Beds: 27
Private/family rooms: None
Single rooms: None
Private bathrooms: None
Affiliation: Hostelling International-Canada
Extras: Lockers, campfires, hot water, bears, moose, elk, food

This hilltop hostel offers the best of both worlds, set near beautiful Takkakaw Falls—one of Canada's five highest waterfalls—and really close to the ski and social action in Lake Louise and Banff. It's also one of the few hostels in the area that has indoor plumbing, hot showers, and cooking/common areas in the same building as the sleeping quarters. And it gets top ratings for its incredibly friendly manager, Olga, who makes hostellers feel right at home in these big, big mountains.

Best bet for a bite: House pantry

What hostellers say: "Where's the whiskey?"

Gestalt: Jackpot

Hospitality: A

Cleanliness: A

Party index:

The place used to be the former staff quarters for a hotel that was swept away by an avalanche. (So much for great location, huh?) Now the sleeping quarters are divided into three cabins containing nine beds each. The front porch is ideal for wistfully whiling away a few hours watching the cascading falls, which you can see from that very spot. Frequent campfires here also provide further social interaction and are the best places to discuss attainment of the proper shade of brown of a marshmallow. Limited food is also sold here for the hungry; it is a bit of a hike to any town (or grocery) of any size.

This being a national park, there is of course some great hiking to be had nearby, both at Emerald Lake and in the President Range. Rockhounds will get a kick out of the fossils in the Burgess Shale Formation, which has been designated as a world heritage site for its unusual fossils.

Rusticating without being too, too rustic. That's how we like it. You will, too.

Note: Although the hostel is administered by the Southern Alberta Hostelling Association, the listing for it occasionally appears in literature provided by the British Columbia Association. So don't be confused; it's a hostel located in extreme western B.C., but everything's handled over in Banff National Park, across the provincial line.

How to get there:

By car: Drive Trans-Canada Highway (Highway 1) to Field, 27 km (about 15 mi.) west of Lake Louise; then go 13 km (about 8 mi.) west up the Yoho Valley Road from Kicking Horse Campground.

RED GOAT LODGE 

Highway 37, Iskut, British Columbia V0J 1K0

(888) 733–4628; (250) 234–3261

Rates: $15 Canadian (about $11 U.S.) per person
Credit cards: MC, VISA
Office hours: 8:00 A.M.–noon; 2:00–10:00 P.M.

Season: June 1–September 30
Beds: 10
Private/family rooms: Yes; number varies; call for availability
Single rooms: None
Private bathrooms: None
Affiliation: None
Extras: Laundry, canoe rental, meals (sometimes), wood-burning stove

This place is quite a hoof. Literally. Let's put it this way: If you drove (or walked or, say, rollerbladed) north from Vancouver and hit the little dot of Dawson Creek, well, you've gone about 1,000 km (about 600 mi.). And you're still only a little more than halfway to Iskut!

If you make it here, however, you've got wilderness galore to experience. And we mean real wilderness, not mini-golf courses carved out of old farms or something. It's here, in the midst of incredible and unspoiled scenery, that you find Red Goat Lodge.

The hostel is actually part of a larger lodge complex, which also includes a campground on the shore of Eddontenajon Lake and a bed and breakfast with good food. There are only ten hostel beds here, but you do get the use of the building's laundry, drying room, lockers, and showers. Meals can also be had by special arrangement. And, *voilà,* you're a day closer to Alaska—with a pleasant night's sleep under your belt.

But you might not leave the next morning. We mentioned hiking: Iskut is squeezed between two mighty fine provincial parks, Mount Edziza and Spatsizi; strap on shoes, find a buddy, and check out these craters, cones, purple-stained rocks, and more. There's also great canoeing on two local river systems; luckily, canoes can be rented right here at the hostel. An abandoned rail line provides a 400-plus mile (645-km) biking and hiking trail to Prince Rupert with nary a strip mall to be found.

Oh, yeah, and the red goats? There really are some around here—although they're red only because they've gotten some of the local iron ore into their coats.

There. Once again, you've learned while traveling.

Best bet for a bite:
BYO Food

What hostellers say:
"Not baaaaaaaaad."

Insiders' tip:
Bring lots of film

Gestalt:
Kid stuff

Hospitality: A

Cleanliness: A

Party index:

How to get there:

By car: Call hostel for directions.

OLD COURTHOUSE HOSTEL 

7 West Seymour Street, Kamloops, British Columbia V2C 1E4
(250) 828–7991
Fax: (250) 828–2442
E-mail: kamloops@hihostels.bc.ca
Web site: www.hihostels.bc.ca/kam.htm

Rates: $15 Canadian (about $10 U.S.) per Hostelling International member; private rooms $33–$43 Canadian (about $25–$32 U.S.)
Credit cards: MC, VISA
Office hours: 8:00 A.M.–1:00 P.M.; 5:00–10:00 P.M.
Beds: 73
Private/family rooms: Yes; number varies; call for availability
Single rooms: None
Private bathrooms: None
Affiliation: Hostelling International-Canada
Extras: Laundry, lockers, events, TV, music

10%

What hostellers say: "Not guilty."

Gestalt: This old courthouse

Hospitality: A

Cleanliness: A

Party index:

Guilty as charged! We the hostel evaluators find that, yes, this hostel did indeed used to be a provincial courthouse, and, yes, it is guilty of being a really nice place to stay. However, Kamloops itself is guilty of being nothing more than a blah stopover partway between Vancouver and the really big mountains of western B.C. This is our verdict. Ahem.

Sorry about that. Now on to the hostel. Built in 1909, this handsome red courthouse was renovated into a hostel where hostellers now decide less weighty (but still important) issues—like who gets to sleep next to the snoring guy who sleeps in week-old socks. As befits such a venue, the dining area and lounge of this hostel are actually located right in the former courtroom. How do you know it was the courtroom? It still contains the original prisoner's and witness boxes, jury seats, and judge's bench, that's how.

Bunks are housed in other areas of the building. One of the nice touches here is that, last time we checked, the hostel was hosting folk music night the last Sunday of each month. Bravo!

We have to confess that we're not as excited about Kamloops the destination as the hostel managers are, however. The city is located in a sunny, dry, interior area of the province. Great for tanning, OK. And, yeah, there are attractions sprinkled around, like the Kamloops Museum and Archives, the Secwepemc Native Heritage and the Rocky Mountain Rangers Museum. Events like the Kamloops

Old Courthouse Hostel

Kamloops

Powwow, a professional rodeo, and the Alpine Blossom Festival also pop up from time to time.

Passing through during winter? The place is still open, and you can arrange a dogsledding tour or snowshoe Wells Gray Provincial Park. There's a ski (and snowboard and golf) resort called Sun Peaks, if you've got lots of cash on hand. If you don't, the Kamloops Wildlife Park is home to sixty-five species of local and endangered animals, plus many waterfalls and trails.

But you're paying us for our opinions—and our opinion is that we stay in this part of British Columbia only when we're too tired to keep on truckin'. That said, this hostel gets good ratings from everyone we talk with.

Now please do not discuss this verdict outside this courtroom. Lest we admonish you.

How to get there:

By bus: Greyhound stops in Kamloops. From bus depot, take #3 bus to West Seymour Street and Third Avenue; walk 2 blocks west on West Seymour to hostel.

By car: Call hostel for directions.

By plane: Small airport in Kamloops. Take airport shuttle to within 3 blocks of hostel, or take taxi.

By train: VIA Rail stops in Kamloops. From train station, take taxi to hostel.

BUMPS BIG WHITE HOSTEL 

7500 Porcupine Road, Kelowna, British Columbia V1X 4K5
(250) 765–2100

E-mail: bumps@bc.sympatico.ca
Rates: $15 Canadian (about $10 U.S.) per person; private rooms $39 Canadian (about $28 U.S.)
Credit cards: MC, VISA
Office hours: 9:00 A.M.–9:00 P.M.
Season: Varies; contact hostel for season
Beds: 110
Private/family rooms: Yes
Private bathrooms: 4
Single rooms: None
Extras: Laundry, lockers, ski storage, TV, Internet access

This hostel is smack inside the popular Big White resort; the views are great—and you can ski right to the place in winter or walk to any of a number of local watering holes any time of year.

The place has been recently expanded; it now encompasses two buildings: an old ski lodge with room for twenty-four bodies and the first two floors—thirty-eight rooms' worth—of a condominium complex. The room configurations include a coed dorm sleeping twelve hostellers in bunks, a pair of cozier bunkrooms that can sleep four apiece, and two private rooms for couples, among others. Some of these rooms have their own kitchen units; some don't. Rates vary according to time of year and room size.

Best bet for a bite: Mountain Mart

Gestalt: Stacks o' Wax

Hospitality: A

Cleanliness: A

Party index:

The common facilities have been expanded, too. Internet access is a cheap, cheap $4.00 Canadian (about $3.00 U.S.) per hour, and the common room has cable television. There are two useful laundry rooms, ski storage, and other perks, too.

Charlotte, a former nurse, and Tony, a former computer expert, traveled and lived abroad in places like Australia, Mexico, South Africa, and China before coming to the B.C. Rockies. They live at the hostel with two kids, so they're never far away if you need a hand. With a mess of pubs and restaurants within a few minutes' walk of the hostel, this place looks good so far.

How to get there:

By bus: Greyhound stops in Kelowna. From station, take shuttle ($22 Canadian, about $17 U.S.) to hostel or call hostel for transit details.

By car: Call hostel for directions.

By plane: Small airport in Kelowna. From terminal, take shuttle ($22 Canadian, about $16 U.S.) to hostel or call hostel for transit details.

SAMESUN BIG WHITE HOSTEL

7660 Porcupine Road, Kelowna, British Columbia, V1X 4K5

(250) 765-7050

E-mail: samesun@silk.net

Web site: www.samesun.com

Rates: $17 Canadian (about $12 U.S.) per Hostelling International member; private room $60 Canadian (about $45 U.S.)
Credit cards: MC, VISA
Office hours: 8:00–11:30 A.M.; 3:30-10:00 P.M.
Season: October 15–April 15
Beds: 43
Private/family rooms: 1
Single rooms: None
Private bathrooms: None
Affiliation: Hostelling International-Canada
Extras: Hot tubs, pub, restaurant

Note: A new, bigger Big White Hostel will emerge sometime in time for the 2000–2001 ski season. This writeup holds true till then.

The Big White Hostel evolved out of a growing need to house those hostellers seeking the socalled "champagne lifestyle on a beer budget" in the Okanagan. Downtown Kelowna was just too far away from the mountain, so the enterprising (and good-hearted) owners sought out a property in order to fill this request. What you've got is a former ski lodge sitting practically on top of Big White now catering to skiers whose accommodations standards don't require mints on the pillow.

The rather large dorm rooms have been partitioned into smaller areas, with dividers keeping sections limited to two to four people. This partly compensates for the anonymity of the big rooms. There's also one private room that sleeps four folks.

This self-described "best ski hostel on the planet" obviously caters to more of a youthful ski crowd than the partner hostel downtown; its bonus extras include Internet access, a jukebox, three outdoor hot tubs, a restaurant, and a bar. It's party central, we hear—a downright rockin' joint in high ski season. And why not? What better way to spend a winter week in the mountains than to ski right to your bed, jump in a hot tub, crack open a cold brewski, and have someone else cook for you?

OK, reality check: It doesn't always snow up here. And you could find ten or twelve goateed guys in the tub, just waitin' for that lone gal to step right in. But still, this place is happenin'. It's not the spot to catch up on your reading, that's for sure; try the downtown hostel for that.

The "Loose Moose" bar and grill right here is an option for food, albeit a bit pricey. You could keep costs down by cooking yourself, though the only grocery store up here is also high priced due to the high demand and equally high cost of schlepping barrels of salmon up a big mountain. Best to grab a few things at the Safeway in downtown Kelowna, take the hostel shuttle ($10 Canadian one-way; $15 Canadian round-trip) from the downtown hostel to the tub, and soak away.

Best bet for a bite: Cafeteria on premises

What hostellers say: "DUUUUUDE!"

Gestalt: Snow White

Hospitality: A

Cleanliness: B

Party index:

How to get there:

By bus: Greyhound stops in Kelowna. From bus station, take #10 bus to Samesun Travel Hostel door on Bernard Avenue, then take shuttle bus ($10 Canadian one-way, Monday and Wednesday) from downtown hostel.

By car: From Kelowna, drive Highway 33 south approximately 45 km (25 mi.) to the Big White turnoff. The Alpine Center is directly at the top of the Village.

SAMESUN TRAVEL HOSTEL

245 Harvey Avenue, Kelowna, British Columbia V1Y 6P5

(250) 763–9814

Fax: (250) 763–9814

E-mail: samesun@silk.net

Web site: www.samesun.com

Rates: $15 Canadian (about $10 U.S.) per Hostelling International member
Credit cards: MC, VISA
Office hours: 8:00 A.M.–11:00 P.M.
Beds: 80
Private/family rooms: Yes (number varies, call for availability)
Private bathrooms: None
Single rooms: None
Affiliation: Hostelling International-Canada

Extras: Laundry, lockers, bicycle rentals, canoe rentals, TV, VCR, shuttle, tours, jukebox, grill, volleyball, basketball

10%

This place—owned by the same folks who own the Big White Hostel up on top of a nearby mountain—has recently moved to a fixed-up motel right on the highway into Kelowna, one of the capitals of the fertile Okanagan Valley.

The new site comes with some perks: all the rooms now have private bathrooms. Plus they've added a grill, volleyball court, and basketball court. Hostellers have previously reported that the owners are really, really nice people who run a respectable place. Parties do sometimes fire up—summer activities here include pub crawls, houseboat tours, and keggers—but in general this is a slightly quieter place than the Big White juke joint.

Popular diversions include the local lake's sandy beaches, golfing, and mountain biking. During the summer months wine tours leave directly from the hostel—and there's plenty of wine to check out around here. Hey! Stop slobbering all over this book and pull yourself together, willya? If you take the tours, pace yourself, and remember: You're *not* supposed to swallow the wine.

Okay. Lots of restaurants, pubs, cafes, and nightclubs lie within easy walking distance of the place. Summer is the high season for nightlife; fall is the time to hit local harvest festivals and associated stuff; and winter is the time to use the area as a ski base. This hostel is definitely a good place to shack up when you don't want the ski-resort atmosphere of Big White. A shuttle from here takes you up there, just in case you want a little taste.

Nice job, guys.

Best bet for a bite: Safeway

Gestalt: Cheap Kelowna

Hospitality: A

Cleanliness: B

Party index:

How to get there:

By bus: Bus lines run to Kelowna. From bus station, take #10 bus downtown and walk 1 block back toward hostel on highway.

By car: Take Highway 97 to hostel, between McDonald's restaurant and bridge.

NICOL STREET HOSTEL

65 Nicol Street, Nanaimo, British Columbia V9R 4S7

(250) 753–1188

E-mail: gmurray@island.net

Rates: $15 Canadian (about $10 U.S.) per person
Credit cards: None
Office hours: 8:00–11:00 A.M.; 4:00–11:00 P.M.
Beds: 30 (summer); 20 (winter)
Private/family rooms: Yes; number varies; call for availability
Single rooms: None
Private bathrooms: None
Affiliation: None
Extras: Grill, TV, laundry

10%

You'd never think that a hostel right on a busy straightaway of Vancouver Island's main drag would be this cool. But it is.

Moni and John Murray's hostel in Nanaimo has long been a favorite stopover on the way north from Victoria. And it's only getting better: The Murrays have slowly purchased enough surrounding buildings to own what now seems like half a city block. As a result, all this space gives hostellers a wide choice of accommodations: bunkrooms, a cozy private room in the basement called the Sugar Shack, even—in summer—a private room with a television and a peach tree outside the windows.

Best bet for a bite: Wild Roots Cafe for vegetarian

What hostellers say: "Great manager."

Insiders' tip: Nanaimo bars at Scotch Bakery

Gestalt: Block party

Safety: A

Hospitality: A

Cleanliness: A

Party index:

The bunks come in three nice rooms, and the kitchen and common room and patio areas really draw international folks together once the sun goes down. (Bathroom space is a bit limited, however.) Some hostellers like this place so much that they paint their impressions on cinder blocks along one big wall. Pretty neat.

In the morning everything you could possibly need is just five minutes away: bakeries, shops, restaurants, natural-foods stores, clubs, a tidy shopping mall. There are ferries going everywhere from nearby Newcastle and Gabriola Islands—so close you can almost reach out and touch them (when it's not raining, that is)—to North Vancouver. One surprise here in town is the strong Japanese influence; there are lots more sushi houses than usual to pick from, if that's your thing. Also, take advantage of the preponderance of Nanaimo bars, sweet desserts made of layers of chocolate and butter.

Moni has worked hard to set up a number of local discounts for hostellers, and she is as friendly as they come. Things just keep improving here.

How to get there:

By bus: Call hostel for transit route.

By car: From Victoria, drive Canadian Highway 1 north to Nanaimo. Highway 1 becomes Nicol Street just south of downtown. Watch for health-foods store on right; hostel is just after it, also on the right, at #65.

By train: VIA Rail stops in Nanaimo. From train station, walk 3 blocks to hostel.

DANCING BEAR INN HOSTEL

171 Baker Street, Nelson, British Columbia V1L 4H1

(250) 352–7573

E-mail: dbear@insidenet.com

Rates: $17 Canadian (about $13 U.S.) per Hostelling International member
Credit cards: MC, VISA
Office hours: 7:00–11:00 A.M.; 4:00–10:00 P.M.
Beds: 33
Private/family rooms: 3
Single rooms: None
Private bathrooms: None
Affiliation: Hostelling International-Canada
Extras: Laundry, library, TV, VCR, movies, store, lockers, postal and fax service, tea, fireplace

10% $

We've searched the entire North American continent for the near-perfect hostel; many hostels try, but they fail. Ooh, how they fail, honey! The Dancing Bear Inn may have come up with a blueprint for a perfect contemporary hostel: almost like a B&B, but at half the price.

The perfect hostel is one where guests are treated with dignity—not as budget travelers who should get down on their hands and knees in abject thanks to stay there. It's a place where the interior is classy, attractive, and fun; the bedding's comfortable and clean; the managers are thoughtful and provide lots of accurate information about the local area. It's not a place that charges lots for a dinky bunk bed in a room that hasn't been swept in a while; where the kitchen is grungy and missing essential equipment; where the managers radiate bad karma; where blankets are thin and ripped and the bed's got bugs.

Not to worry. The Dancing Bear, a restored inn, must be one of the best hostels in western Canada—maybe all of Canada—and everyone who stays here comes away raving about the beautiful

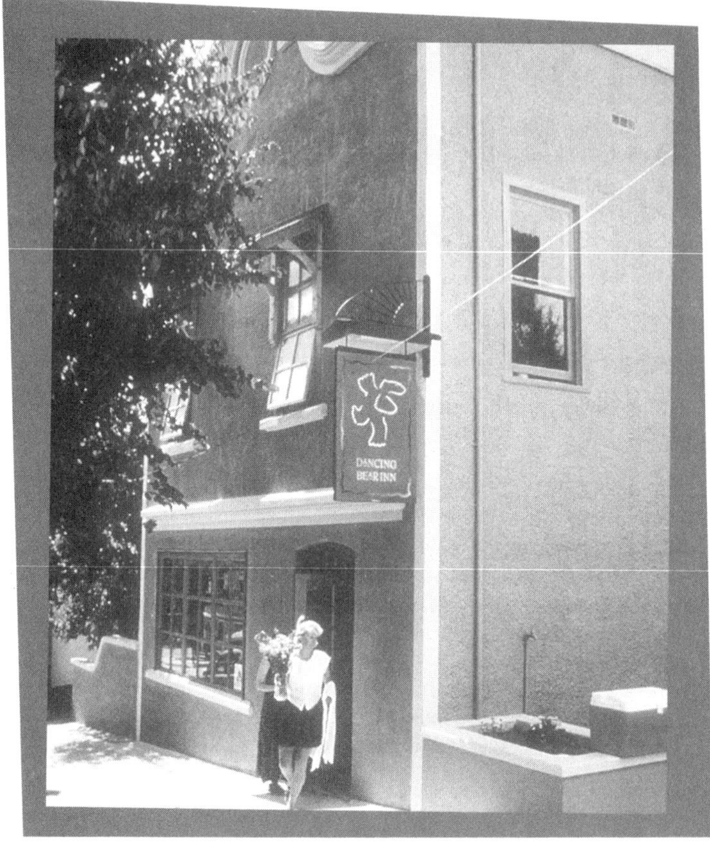

Dancing Bear Inn Hostel
Nelson
(photo courtesy HI-Canada)

restoration job that owners Brooke and Sandi Leatherman have done since purchasing the building.

Bunkrooms are small, and the double rooms here are a sheer pleasure—with a reasonable price—in varying degrees of accommodation: There's one room for a couple, one for a family or group of three, and one for a family or group of four. Beds are furnished with "fab" (as one hosteller put it) duvets; family bunks are wide on the bottom, with a single bunk on top, and seem to have enough headroom for an average-size adult.

The inn offers incredible support services as well, like a small regional travel center, postal and fax services, and tour and educational programs that change according to the season. The owners sell a few items, too. What's more, you get to share a gorgeous common space (with fireplace) and library that feature decorations, art, and furnishings by local woodworkers and artists. Games and a VCR are available in the common room, too. As far as meals goes, you can take a complimentary afternoon tea here, and continental breakfast is also an option for $5.00 Canadian (about $4.00 U.S.).

And Nelson is actually a really nice town to get stuck in for a few days. You wouldn't be too familiar with it, though—not unless you've seen that Steve Martin film about the fire chief with the huge nose, *Roxanne*. Yep, it was filmed here! That's why you've seen this place before. Nelson was also recently declared the top arts town in Canada, so if you're into oil paint and pottery, this is your place.

Pretty little Nelson also boasts more than 350 restored buildings, including the hostel. That's almost as many as there are in Victoria—probably more historic buildings per capita than anywhere else in Canada—and they include a Frank Lloyd Wright building. Nearby, adventurous hostellers might investigate the ghost town of Sandon, observe the annual fall salmon spawn in Kootenay Creek, spelunk in local caves, or take a dunk in the Ainsworth Hot Springs. There's great hiking in the Valhalla and Kokanee provincial parks, too, we've heard. Just remember that during high season, a maximum stay of five days is imposed.

This is a great hostel, so stay here and relish it before the word gets out. Places like this don't just fall off trees, ya know.

Best bet for a bite: These four walls

What hostellers say: "This is a hostel?!"

Insiders' tip: Hot springs nearby

Gestalt: Full Nelson

Hospitality: A

Cleanliness: A

Party index:

How to get there:

By bus: Greyhound stops in Nelson. From bus depot, turn right on Front Street (which becomes Ward Street), go right on Baker Street, and walk 4 more blocks. Hostel is on right.

By car: Call hostel for directions.

HOSTELLING INTERNATIONAL—PENDER ISLAND

Cooper's Landing, RR #1, Pender Island, British Columbia

V0N 2M0

(888) 921-3111; (250) 629-6133

Fax: (250) 629-3649

E-mail: bob_cooper@gulfnet.pine.com

Rates: $18 Canadian (about $12 U.S.) per Hostelling International member

Credit cards: MC, VISA

Office hours: 24 hours
Beds: 18
Private/family rooms: Yes
Affiliation: Hostelling International-Canada
Extras: Kitchen, lockers, bike rentals, meeting room

We're giving the early thumbs-up to this place, which just opened in the spring of 1999. They've only got eighteen beds so far, but good management seems bent on making it a better and better place over time. Among the stuff already in place: lockers, a kitchen, bikes for rent, and a room that can be sectioned off for meetings when necessary. There are private rooms available, too.

Best bet for a bite: Southbridge Farms store

Gestalt: Bender

Hospitality: A

Party index:

Plenty of hikes, swims, and other outdoor fun await. But we really like the laid-back atmo of this island, which like other Gulf Islands in the area has attacted a mixture of hippies, Americans, and others. It's easy to find natural foods, for instance, which is a big plus.

How to get there:

By car: Call hostel for transit route.

By ferry: Call hostel for transit route.

PENTICTON HOSTEL 

464 Ellis Street, Penticton, British Columbia V2A 4M2
(250) 492–3992
E-mail: penticton@hihostels.bc.ca
Web site: www.hihostels.bc.ca/pen.htm
Rates: $14.50 Canadian (about $11.00 U.S.) per Hostelling International member; private rooms about $35.00 Canadian ($26.00 U.S.)
Credit cards: JCB, MC, VISA
Office hours: 7:00 A.M.–noon; 5:00–11:00 P.M.
Beds: 47
Private/family rooms: 7
Single rooms: None
Private bathrooms: None
Affiliation: Hostelling International-Canada
Extras: Laundry, lockers, grill, bicycle rentals, grill, TV, patio

Move over Georgia and South Carolina; Penticton is the real "Peach City." At least, that's what proud Canadians will tell you—and

Penticton uses a giant talking peach to promote itself. "Pick me!" cries the succulent fruit. And why not? The temperate climate of British Columbia's interior Okanagan Valley makes this area the fruit belt of Canada. Peaches, pears, grapes, they're all here. If you want to work the summer and fall harvests to make some extra bucks, save that European plane fare and pick Penticton instead.

The hostel here in Penticton, though ideally suited for those seeking temporary work in the fruit-picking industry, welcomes everyone else who wants to savor this region of B.C. It's a two-story former bank building with a bright red roof. Hostellers love the small rooms; they sleep no more than six people.

Best bet for a bite: Orchards galore

What hostellers say: "Pick me!"

Gestalt: Good pick

Hospitality: A

Party index:

The private rooms can fit various combinations of people. Some are just small dorms and have bunk beds that sleep one to two friends, while others are considered family rooms (they're equipped with a double bed plus a single). Finally, one has just the simple double bed that couples without kids require. As with many of western Canada's hostels, package deals are offered to encourage longer stays; you're given a discount for a three-day or one-week visit, for instance.

Summertime is the right time to visit the Okanagan. Not only are the fruit trees in bloom, but the beaches of Okanagan Lake are a major draw. Anything and everyone goes in the water: boaters, water-skiiers, windsurfers, and parasailers. Surrounding the lakes are orchards, vineyards, and wineries, which give lots of tours and tastings.

The Peach Blossom Festival conjures up more summer fun, and so does the annual Wine Festival. Gearheads and hardbodies blow into town for some serious carbo-loading, followed by the Ironman Canada Triathlon—a true test of strength and endurance. Other points of cultural interest include the En'owkin First Nations' Cultural Center, a newly opened Wine Center, and the Dominion Radio Astrophysical Observatory.

To summarize, this valley is a popular tourist area among Canadians, and hostellers seem to really enjoy this hostel. Tell 'em the giant peach sent ya.

How to get there:

By bus: Greyhound stops in Penticton. From station, walk 1 block south on Ellis Street. Hostel is on left.

By car: Drive Route 97 to Penticton. Go straight onto Eckhard Avenue, then turn north several blocks later onto Ellis Street. Hostel is on right.

By plane: Small airport in Penticton. From airport terminal, walk south to Skaha Lake Road. Catch #206 bus downtown and get off at the 400 block of Main Street; walk east to Ellis Street, then follow

Ellis to hostel. The #206 Crosstown bus runs every hour at eighteen minutes past the hour, from 8:18 A.M. to 4:18 P.M.

FIDDLEHEAD FARM HOSTEL

Box 421, Powell River, British Columbia V8A 5C2

(604) 483–3018

Fax: (604) 485–3832

Web site: www.fiddleheadfarm.org

Rates: $32 Canadian (about $24 U.S.) per Hostelling International member; $20 Canadian (about $15 U.S.) fare for boat ride *not* included
Credit cards: None
Office hours: Vary; call
Beds: 18
Private/family rooms: Yes; number varies; call for availability
Single rooms: None
Private bathrooms: None
Affiliation: Hostelling International-Canada
Extras: Laundry, sauna, piano, canoes

Granola alert: This is a place you'll either love or hate—and either way, you're stuck for a week. So think carefully.

The hostel's poster tips you off right away. It features photos of some fuzzy, felt-hatted guy looking goofy (Just wondering: Did he sign a model release?), plus other sylvan shots of outdoorsy types and farm work. Right away you get the idea that this place is a little, um, different. And boy, is it.

Best bet for a bite: No choice

What hostellers say: "All they had was turnips!"

Gestalt: Funny farm

Hospitality: B

Party index:

The deal is this. The hostel owner runs a homesteader's organic farm on eighty acres of land along B.C.'s Sunshine Coast, a hard-to-reach but gorgeous stretch north of Vancouver. In fact, you take two ferries to reach this place—one to Powell River, and then a hostel-run speedboat up a small river. The boat runs once a week, and you pay an extra $20 Canadian (about $15 U.S.) for it. While here, you participate in farm life in every way. (More on this in a moment.) Meals are said to be fixed from the on-site produce, dairy, and meat, which is a nice touch when it succeeds.

All the buildings here were built by loving hands. There's a six-bedroom guesthouse with a common area, a bathhouse with a wood-fired sauna, and a large dining room and kitchen area. A large log meeting building here can accommodate groups of up to thirty, in case you've got lots of friends. For fun, there's lots of room to roam. Use of the canoes is included with your fee, so go ahead and canoe to your heart's content. Or steam away in the sauna.

If you've got time, that is, between chores. Some of the hostellers really enjoy the work exchange, getting a chance to bake bread and chop wood and haul water and all that other farm stuff they've heard about but never done before. Great if you're looking for a little fresh air. However, we've heard a few grumbles about the administration of this work program. Our advice: If you're being promised a discounted stay in exchange for extra chores, we'd recommend you get the work-for-pay agreement down on paper before you arrive. Not that it will help you get out earlier—remember, it's a week at a time—but it might prove useful later if someone disagrees with someone else's interpretation of things.

We know, we know, you're coming to get away from bureaucracies and red tape and all that. OK. Just don't come whining to us if you end up paying full price to eat turnips and chop wood all day long.

That said, some hostellers reported that the place was so wonderful they never wanted to leave! So this hostel, maybe more than any other in North America, is really what you make of it.

If you're coming, take note that the hostel's phone is a radio phone. So you need to let it ring at least ten times and, if you get through, speak V-E-R-Y C-L-E-A-R-L-Y. Then get ready for days of fresh air.

How to get there:

By ferry: From Vancouver, take bus ($26.00 Canadian, about $19.00 U.S.) to Powell River. From Victoria, drive to Comox area; take ferry from Little River to Powell River ($7.00 Canadian, about $5.00 U.S.). Hostel will then pick up hostellers from ferry waiting room ($20.00 Canadian, about $15.00 U.S.).

KEY TO ICONS

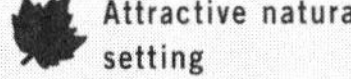
Attractive natural setting

Romantic private rooms

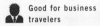

Good for business travelers

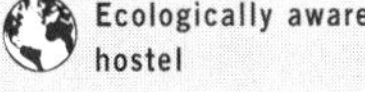
Ecologically aware hostel

Comfortable beds

Especially well suited for families

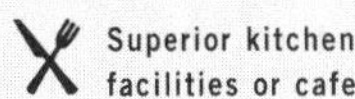
Superior kitchen facilities or cafe

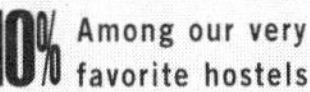
Among our very favorite hostels

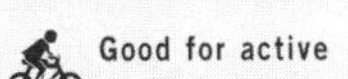
Good for active travelers

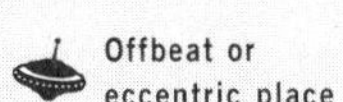
Offbeat or eccentric place

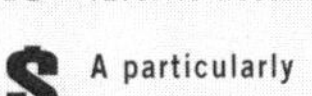
A particularly good value

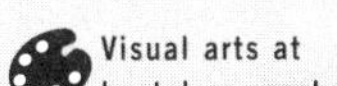
Visual arts at hostel or nearby

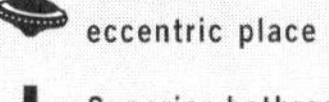
Superior bathroom facilities

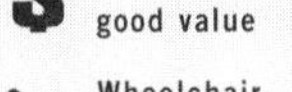
Wheelchair-accessible

Music at hostel or nearby

DANIEL'S GUEST HOUSE

313 First Street East, Revelstoke, British Columbia V0E 2S0

(250) 837–5530

Rates: $15 Canadian (about $11 U.S.) per person; private rooms $30 (about $21 U.S.)
Credit cards: MC
Office hours: Vary; call
Beds: 18
Private/family rooms: Yes; number varies; call for availability
Single rooms: None
Private bathrooms: None
Affiliation: None
Extras: Laundry, free pickups, TV, games

This hostel, another one of those tucked into the many mountain ranges of western B.C., sits in a two-story house with views of the mountains. The house features a wraparound porch with couches for major-league crashing; there's a picnic table for alfresco dining, too.

Inside, there are two dorms with six beds apiece. There's one family room, a "honeymoon suite" with a big double bed, and two other rooms with a single pair of bunk beds each. The kitchen area contains two refrigerator/freezers, a stove, double sink, and—yes—a second picnic table. Finally, the hostel's common room features cable TV, a very small library, and some games.

Best bet for a bite: Southside Grocery

Gestalt: Picnic

Hospitality: D

Party index:

For fun? Hike in the woods or take a tour of a huge hydroelectric dam on the nearby Columbia River. Revelstoke isn't real big, you understand, but you do have access to a number of outfitters who run heliskiing, horseback riding, or mountain bike rental operations.

How to get there:

By bus: Bus lines stop in town. From bus station, walk through one set of lights and underneath railroad bridge; continue 1 km (0.6 mi.) up road to corner of Victoria and First.

By car: Call hostel for directions.

REVELSTOKE TRAVELLERS HOSTEL

400 West Second Street, Revelstoke, British Columbia V0E 2S0

(250) 837–4050

Fax: (250) 837–6410

E-mail: roman@junction.net

Web site: www.revelstokecc.bc.ca/mountns/hostel.htm

Rates: $14.00–$19.75 Canadian (about $11.00–$15.00 U.S.) per Hostelling International member
Credit cards: MC, VISA
Office hours: 1:00–11:30 P.M.
Beds: 62
Private/family rooms: 25
Single rooms: None
Private bathrooms: None
Affiliation: Hostelling International-Canada
Extras: Laundry, lockers, TV, fax, games, breakfast, free Internet access, camping, garden, bike storage

Owners John and Melody Romanchuk recently finished a $300,000 renovation job at this hostel that brought new oak floors, new kitchen and bathroom facilities, and additional private rooms. It sounds good—and it is especially nice for folks who don't like to be crammed into a huge room with thirty other bodies.

For instance, the maximum number of beds in any dorm room is just four, which goes well with the new trend toward smaller rooms. And each private room in this place shares a bathroom and kitchen with just two or three other private rooms. That's right: There are eight kitchens and eight bathrooms in a hostel with only fifty-six beds. That might be some sort of a record for CRTHR (clean-rangetop-to-hosteller ratio) and the all-important WTTHR (working-toilet-to-hosteller ratio).

Best bet for a bite: Try here

Gestalt: Stoked

Hospitality: A

Party index:

Those private rooms are an especially good deal, coming with picture windows and double and bunk beds. Bathrooms and kitchens are located directly outside of each room, which sounds mighty convenient to us. The common room, located directly off the main lobby, comes with a television.

Here's something else to like. Pay a few bucks extra for the breakfast option and you get fruit-topped Belgian waffles—with a choice of cappuccino, fresh-squeezed orange or carrot juice, and coffee—at a nearby sidewalk cafe.

Wedged among spectacular mountain ranges, the town is considered a good base for visiting Glacier and Mt. Revelstoke National Parks, with all the hiking, river rafting, climbing, fishing, and so on you could possibly need. Want to really get close to nature? The Romanchuks run a small camping operation on the side; campers get full kitchen and bathroom privileges, a welcome privilege out here in the sticks.

We like what we've heard about this hostel, and it just seems to be improving.

How to get there:

By bus: Call hostel for transit route.

By car: Drive Victoria Road to the 7-Eleven store, turn onto Boyle Avenue, and drive 1½ blocks farther to corner of Second Street. Check in at hostel office, at #403; hostel itself is across street, at #400.

MOUNTAIN SHADOW HOSTEL 

2125 Columbia Avenue, Rossland, British Columbia V0G 1Y0

(250) 362–7160; (888) 393–7160

Fax: (250) 362–7150

E-mail: mshostel@kootenay.net

Web site: www.pagehost.com/mshostel/index.html

Rates: $17.00 Canadian (about $12.00 U.S.) per Hostelling International member; private rooms $37.50 Canadian (about $26.00 U.S.)

Credit cards: MC

Office hours: 7:00–11:00 A.M.; 4:00–10:00 P.M.

Beds: 40

Private/family rooms: 2

Single rooms: None

Private bathrooms: None

Affiliation: Hostelling International-Canada

Extras: Laundry, TV, VCR, tours, lockers, ski storage

We didn't get to sneak a peek at the Mountain Shadow, a recent addition to Hostelling International-Canada's already stellar lineup of associate hostels in B.C. But if it's anything like its *compadres,* it's a combination of good times, good meals, good management, and gnarly skiing. The building here features a large kitchen, TV room, and laundry—in short, everything you've come to expect from a solid hostel. We were glad to hear that French, German, and Italian are all spoken here; European hostellers will certainly find this heartening.

What hostellers say: "Peak experience."

Gestalt: Shadowland

Hospitality: A

Cleanliness: B

Party index:

Lodgings consist of two rooms with four bunks each, two rooms with three apiece, one room with two bunks, and a pair of private rooms. Each private room contains a double bed plus a bunk bed, perfect for families. There's a dining room, reading room, and lounge, too. Downstairs from the hostel, in a retail complex, are a grocery store, one-hour photo lab, and combination bicycle/snowboard store with repair facilities.

The terrain out here in south-central British Columbia is good for outdoorsy types—lots of sun in summer and snow in winter. Red Mountain Resorts, just 3 km (2 mi.) away, snags some 7-plus meters (27-plus feet) of snow annually, for instance. Sounds promising.

How to get there:

By car: Call hostel for directions.

SALT SPRING ISLAND HOSTEL 

640 Cusheon Lake Road, Ganges (Salt Spring Island), British Columbia V8K 2C2

(250) 537–4149

E-mail: hostel@saltspring.com

Web site: www.beacom.com/ssihostel

Rates: $15.50 Canadian (about $11.00 U.S.) per member, private rooms $40.00–$60.00 Canadian (about $30.00–$45.00 U.S.)
Credit cards: MC
Office hours: 9:00–10:30 A.M.; 5:00–8:00 P.M.
Beds: 28
Private/family rooms: 4
Single rooms: None
Private bathrooms: 1
Affiliation: Hostelling International-Canada
Extras: Grill, bicycle rentals, tepees, tree house, waterfall, kayak, tours, volleyball

What do you get when you cross a beautiful island, friendly folks, and an innovative hostel? Paradise for the weary traveler, that's what.

The Salt Spring Island Hostel's managers, Mike and Paula, have developed such a convivial place that it would be worth ten times the price. Mike's quite a character, a walking dictionary of things to do in the area—from hang gliding (he's reportedly the only such pilot on Salt Spring), to whale watching, to kayaking under a full moon, he's done it. If he hasn't done it, he'll try it. And Paula's artistic tendencies—she's a former professional photographer—are reflected all over the place, in touches like a little luggage house or the Pooh motifs or the dolphins that turn up here and there. These folks love to play and build, and it shows!

You start out by picking from the various accommodations—good clean hostel bunkrooms, nice woodsy tent sites, big funky (and popular!) tepees with views of the stars, two superb family rooms, or—couples only, please—a super-romantic, spic-and-span new

Salt Spring Island Hostel

Salt Spring Island

(photo courtesy Salt Spring Island Hostel)

tree house with a big trunk growing right up through the middle, furnished in Contemporary Winnie-the-Pooh style. Plans call for a second tree house as well, and maybe some gypsy caravans someday soon. Now this is living.

Supper is prepared in an immaculate and well-stocked kitchen sharing the common area; unfortunately, the sheer popularity of this place can be a drawback at suppertime, but otherwise everything is nicely kept and homespun. This place's most wonderful feature is its collegial atmosphere: As befits such a wonderfully laid-back island, the hostel's layout encourages get-togethers rather than discouraging them. At the end of an active day exploring parks and beaches, spontaneous friendships form each night by the firelight and the grill. Outdoor chairs and tables are used by everyone as darkness slowly falls.

You won't have any trouble finding things to fill your days on this island. The staff will happily rent you a bike, and this is a superb place to explore with two-wheelers, though again the popularity can occasionally mean you'll be shut out for a day. No matter; you're within hailing distance of a nice ocean beach, and an oceanfront park, and hitching a ride (if you tried) could get you to a tall cliff or downtown, too. There's a good Saturday farmers' market in the only town of consequence, Ganges; and arts, crafts, and coffee galore.

Most folks get here by arriving at one of three ferry landings, depending on where they're coming from (Vancouver, Victoria, or Crofton, British Columbia). They extend their left thumb skyward by the roadside; most get a ride within minutes. It's that kind of island, believe us. The driver might take you on a brief tour that begins to hint at the island's treasures—rolling pastures, sheer cliffs, ocean beaches, and more than a few lakes—before depositing you at the hostel. Now, we're not recommending that you hitchhike. Not us. We're way too responsible to do that. No, we're merely reporting what we've seen, in the public interest. We'd never try it. Not us. No way.

Best bet for a bite: Ganges fish market

What hostellers say: "Heavenly."

Insiders' tip: Ruckle Park

Gestalt: Salt of the Earth

Hospitality: A

Cleanliness: A

Party index:

Elsewhere on the island lie a trim little town that eats and shops surprisingly well, a fishing village, farmland . . . all taken in at a slowed-down, appreciative pace. Plus temperate weather. What else could a hosteller want? This is one of the best two or three hostelling experiences we've ever had, hands-down. Go, if you can find room to stay.

SQUAMISH INTERNATIONAL HOSTEL

38490 Buckley Avenue, Squamish, British Columbia

V0N 3G0

(800) 449–8614 (from British Columbia only);

(604) 892–9240

E-mail: hostel@mountain-inter.net

Rates: $15 Canadian (about $10 U.S.) per person; private rooms $30 Canadian (about $21 U.S.)
Credit cards: MC, VISA
Office hours: Vary; call hostel for hours
Beds: 16
Private/family rooms: 2
Single rooms: None

Private bathrooms: None
Affiliation: None
Extras: Grill, patio, tours, climbing wall, TV, VCR, store

"There is so much to do here, it's unbelievable," exclaimed the stand-in manager of the Squamish Hostel when we popped in to have a look. He's right. About the area, that is. And the hostel, while not exactly the Ritz, is certainly a cheap option for the legions of adventure travelers who find themselves here just about any time of year.

The unlikely-looking building formerly housed a video store, of all things, and it's easy to drive right by without noticing the hostel sign. Plans are in the works to continue to expand and upgrade the hostel's capacity. This is a good idea—it still carries a rather funky smell, weird stonework out back, and some other vestiges of its former life. We're hoping the work comes along promptly.

Best bet for a bite: Groceries aplenty

What hostellers say: "Got any toprope?"

Insiders' tip: Local brewpub has good deals

Gestalt: Squeamish

Hospitality: A

Cleanliness: C

Party index:

The kitchen did catch our eye, 'cause it was sparkly and clean, with well-marked cabinets and drawers clearly explaining the contents within. Good job, guys. Rooms are haphazardly scattered about the place; private rooms, although adequate, don't seem private enough—one of them serves as a walk-through toward the other. Bunkrooms appear comfortable enough and sit close to the all-important kitchen. Common areas and hallways are slightly disheveled, though, furnished with garage-sale–type furniture, and clearly well used.

If you're somehow stuck for something to do, owner-manager Gordon Addison has stocked the place with a couple of televisions and constructed a climbing wall for practicing; we didn't take a whack at it. Travel books and other related paraphernalia are also sold here in case you start dreaming of far-off lands.

Perhaps the most striking decorative touch at the hostel is the professional-quality photographs taken on safaris in Africa and other far-flung locales by Gordon and his buddies. This guy is obviously well traveled. It helps when a hostel owner has been in your hiking boots.

It's not spotless here. But we've definitely seen hostels in more dire straits than this one. What makes it even more appealing is the nonsmoking policy inside the house, a welcome rule indeed. Last we checked, doing your laundry was apparently free of charge, too.

About the crowd: The guys and gals who come here seem earnest enough about engaging in the local activities, and why not? This is a gearhead's paradise. Squamish—it's a native word that means "Mother of the Wind," since you asked—is renowned as one of the best rock-climbing locations in all of North America. The hostel manager claims that there are hundreds of climbing routes within easy walking distance of the hostel. The very experienced might climb straight up the face of the Big Chief—that granite monolith looming over the town—but the rest of us will hike around the back and get the same views from the top, thanks very much. (Gordon offers climbing classes if you're serious about that big-rock stuff.)

Mountain bikes can be rented in town; Canada's best windsurfing is here on Howe Sound; a couple of outfits run rafting trips over local rapids; and nearby Shannon Falls is one of Canada's highest waterfalls. At Murrin Park you can scale the rocks (hey, it's a lot easier than climbing the Chief) or watch the fish flop around catching flies. And nature-lovers will absolutely flip: Besides the views, this is bald-eagle turf. In winter as many as 4,000 birds might show up here.

Food choices aren't as bad as they seem when you approach the town, either. While it seems at first glance as though every fast-food restaurant ever conceived has set up shop here, there's also a little natural-foods store and a big mainstream grocery store if you want to cook your own grub.

Can't make it to Whistler? This is a lowbrow and threadbare place but, we guess, an acceptable option.

How to get there:

By bus: Maverick Coach Lines runs to Squamish ($7.50 Canadian/about $6.00 U.S.). If bus stops at Dentville Stores, get off there; hostel is in complex; otherwise, get off bus downtown. Walk up Route 99 to McDonald's, turn east on Cleveland Avenue, then walk to first light and turn right. Hostel is 100 meters (300 feet) on right.

By car: From Vancouver, drive north on Highway 99 approximately 70 km (50 mi.) to Squamish. Turn left onto Cleveland Avenue at McDonald's. Continue to first traffic light, turn right on Buckley Avenue, then go 100 meters (300 feet) more. Hostel is on right, just past school.

SQUILAX GENERAL STORE HOSTEL

Highway 1, Chase (Squilax), British Columbia V0E 1M0

(250) 675–2977

E-mail: squilax@jetstream.net

Rates: $14 Canadian (about $10 U.S.) per Hostelling International member; private rooms $32 (about $24 U.S.)
Credit cards: VISA
Office hours: 8:00–10:00 A.M.; 5:00–10:00 P.M.

Beds: 23
Private/family rooms: 2
Single rooms: None
Private bathrooms: None
Affiliation: Hostelling International-Canada
Extras: Laundry, store, gym and sauna membership, VCR, movie rentals, game room

10%

This has got to be one of the most intriguing hostels in western Canada. Blair Acton, the enthusiastic manager, packed in her corporate life back east and set up shop in central British Columbia. What she's got going on now is a unique hostel, general store, and bat study center.

The hostel has claimed three orange cabooses, formerly part of a Canadian National freight train, once living quarters on freights. That's where you sleep, believe it or not—on the train! Each rail car sleeps six and contains a toilet, kitchenette unit, and sitting area; a two-seat cupola in each car divides these areas from the bunk section (and also makes a great spot to sit watching the river on the property). Showers are in a separate building that's been modeled to look like a little train station.

Best bet for a bite: It's a store

What hostellers say: "All aboard!"

Insiders' tip: Bluegrass festival in area

Gestalt: Bat cave

Hospitality: A

Party index:

The main building, an honest-to-goodness heritage building, houses the hostel office and a lounge—and a grocery store. This store is nifty: You can choose from a selection of health foods, for once, instead of fried or processed junk. Its shelves emphasize locally produced foods, including organic veggies, local honey, green eggs (!), and other dairy products. In the same building are two private rooms. One has two twin beds, while the other has that double-bed/single-bed combination that's perfect for couples or families with children. These two rooms share a kitchen and washroom with the hostel's two live-in staffers.

Then there's the question of what to do while you're here. For fun, an old Union 76 garage has been converted into a combination game room/meeting room. That's one possibility. July brings the annual First Nations powwow, a gathering of tribes where you can watch dancers and try new foods. That's another. Salmon begin their annual spawning in the fall, so you can watch these beautiful silver-scaled fish do their thing close by.

Don't forget the big selection of videos that you can rent, either. The videos are chosen from a local video club's vast library, and there's a VCR in the main lounge. Other amenities include a large wharf on the river, a campfire pit, and an outdoor games area. Coming soon: a sweathouse made of bales of straw. Should make an interesting place even more unique.

And, of course, there are the bats. It seems that back when Blair purchased the property, she discovered an entire colony of Yuma bats hanging out (literally) in the abandoned building. Instead of screaming and running out the door like most people would, she decided to learn what makes these critters tick and set up an education center. And so, yup, the bats still reside in the general store.

But that's not to say this hostel is completely batty. Far from it. In fact, people seem to like the friendliness and novelty of staying here and sleeping in the blaze-orange rail cars. We're always in favor of alternative transportation, and so, in this case, we'll take the train, too.

How to get there:

By car: Call hostel for directions.

WHALERS ON THE POINT GUESTHOUSE HOSTEL

West Street and Grice Road, Tofino, British Columbia V0R 2Z0

(604) 684–7101

Fax: (604) 684–7181

E-mail: info@tofinohostel.com

Rates: $22 Canadian (about $15 U.S.) per Hostelling International member, doubles $66 Canadian (about $44 U.S.)
Credit cards: MC, VISA
Office hours: 7:00 A.M.–noon, 5:00–11:00 P.M.
Beds: 60
Private/ family rooms: Yes
Affiliation: Hostelling International-Canada
Extras: Kitchen, laundry, lockers, Internet access, bike rentals, sauna, game room, meeting room, grill, patio, fireplace

In a country full of superlative spots, Tofino's got one of the best: right at the edge of the Pacific, this fishing town is wedged between green, green mountains and pounding surf and long white beaches that go on for miles. And this hostel, at the foot of Tofino's main street, has superb position and facilities—making up for some recent losers in this town.

Inside a cedar-sided, two-story house, they've got doubles, triples, a quad room, and a five-bedded room—some with bathrooms. There's Internet access in the common room, a kitchen, and incredible views of the ocean from the dining and living rooms—not to mention a gas fireplace, laundry, game room, and patio with a barbecue. Perfect. As long as it isn't raining—which it might well be. Ah, so that's why everyone from L.A. hasn't picked up stakes and moved here yet . . .

Best bet for a bite:
Common Loaf Bake Shop

What hostellers say:
"Amazing area."

Gestalt:
No idle coast

Party index:

The town of Tofino (say Toe-feen-oh) itself isn't scenic, but the various boat cruises, bike rides, and swims you can take from here are incredible. Check at the hostel reception or the local tourism office for more info on the many offerings, which include a rugged trail down the Pacific Coast, a dip in a nearby hot springs, and a tour through huge, primeval stands of virgin forest.

How to get there:

By bus: From Vancouver, take ferry to Nanaimo and switch to Laidlaw bus to Tofino. From Victoria, take train to Nanaimo and switch to Laidlaw bus for Tofino.

By car: From Victoria, drive north on Route 1 to Parksville, then turn left onto Route 4. Continue to end of route in Tofino.

BORDERLINE RANCH HOSTEL NR

Box 434, Valemount, British Columbia V0E 2Z0

(250) 566–9161

E-mail: borderline@valemount.com

Rates: $6.00–$15.00 Canadian (about $4.00–$10.00 U.S.) per person
Credit cards: None
Office hours: Vary; call hostel for hours
Season: May 15–October 15
Beds: 16
Private/family rooms: None
Single rooms: None
Private bathrooms: None
Affiliation: None
Extras: Horse trips

Itchin' for a big Rocky Mountain experience without the crush at hostels just over the borderline mountain pass? Located on a seventy-six–acre ranch, the ranch claims the sunny side of a mountain slope with valley views. It is just over an hour by bus or train from Jasper. This horsey hostel might do in a pinch, though we can't vouch for the quality of the experience.

Accommodations are slightly irregular. There are indoor bunks, yet all kitchen and washroom facilities are outdoors—making clear why this place operates just from May to October. The real draw here is the guided horseback rides, which allows hostellers a close-up look of the magnificent mountains; they're a bit expensive, but do ask about the fee schedule if you're interested. You might even get a chance to see the top of the magnificent white dome of Mount Robson, the highest mountain in the Canadian Rockies, which is said to be visible only on about two clear days all year. It's a beautiful sight.

Gestalt: Headed for the border

Hospitality: A

Party index:

How to get there:

By bus: Bus stops in Valemount. From depot, call hostel for transit route.

By car: Call for directions.

By train: VIA Rail stops in Valemount. From train station, call hostel for transit route.

C&N HOSTEL NR

927 Main Street, Vancouver, British Columbia V6A 2V8

(888) 434–6060; (604) 682–2441

E-mail: backpackers@sprint.ca

Rates: $12.00–$30.00 Canadian (about $8.00–$20.00 U.S.) per person; double rooms $35.00 Canadian (about $24.00 U.S.)
Credit cards: AMEX, DISC, MC, VISA
Office hours: 8:00 A.M.–11:00 P.M.
Beds: 100
Private/family rooms: Yes
Private bathrooms: None
Affiliation: None
Extras: TV, VCR, laundry, bike rentals, Internet access, kitchen, patio, lockers, shuttle, store

This hostel has changed hands since the last edition of *Hostels Canada,* and new management promises improvements. Its former incarnation was not too impressive—a turkey in fact. We're wondering what the near future will bring for this former hotel with a yucky street in front and a tennis court in back.

The place is well situated in one way only: It's very close to Vancouver's train station and bus depot. But don't consider that a good thing, necessarily; it also sits beside a club that once advertised GIRLS GIRLS GIRLS. Yup, seedy city. At least it's near Vancouver's main Chinatown area, meaning tons of

Best bet for a bite: Han's, in Chinatown

What hostellers say: "Hmm, I dunno . . ."

Gestalt: Risqué business

Safety: D

Party index:

VANCOUVER-AREA HOSTELS: A Summary

	RATING	PROS	CONS	COST	PAGE
Vancouver Downtown		location, features		$19.95	p. 228
Jericho Beach Hostel		location	slacker crowd	$21.50	p. 224
Globetrotter's Inn		location	upkeep	$18.00	p. 222
Cambie Hostel		free breakfast	grunge crowd	$20.00–$25.00	p. 220
C & N Hostel	NR		unsafe area	$12.00–$30.00	p. 219
New Backpacker's Hostel			unsafe area	$10.00	p. 227

affordable and interesting food is pretty close at hand. A few minutes lost in that sea of humanity can make you forget where you're staying. Almost.

The building itself, while appearing shabby, actually has some decent rooms—bigger and better furnished than expected. Claudia and Nasser, the C&N in question (one African and one Iranian), claim they've made things better than before and that the young, grungy crowd that used to dominate the postage-stamp kitchen and dirty bathrooms is no more.

We'll see.

How to get there:

By bus: Bus lines stop in Vancouver. From bus depot, call hostel for directions.

By car: Call hostel for directions.

By train: VIA Rail stops in Vancouver. From train station, call hostel for directions.

CAMBIE INTERNATIONAL HOSTEL 

300 Cambie Street, Vancouver, British Columbia V6B 2N3

(604) 684–6466

E-mail: cambie@dowco.com

Rates: $20.00–$25.00 Canadian (about $16.00 U.S.) per hostel association member; $26.35 Canadian (about $18.00 U.S.) per nonmember
Credit cards: MC, VISA
Office hours: 24 hours
Beds: 50
Private/family rooms: Yes; number varies; call for availability
Single rooms: None
Private bathrooms: None
Affiliation: None
Extras: Laundry, bar, free breakfast

"If you bunk it, they will come." That's the theory, anyway, that's driving a number of recently opened urban hostels around North America—including this one smack in the heart of downtown Vancouver. It isn't the worst place in town, and it isn't the best. "An option" is what it is when you've been shut out of the good guys.

First off, you've got to wonder about a place with PARTY HERE TONIGHT painted in huge red letters on the side. Maybe that's because this place has always been a watering hole; located inside an old brick hotel, it claims to be the city's oldest pub.

The ground floor of the building is dominated by a bar with a wacky gate to deal with strange city liquor laws. At 11:00 P.M. the bar half closes and everyone slithers through the gate to the restaurant side. That part serves liquor until around 1:00 A.M., but there's a catch: You've gotta order food. Either way, it's a raucous scene down there. Every pierced, braided, and space-suited disaffected youth in the city appears to show up and engage in cigarette-smoking marathon contests with his/her/its buddies.

Fortunately, this scene is insulated a bit from the second-floor hostel by extra-high ceilings. Still, smoke, noise, and the perfumed scent of frying grease waft through the hallways all night long.

That said, the owner has actually done a pretty good job of renovating the hundred-year-old hotel into a hostel. The fixes include fresh coats of paint, a laundry, lockers in the rooms, a slow eviction of longtime tenants, and brand-new bunk beds so wide that you could probably drive a (compact) car onto them.

This isn't the greatest neighborhood, but the staff has done a good job with security: You need three, count 'em, three different keys to open three separate locked doors before you're in your room. Four if the front door's locked, which it might be late at night.

Best bet for a bite:
Chinatown

What hostellers say:
"Just one more beer, dude?"

Insiders' tip:
SeaBus is nearby!

Gestalt:
Can't-be

Safety: B

Hospitality: C

Cleanliness: B

Party index:

Come morning you get one free breakfast at the bakery next door. Nice touch. Too bad there isn't a kitchen for other meals; you're stuck with the drab Gastown neighborhood for food and fun. Unless you like hokey T-shirts and overpriced Italian food, you're probably not gonna feel like it's hosteller heaven around here.

How to get there:

By bus: Greyhound stops in Vancouver. From depot, call hostel for directions.

By car: Call hostel for directions.

By plane: Airport outside Vancouver. From airport, call hostel for transit route.

By train: VIA Rail stops in Vancouver. From station, call hostel for transit route.

GLOBETROTTER'S INN INTERNATIONAL HOSTEL

170 Esplanade West, North Vancouver,
British Columbia V7M 1A3
(604) 988–2082

Rates: $18 Canadian (about $13 U.S.) per person; private rooms $45 Canadian (about $32 U.S.)
Credit cards: None
Office hours: 8:00 A.M.–11:00 P.M.
Beds: 32
Private/family rooms: 4
Single rooms: None
Private bathrooms: 2
Affiliation: None
Extras: Pool table, laundry, piano, TV, grill

A pale-yellow stucco building wedged between a Thai restaurant and a community-resource center, this hostel provides clean and relatively comfy digs away from the hustle of downtown Vancouver—yet easily accessible to the city via the SeaBus, a ferry that deposits you just a block from the place. Too bad it's slated to change from a hostel to a hotel in a couple of years.

This is a decent enough place, despite the slacker, live-in crowd and loud music that occasionally vibrates the walls and teeth. Rooms come in varying degrees of privacy, with a mix of metal family-style bunks and wooden bunks outfitted with futon mattresses. Some add an en-suite bathroom or a desk, while spacious closets offer enough space for a couple of big backpacks.

We also like the bathroom setup; there are two single-sex showers on each floor, separate from the washroom facilities, making the morning grooming routine much easier to navigate. Other nice touches in the place include Native paintings, houseplants, and kitschy felt souvenir banners from such far-flung places as tiny Point Roberts, Washington, and the fruitful Okanagan Valley.

The manager is trying to renovate a building that was definitely beginning to deteriorate. Lots of renovation means the smell of paint might be wafting through the halls. Some rooms are in a state of partial improvement. The kitchen suffers from a balky stove. And so on.

The biggest drawback here is the crowd; this is another one of those places where guests have a tendency to become permanent residents. When most of the pictures on the wall feature guests who you've just seen yakking in the TV room, months (or years) after the snapshots were taken, it's not a good sign. This kind of hostel can create a problem between two different kinds of people sharing space—the short-termers and the long-termers—as the long-termers often claim the kitchen and television as their own, to the detriment of passers-through.

On the upside, though, this place is smoothly run, and it's in a terrific neighborhood away from the craziness of downtown Vancouver. There's a street (Lonsdale) with everything one could need to buy; an indoor market (Lonsdale Quay; pronounce it *key* or sound like an outsider) with fruit, fish, good cheap restaurants and everything else you could need to eat; and a quick public transit shot over to Vancouver itself. Also, great parks lie here in North Van, where the mountains rise high above the city. Try Lynn River Canyon Park for a suspension bridge that's more interesting, narrower, and deeper than the famous tourist-trap one at Capilano. Still not convinced? This one is free! You can swim here, too.

We could say lots more about North Van, but you get the point. It's a good escape, and this hostel delivers as a solid third choice when the two Hostelling International joints across the water are booked solid.

Best bet for a bite: Lonsdale Quay market

What hostellers say: "Whose turn is it to cook tonight?"

Insiders' tip: Lynn River Canyon Park

Gestalt: World party

Safety: A

Hospitality: A

Cleanliness: B

Party index:

How to get there:

By bus: Greyhound stops in Vancouver. From depot, call hostel for directions.

By car: Call hostel for directions.

By ferry: Take SeaBus ferry ($2.25 Canadian/about $1.50 U.S.) from waterfront station in Vancouver to North Vancouver. From station, walk uphill 1 block to Esplanade; turn left and walk 1 block west. Hostel is at #170.

By plane: Airport outside Vancouver. From airport, call hostel for transit route.

By train: VIA Rail stops in Vancouver. From station, call hostel for transit route.

JERICHO BEACH HOSTEL

1515 Discovery Street, Vancouver, British Columbia V6R 4K5

(604) 224–3208

Fax: (604) 244–4852

E-mail: van-jericho@hihostels.bc.ca

Web site: www.hihostels.bc.ca/van-jer.htm

Rates: $21.50 Canadian (about $16.00 U.S.) per Hostelling International member; private rooms $47.00–$61.00 Canadian (about $33.00–$43.00 U.S.)
Credit cards: JCB, MC, VISA
Office hours: 24 hours
Private/family rooms: 9
Single rooms: None
Private bathrooms: 2
Affiliation: Hostelling International-Canada
Extras: TV, laundry, cafe, courtesy phone, shuttle

Close by the University of British Columbia campus, the Jericho Beach Hostel is a great place to kick back. The dorms here are pretty nice, considering how many folks they need to pack into this popular stop (it was once a former military barracks).

The private rooms are a surprising treat, too: They're beautiful. Various combinations exist, which is nice—some contain private bathrooms, a sink, a bureau, some dishes, picnic supplies (like bug juice and sandwich bags), and shared kitchenettes. Some have dazzling views of downtown Vancouver, which lights up at night against a backdrop of misty mountains and water.

Finally, this place is blessed with a truly great hostel staff. They're helpful and patient with hosteller inquiries as simple as "When's the bus get here?" or as complicated as "I wanna go to Australia this weekend. . . ." (No, we didn't make that one up; they get it about once a week.)

As we say, what a spot for chillin' out. As befits the name of this hostel, there is indeed a beach—a half-dozen, in fact—within a surprisingly short distance; you can literally walk out the front door to them. One of them, rocky Wreck Beach, is famous because it's clothing-optional; others, like Kits Beach, have better sand, views, parking, and changing facilities, but you're always close to some sort of water.

Jericho Beach Hostel

Vancouver

(photo courtesy HI-Canada)

Green athletic fields across the street make a prime place for whipping around your choice of flying disc. For culture vultures, the community theater next door presents performances throughout the summer months as well. Get a map or directions from the front desk if you need 'em.

The university campus is also a big place to roam around. There's a world-renowned museum of anthropology and some wonderful Japanese gardens, both of which charge admission. And boundless kilometers of hiking trails ramble through the sprawling grounds, if you know where to look; again, get a map at the hostel or university. Commune with nature as long as you want—it's free, it's beautiful, and it sure beats wrestling for counter space with the latest London fashion statement.

The only drawback here is the lack of good common space. A huge TV room occupies lots of folks, but you can't really talk there. As for the kitchen scene, well, it's just plain crazy—lots of hostellers elbowing for very few burners, all at the same time, stealing and breaking equipment, dumping mounds of dirty dishes in the deep army-issue steel sinks. Our advice: Eat out on the town, or else schedule your cooking for off-hours. The hostel maintains a small cafe on the premises, and it's a good place to sip a beer and write meaningful poetry, even if the food isn't always top-drawer.

Best bet for a bite: Anything on Broadway

What hostellers say: "Which way to the nude beach?"

Insiders' tip: Pacific Spirit Park

Gestalt: Beach ball

Safety: A

Hospitality: A

Cleanliness: B

Party index:

Oh, and one other complaint we kept hearing: You can stay up to three months at a time, which means lots of dead-enders basically wind up living here—especially during the shoulder seasons—while they look for work, read about housing, or just slack off smoking butts and generally acting like jerks. Maybe that stay policy could be rewritten.

But back to the positives. This is easily the best place in town for relaxing out-of-doors rather than exploring the bustle of the city. Tired of looking at so many beautiful hills and skyscrapers? Free shuttle buses run downtown from the hostel door all day (and night, in summer) if you want to dive back into the craziness.

How to get there:

By bus: Bus stops in Vancouver. From station, take Skytrain west two stops to Granville stop. Walk to bus stop on Granville Street (outside Holt Renfrew Store) and take #4 bus to NW Marine Drive. Walk downhill and turn right on Discovery Street. Hostel is second building on left.

KEY TO ICONS

 Attractive natural setting

 Ecologically aware hostel

 Superior kitchen facilities or cafe

 Offbeat or eccentric place

 Superior bathroom facilities

 Romantic private rooms

 Comfortable beds

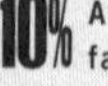 Among our very favorite hostels

$ A particularly good value

 Wheelchair-accessible

 Good for business travelers

 Especially well suited for families

 Good for active travelers

 Visual arts at hostel or nearby

 Music at hostel or nearby

By car: Drive Route 99 into Vancouver. At Fourth Avenue, turn left and continue west to stoplight for NW Marine Drive. Bear right and follow NW Marine to first right. Turn right onto Discovery; hostel is second building on left.

By plane: Large airport outside city. Take #100 bus to Seventieth and Granville; change to #20 bus, take to Sixth Avenue. Cross street using underpass and take #4 bus to NW Marine Drive. Walk downhill; take first right into Jericho Park. Hostel is second building on left.

By train: VIA Rail stops in Vancouver. From station, take SkyTrain west two stops to Granville stop. Walk to bus stop on Granville Street and take #4 bus to NW Marine Drive. Walk downhill and turn right on Discovery Street. Hostel is second building on left.

NEW BACKPACKER'S HOSTEL

347 West Pender Street, Vancouver,

British Columbia V6B 6T3

(604) 688–0112

Rates: $10.00 Canadian (about $8.00 U.S.) per person; $20.00–$35.00 for private rooms ($14.00–$25.00 U.S.)
Credit cards: None
Office hours: 10:00 A.M.–midnight (earlier in winter)
Beds: Number varies; call for availability
Private/family rooms: 10
Single rooms: None
Private bathrooms: None
Affiliation: None
Extras: Laundry, bicycle rentals, kitchen, video games, lockers, stereo

Nothing new here despite the name—except that it appears some "dudes" have taken the place over and may be are managing it slightly better. This is still a cheap bed for the night with no extras, although if you call for info on the place, you'll have to endure a ten-minute recording of "Hotel California" interpersed with that hotel data. This hostel seems to be a haven for smokers, despite the nice coffee shop downstairs. There's a tiny kitchen, somewhat tacky common room, and yellowing wallpaper. At least the former hostel can boast (?) of an extremely whimsical layout; rooms, windows, and bathrooms are arranged apparently at random.

The supposedly hip (yawn) Gastown neighborhood is situated about a block away.

Best bet for a bite:
Chinatown

Insiders' tip:
Leave window open to avoid smash

Gestalt:
Smoke show

Safety: D

Hospitality: C

Cleanliness: D

Party index:

Chinatown is fairly close as well, so there's plenty of incentive to get out and explore the surroundings. You might want to do that—if you really feel you must stay—but we'd think once, twice, and three times hard before sticking around here, even though management promises good times with keg nights with dancing and DJ. Especially when there are two great Hostelling International joints in town.

How to get there:

By bus: Greyhound stops in Vancouver. From bus station call hostel for directions.

By car: Call hostel for directions.

By plane: Airport in Vancouver. From airport, call hostel for transit route.

By train: VIA Rail stops in Vancouver. From train station call hostel for transit route.

VANCOUVER DOWNTOWN HOSTEL

1114 Burnaby Street, Vancouver, British Columbia V6B 1P1

(604) 684–4565

Fax: (604) 684–4540

E-mail: van-downtown@hihostels.bc.ca

Web site: www.hihostels.bc.ca/van-downtown.htm

Rates: $19.95 Canadian (about $14.00 U.S.) per Hostelling International member
Credit cards: MC, VISA, JCB
Office hours: 24 hours
Beds: 223
Private/family rooms: 23
Single rooms: None
Private bathrooms: Yes; number varies
Affiliation: Hostelling International-Canada
Extras: Laundry, game room, meeting room, TV, library, bicycle rental, information desk, shuttle

10%

Hostelling International should be right proud of their newest hostel in Vancouver, an addition made necessary by the crush at the Jericho Beach Hostel and the demand for a downtown facility. This is one classy place, in a safe and classy neighborhood, and a steal at the price.

Once a Catholic nursing home, the hostel consists of newly renovated rooms and facilities that are a joy to be in—like a really nice hotel. No dorm room has more than four beds in it, we're told, which is just not the kind of luxury you usually get for these prices. And the other amenities at this place are equally amazing: a free information kiosk to steer wayward travelers around the city's some-

Vancouver Downtown Hostel

Vancouver

(photo by Martha Coombs)

times confusing streets; a well-stocked library; a TV lounge that's nicer than many; a backyard patio with soft benches and a hammock; a great kitchen; a meeting room.

Bunkrooms are narrow but certainly adequate, usually stocked with just two sets of bunks each. Private rooms are more interesting, coming in various shapes and sizes but usually including a closet and desk or dresser.

There's a courtesy phone in the lobby, so you can receive incoming calls; and a free shuttle over to Jericho Beach, where you find all the views, sunbathing (when the sun's out, that is), and hiking action. This shuttle runs day and night during the summer, daytimes only during the winter months.

You won't want to leave the hostel at first, but what to do once you do? Well, this is Vancouver, so there's no shortage of eats and sights and clubs. There's a nice little beach very close at hand, a few blocks down the street. Davie Street is chock-full of

Best bet for a bite:
Ten Thanks, on Davie

What hostellers say:
"I'll be here awhile."

Insiders' tip:
Great bulletin board

Gestalt:
Heaven-sent

Safety: A

Hospitality: A

Cleanliness: A

Party index:

every sort of restaurant you'd want to try. There's plenty of shopping in the West End, on Robson Street.

A little farther afield—but not much—The Granville Island public market is a must-visit. Stalls brim with fresh B.C. produce, meats, cheeses, chocolates, and much more. There's a neat microbrewery on the island, too. Get there by a free barge ride or a short drive.

How to get there:

By bus: Greyhound stops in Vancouver. From bus station, take SkyTrain west two stops to Granville station. Walk out front door to bus stop on Granville Street and take #8 bus to Thurlow Street. Cross Davie Street, walk 1 block south on Thurlow; hostel is on right, at corner of Burnaby.

By car: Call hostel for directions.

By plane: Large airport outside city. From airport, take shuttle bus ($9.00 Canadian/about $7.00 U.S.; runs every half-hour) to Parkhill Hotel on Davie Street. Walk east on Davie to corner of Thurlow; walk 1 block south on Thurlow; hostel is on right, at corner of Burnaby.

By train: VIA Rail stops in Vancouver. From station, take Skytrain west two stops to Granville station. Walk out front exit to bus stop on Granville Street and take #8 bus to Thurlow Street (outside drugstore). Cross Davie Street, walk 1 block south on Thurlow; hostel is on right, at corner of Burnaby.

BACKPACKERS HOSTEL 

1418 Fernwood Road, Victoria, British Columbia V8V 4P7

(250) 386–4471

Rates: $12.00 Canadian (about $9.00 U.S.) per person; $35.00–$40.00 Canadian ($25.00–$28.00 U.S.) for private rooms

Credit cards: None

Office hours: Vary; call

Beds: Number varies; call for availability

Private/family rooms: None

Single rooms: None

Private bathrooms: None

Affiliation: None

Extras: Um . . .

This is a crash pad, simply put: the kind of place where sweaty backpackers and packs pile up in the corners, and where cleaning isn't necessarily a priority.

Otherwise, there isn't a whole lot to say about this hostel, except that the layout is extremely, er, interesting—befitting the old house it's in—with stairways and fire escapes and rooms appearing and disappearing, seemingly at random, throughout the hostel. Rooms are serviceable for catching a few winks, if cramped. The roof is a

VICTORIA-AREA HOSTELS: A Summary

	RATING	PROS	CONS	COST	PAGE
Ocean Island Backpackers		fun	loud	\$16.00–\$19.50	p. 233
HI-Victoria		right downtown	crowded	\$16.00	p. 231
Selkirk Guesthouse		riverside location	cluttered	\$18.00	p. 235
Backpackers Hostel		neighborhood	shabby	\$12.00	p. 230

cool place to hang out to get away from it all, though lots of smokers seem to find it. Come to think of it, people smoke inside, too. You can't escape the nefarious curling of cigarette smoke; it will hunt you down and find you.

This hostel's lone saving grace is a really nice residential neighborhood. Fernwood is a real place where real Victorians live—a far cry from the downtown tourist experience most folks get of the city—and a good place to meet people. There's a cluster of theaters, restaurants, and bars nearby; the area is safe, friendly, and a mixture of bohemian and upwardly mobile. Lots of young people live here, maybe the only section of Victoria that can make such a claim.

Gestalt: Crash-test dummies

Safety: D

Hospitality: D

Cleanliness: F

Party index:

How to get there:

By bus: Greyhound stops in Victoria. From depot, take #10 bus (at Douglas and Fort) to hostel on Fernwood.

By car: From U.S.A., take ferry from Port Angeles, Washington, to Victoria. From ferry terminal, call hostel for directions.

HOSTELLING INTERNATIONAL-VICTORIA

516 Yates Street, Victoria, British Columbia V8W 1K8

(250) 385-4511

Fax: (250) 385-3232

E-mail: victoria@hihostels.bc.ca

Web site: www.hihostels.bc.ca/vic.htm

Rates: $16 Canadian (about $11 U.S.) per Hostelling International member
Credit cards: JCB, MC, VISA
Beds: 110
Office hours: 7:30 A.M.–midnight
Private/family rooms: 3
Single rooms: None
Private bathrooms: 1
Affiliation: Hostelling International-Canada
Extras: Laundry, lockers, TV, game room, ride board, video games, courtesy phone, intercom, events, fax service, store, pool table, pinball

This hostel, located right in the hub of Victoria's bustling, historic waterfront district, couldn't be better located. The very location, however, may ultimately turn out to be a curse: The place has become so popular, and downtown real estate so expensive, that this fine hostel is suffering some serious growing pains.

Best bet for a bite: Chinatown, a block away

What hostellers say: "Get a bigger building."

Insiders' tip: Ride board/for-sale board

Gestalt: Fish and chips

Safety: A

Hospitality: A

Cleanliness: C

Party index:

The hostel tries hard, though. There's a locker in every room; locks and keys can be purchased at the front desk, along with a few basic travel supplies. There are almost-unheard-of services, like an intercom and incoming courtesy phone; you can receive calls, pages, or even faxes (for a fee). Coed dorms? Yup, they've got 'em.

Let's back up a second. The first thing you notice upon entering is the way the place's extraordinarily friendly staffers—who seem to hail from every imaginable corner of the globe—know just where to snag the best grub (Chinatown); beer (North America's first brewpub is a fifteen-minute walk away); and sights like Wharf Street, Parliament, the awesome Royal British Columbia Museum, and the picture-postcard harbor. It's just steps from the bus and train stations and the ferry depot, too, a great boon for international travelers.

But if it's solitude you want, this ain't the place. The men's dorm, in particular, feels very much like a cattle call. Mornings can get hairy as dozens of sleepy guys line up for next shot at the first available shower, sink, or stall. The women's dorm has a private room right inside it (!), but an enormous bathroom somewhat compensates.

The kitchen handles the overload pretty well most of the time, but it, too, can get awfully crowded. Still, it is a very big, if narrow, kitchen that features acres of prep space. Three sinks, two refrigerators, a freezer, five microwave ovens (gotta love modern culture), four stoves . . . you get the drift. There's also some gadget called a "Snack Factory™." Too bad the floor gets sticky and dirty quite easily.

Fortunately, the staff here are very helpful with information. They even have a volunteer staff an extra desk sometimes to dispense additional wisdom about everything to do in the area. And there's also a handy upstairs game room to relieve pressure when the crush is on, with plenty of distractions: a nice television, two video-game machines, foosball, a pool table, pinball, and—this being England (practically)—a dartboard.

Our advice? This place is fine for a short stay. Just make sure and ask the front desk what to do around town; you won't, you'll soon discover, need to spend much time packed like a sardine in a tin in your bed after all.

How to get there:

By bus: Pacific Coach Lines runs from Vancouver. From depot, walk north up Douglas Street to Yates Street. Turn left on Yates and walk 2 more blocks. Hostel is on right.

By car: From U.S.A., take ferry from Port Angeles, Washington, to Swartz Bay. From ferry terminal, follow signs to Pat Bay Highway and drive approximately 30 km (20 mi.) to Victoria. Expressway becomes Blanshard Street; make a right onto Yates Street in city and proceed nearly to water. Hostel is on right. From southern Vancouver, B.C., take ferry to Swartz Bay. From ferry terminal, follow signs to Pat Bay Highway and drive approximately 30 km (20 mi.) to Victoria. Expressway becomes Blanshard Street; make a right onto Yates Street in city and proceed nearly to water. Hostel is on right. From North Vancouver, B.C., take ferry to Nanaimo. From Nanaimo ferry terminal, drive Highway 1 south to Victoria. Highway 1 merges with Douglas Street; then turn right onto Yates and proceed nearly to water. Hostel is on right.

By ferry: From U.S.A., take ferry from Port Angeles, Washington, to Swartz Bay; from southern Vancouver, B.C., take ferry to Swartz Bay. From Swartz Bay terminal, take #70 bus to Johnson Street, and walk 3 blocks to hostel.

By plane: Airport in Victoria. Call hostel for transit route.

By train: VIA Rail runs to Victoria from Nanaimo, once per day. Train station is 1 block from hostel.

OCEAN ISLAND BACKPACKERS INN

791 Pandora, Victoria, British Columbia V8W 1K8

(888) 888–4180

E-mail: get-it@oceanisland.com

Rates: $16.00–$19.50 Canadian (about $11.00–$13.00 U.S.) per person, doubles $39.50 Canadian (about $27.00 U.S.)

Credit cards: AMEX, MC, VISA
Office hours: 24 hours
Beds: 112
Private/family rooms: Yes
Affiliation: None
Extras: Pickups

♫

Victoria's newest entry in the hostelling sweepstakes was badly needed, and it looks good so far. Kevin and Daniel, the two young men from back east who opened the place, report that they enjoy the west coast's pace of life. The hostel shows it.

Their blue-and-white building, once a hotel, dates from 1893, and it's decorated with an attractive rain forest mural outside; inside, the floors are refurbished hardwood. They've got plenty of dorms here, plus two private rooms with their own bathrooms. Another twenty-one bathrooms handle the rest of the guests, so you won't be standing in a long lineup.

Best bet for a bite:
Barb's Fish and Chips

What hostellers say:
"Fun."

Gestalt:
Victoria is ours

Hospitality: A

Cleanliness: B

Party index:

The perks include a big kitchen; TV room that never closes; music room with guitars, drums and other jamming equipment; a game room with pool table and video games; Internet, computer, and fax access; a cafe serving meals and drinks; a small supplies store; and plenty of activities such as pub-crawling, beach trips, hikes, and more.

Location is good and central, near what passes for shopping and excitement (yeah, right) in Victoria; the staff especially recommends the city's thrift stores, and indeed there's one right next door selling hiking gear, boots, and other stuff at low prices. You're also quite close to shops, the Inner Harbour, the city's tiny Chinatown, the Royal British Columbia Museum, pubs and lots more stuff—including, of course, the Parliament Buildings that everyone seems to want to see.

Good effort, with twenty-four–hour reception and fun staff, so far. Keep it up!

How to get there:

By bus: From bus station, call hostel for pickup.

By car: Call hostel for directions.

By ferry: From Swartz Bay ferry terminal (from Vancouver), take #70 bus to Pandora and Douglas Streets. Walk 1 block east to Blanchard; hostel is at corner of Pandora. From Ogden Point ferry terminal (from Seattle), take #30 or #31 bus to Pandora and

Douglas Streets. Walk 1 block east to Blanchard; hostel is at corner of Pandora.

By train: Call hostel for transit route.

SELKIRK INTERNATIONAL GUESTHOUSE

934 Selkirk Avenue, Victoria, British Columbia V9A 2V1

(250) 389–1213

Rates: $18 Canadian (about $13 U.S.) per person; private rooms $40–$70 Canadian (about $28–$49 U.S.)
Credit cards: MC, VISA
Office hours: 4:00–11:00 P.M.
Beds: 22
Private/family rooms: 2
Single rooms: None
Private bathrooms: 1
Affiliation: None
Extras: Hot tub, laundry, breakfast, dock, trampoline, TV, canoe rentals, boats

Of all the hostels in Victoria, we might pick Selkirk as our first choice. It's set in the nicest location, off the beaten track, and you get a nice, grassy view of a peaceful tidal river. Where else are you gonna get that? As long as you don't mind a bit of crowding or clutter, this is a pretty nice place.

The hostel occupies the house of Norm and Lyn Jackson and their family, and it's a nice place. Their dock on the river allows for swimming and boating, there's a hot tub for soaking—and, get this, a trampoline for springing up and down on. Or try biking or walking downtown alongside the water, a nice way to get there, if a bit of a trek.

The private rooms are the real steal here. One of them is among the very nicest we've seen anywhere in a hostel—a bona fide suite with a beautiful bed and the best views in the house. It comes with special kitchen and bathroom privileges, too—as well as a price to match. But if you're gonna splurge with your sweetie, we'd do it here.

Best bet for a bite: Doughnuts at Robin's

What hostellers say: "Try the trampoline."

Gestalt: Victoria's secret

Safety: A

Hospitality: B

Cleanliness: C

Party index:

How to get there:

By bus: Bus stops downtown. Call for transit route.

By car: Call hostel for directions.

By ferry: From downtown at Douglas and Yates, take #14 bus to Tillicum stop. Walk 1 block north on Tillicum to Selkirk Avenue; turn right, walk less than 0.5 km (0.25 mi.). Hostel is on right.

By train: Train stops downtown. Call for transit route.

HOSTELLING INTERNATIONAL-WHISTLER

5678 Alta Lake Road, Whistler, British Columbia V0N 1B0

(604) 932–5492

Fax: (604) 932–4687

E-mail: whistler@hihostels.bc.ca

Web site: www.hihostels.bc.ca/whi.htm

Rates: $18.50 Canadian (about $13.00 U.S.) per Hostelling International member
Credit cards: JCB, MC, VISA
Office hours: 8:00–11:00 A.M., 5:00–10:00 P.M. (summer); 7:00–11:00 A.M., 5:00–11:00 P.M. (winter)
Beds: 32
Private/family rooms: 1
Single rooms: None
Private bathrooms: None
Affiliation: Hostelling International-Canada
Extras: Bicycle rentals, piano, guitar, lockers, rowboat, sauna, canoes, inner tubes, store

10%

Recently voted the best ski town in North America, Whistler is hot. Construction of accommodations is overwhelming this relatively small hamlet tucked among towering mountains in western B.C. But you can still get away from it all by booking a bed—well in advance during the winter, mind you—at this hostel set away from the madness, across serene Alta Lake.

WHISTLER-AREA HOSTELS: A Summary

	RATING	PROS	CONS	COST	PAGE
HI-Whistler		location, fun	ways from town	$18.50	p. 236
Shoestring Lodge		great rooms	smoky	$20.00	p. 239
Whistler Backpackers		central	shoddy	$15.00	p. 241

Hostelling International-Whistler
Whistler
(photo courtesy HI-Canada)

As you drive up the curvy road to the hostel, its location is not immediately apparent. Don't bring too much luggage: To get there, you must park and then descend (and, eventually, when you leave, ascend) a long, fifty-step Escherian staircase to a set of train tracks.

Working train tracks. That's right, trains roll through here with amazing regularity. A sign posted below tells you to stop, look, and listen for the whistle. The train doesn't always blow that whistle, however; and, if it's snowing, be extra cautious. Once you overcome this obstacle, though, you're home free. (Hey, things aren't all that bad. If you take the pricey B.C. Rail run from Vancouver, for instance, you'll get dropped right at the hostel door! What a way to arrive.)

Entering the mudroom, you're asked to remove your shoes, a policy no doubt enforced to lengthen the lovely luster of the pine floors in the common room. You'll immediately note the informative display that explains the colorful origins of the hostel, once a lodge. The great common area succeeds fabulously in providing lots of cozy places to curl up with a dog-eared paperback next to the roaring fireplace or just to gaze out onto the lake. This is definitely one of the more fun common rooms we've seen: A pool table, piano, and guitar all present options; and the wide-open space makes conversing with new friends a snap.

The place isn't perfect. Bunks are old-fashioned, some of the four-bed bunkrooms are drafty, and all are pretty dimly lit. Still, some come with a desk and chair, which is really nice. The views, too, are breathtaking. Bathrooms are interesting—two single-sex bathrooms accommodating sixteen people have one toilet each. At least there are plenty of sinks; the women's bathroom even has one inside the toilet stall! Keys are issued here with a $10.00 Canadian (about $8.00 U.S.) deposit; you get it back when you check out.

The kitchen is decent, and the chipper and helpful hostel staff have thoughtfully added a loaded spice rack for which a small donation is asked. Pots and pans are serviceable, and there's quite a large prep space, allowing easy transfer of food to the two-burner gas stoves. Recycling is strongly encouraged; there's even a note posted in the dorm rooms telling you what goes where.

Best bet for a bite: Cafes in town

What hostellers say: "Stop, look, listen."

Insiders' tip: Snow muffles sound of train whistle

Gestalt: Whistler stop

Hospitality: A

Cleanliness: A

Party index:

This hostel is refreshingly free of the usual Hostelling International rules; we noticed beer being responsibly consumed by some of the many Aussies staying here. Although there's no curfew, the door is locked at 10:00 P.M.

Other cool stuff? You can launch a canoe right from the hostel's back lawn on Alta Lake. (The canoes are free, though you must sign a liability waiver first.) The rustic back porch comes complete with a you-start electric sauna, quite pleasing. And basic food items like eggs, milk, soup, candy, and so forth are cheerfully sold at the desk, at very reasonable prices.

Once provisioned, whatcha gonna do in the area? C'mon, give us a break. Hike, ski, swim, gawk at some of Canada's best scenery—heck, do anything you want. Just don't sit around all day griping about inaccuracies in hostel guidebooks. Need food? It's a hike. Bring that heavy wallet, too: The demand is clearly greater than the supply around here, and prices are higher as a result. But you can even buy hand-made Cuban cigars there (along with your copy of *Smoke* magazine, if you're hip and trendy) at the local IGA. Is this progress? Hmmm. . . . Maybe we need to find someplace a little less, um, appreciated.

We really like this hostel, though perhaps the accommodations could be updated. This ain't 1939. Otherwise, it's a great place.

How to get there:

By bus: From Vancouver, take Maverick bus line to Whistler. From bus stop, walk north along lakeside trail about 4 km (2.5 mi.) to Rainbow Park; follow road to left and walk 400 more meters (about 0.25 mi.).

By car: Drive approximately 125 km (80 mi.) north of Vancouver on Route 99. Just after entering Whistler limits, make a left onto

Alta Lake Road. Continue 5 km (about 3 mi.); hostel parking lot is on right.

By train: BC Rail runs from Vancouver to Whistler. Bus stops right at hostel on request.

SHOESTRING LODGE 

7124 Nancy Greene Drive, Whistler, British Columbia
VON 1BO
(604) 932–3338
E-mail: shoestring@whistler.net
Web site: www.whistler.net/boot/string.html
Rates: $20 Canadian (about $15 U.S.) per person; private rooms $70 Canadian (about $49 U.S.)
Credit cards: MC, VISA
Office hours: 24 hours
Beds: 110
Private/family rooms: 15
Single rooms: None
Private bathrooms: 15
Affiliation: None
Extras: Pub, liquor store, video games, pool table, restaurant

If you're not in the eighteen- to twenty-two–year male demographic, then pretend for a minute that you are. Imagine an accommodation not unlike a college dorm, where the beer flows freely, there are lots of cool people, and so on. But wait, it gets better.

Shoestring Lodge not only provides all of the above, but there's more. In college you might have had to deal with curfews, RA supervisors, dweeby campus cops hassling you for lighting up, one television for 200 people to share, bland food, and no dancing girls. At the Shoestring, you get a TV in each room; smoking is allowed everywhere; there's no curfew; a serviceable restaurant is on the premises; and a bar and liquor store are attached! They sometimes even bring in "girls" to dance at the bar.

If you're a college-age guy, you're probably not even reading this paragraph. You probably just dropped this book on the floor; threw a few pairs of clean underwear, skis, and, we hope, some kind of precautionary devices (if you know what we mean) into your pack; and are now on your way to Whistler by any means necessary. It just seems too good to be true.

Well, if you happen to be at that age where you can party at the drop of a hat, then this is definitely your place. You don't even have to ski to stay here. In fact, judging by the amount of smokers lounging about in the waiting room, not a lot of physical activity is exerted here. Just a lot of young'uns nursing hangovers and planning the next bladder buster.

Best bet for a bite: IGA Plus

What hostellers say: "How was *your* party?"

Insiders' tip: Great van deals on bulletin board

Gestalt: The Shoe fits

Hospitality: B

Cleanliness: B

Party index:

But seriously. As far as accommodations go, you'll be verrrrry comfortable here. The rooms are exceptionally big, clean, and well suited to a youth-oriented facility. There are no more than six bunks per room—almost all contain four or less—and every single durn one of 'em has its own washroom. Televisions are provided in each room, complete with cable and remote. So, unfortunately, are ashtrays. There are more-expensive private rooms with queen-size beds, but they're still cheaper than some of the big hotels in the area.

Keep in mind that this is a real happenin' town, so it's essential that you book wayyyyy ahead in winter—and in summer, too, if possible. Heck, even fall can be tough as dozens of slackers pile in and light up, waiting not-so-anxiously for job fairs at the two big local ski hills to begin.

One real bonus here is that you're just a five- or ten-minute stroll to the busy town and marketplace: Development Hell, absolutely, but it's where you've got to go to battle Muffy and Brad for eats. Unless you want to chow down in the Shoestring-owned Gaitor's restaurant, that is. You get a 15 percent discount, there, though we can't vouch for the food quality at the place, 'cause we couldn't afford it.

The tiny hostel kitchen—located in a different building and up some stairs and down a back hall, by the way—is obviously well used but not terribly well cleaned. The staff claim that if dirty dishes and messes are not handled by the hostellers themselves, the offenders will be given a "sound verbal thrashing." Yeah, right. Still, all in all this is a nicely outfitted place in a drop-dead location—if you can stand all that smoke, the incredibly slacker crowd, and, alas, the occasional appearance of those dancing girls.

Looking for nature and quiet? Head for the beautiful Hostelling International joint on Alta Lake. Want to rage all night? This is your place.

How to get there:

By bus: Take Maverick bus from Vancouver to Whistler, then call hostel for directions.

By car: Call hostel for directions.

WHISTLER BACKPACKERS HOSTEL 

2124 Lake Placid Road, Whistler, British Columbia V0N 1B2

(604) 932–1177

Rates: $15 Canadian (about $10 U.S.) per person
Credit cards: None
Office hours: Vary; call
Beds: 30
Private/family rooms: Yes
Single rooms: None
Private bathrooms: None
Affiliation: None
Extras: Laundry, sauna, TV

When we saw the metal palm trees on the front lawn of this place, we knew it was going to be a little strange. Then we learned that the hostel was another in the, um, legendary chain of "Vincent's" hostels that operate in British Columbia and Washington state. Ahhhhh. That explains it. Never a dull moment at a Vincent's.

The junked cars out front nearly frightened us away, but we did stick around long enough to get the basics. The place is basically a crash pad (How many times have we seen that before? Too many). And it seems to have been stocked with lots of slacker-friendly extras, like a sauna, TV, and laundry that we're sure gets maximum use. This hostel's prime advantage is its location right in the center of the populated village of Whistler Creek. You're certainly close to the ski resorts, the gas station, and beautiful Alta Lake.

On the other hand, hosteller reports about the place aren't so hot. This hostel offers a discount for monthly stays, and maybe that's part of the problem: Fellow hostellers who are getting to be just too familiar as they go through the daily routine of a smoke, a soap opera on the telly, more smokes, some mac and cheese, maybe a sauna . . . There are two really nice hostels in Whistler. This is the *other* one.

What hostellers say: "Strange."

Gestalt: Whistler's other

Hospitality: C

Cleanliness: D

Party index:

How to get there:

By bus: Maverick Lines runs to Whistler ($17 Canadian/about $12 U.S. one way). Hostel is located across from bus stop, less than 1 block down Lake Placid Road.

By car: From Vancouver, drive Route 99 approximately 120 km (85 mi.). At Husky gas station, turn left onto Lake Placid Road. Hostel is less than 1 block down, on the left.

YUKON TERRITORY

Each summer thousands of travelers feel the irresistible pull of the Yukon. Vast, unspoiled, and drop-jaw beautiful, the place is experiencing something of a boom lately in ecotourism. Hip back-to-the-landers are also rediscovering Whitehorse and Dawson City as places to put down stakes.

Hostellers have only one choice here, so far as we know—an extremely rustic but well-situated joint across the river from Dawson City. You can get there two ways: Drive northeast from Tok ("Yes, I'm pronounced *toke*") Alaska, or head northwest from Whitehorse.

DAWSON CITY RIVER HOSTEL 

P.O. Box 32, Dawson City, Yukon Territory Y0B 1G0

(867) 993–6823

Rates: $13 Canadian (about $10 U.S.) per Hostelling International member; private rooms $30 Canadian (about $23 U.S.)
Credit cards: None
Office hours: 9:00 A.M.–noon; 4:00 P.M.–midnight
Season: May 15–October 1
Beds: 30
Private/family rooms: Yes; number varies; call for availability
Single rooms: Yes; number varies; call for availability
Private bathrooms: None
Affiliation: Hostelling International-Canada
Extras: Canoe rental, bicycle rental, games, free pickups, store

This rustic hostel certainly has the advantage of location: It's situated on the banks of the Yukon River, only 250 km (about 150 mi.) from the Arctic Circle, in the incredible Yukon Territory.

The setup is very simple: a series of cabins with two to six beds apiece. There are kitchen facilities as well, a nice bonus, and—since this hostel sees nearly twenty-four hours of daylight during June and July—the outdoor firepit must get lots of use, too.

However, be prepared to rough it a bit. Outhouses are the rule of thumb here, there's only a "prospector's bath" (does that mean river water in a tub?), and manager Dieter Reinmuth cheerfully advertises "icy cold showers" and "no electricity" among the so-called amenities.

At least you'll find plenty to do in this wilderness wonderland. You might rent a bicycle, for instance, and go nuts in the hills or just tool around Dawson City. This ain't Manhattan, obviously, but the place has a growing cultural scene as a new generation of young folks discover the Yukon and infuse it with a fresh new spirit.

Alternatively, you could check out the "sweat lodge" here. Or—this is pretty wild—it seems you can book a one-way canoe to the little hamlets of Eagle and Circle, Alaska. They're way out there in the bush; sounds interesting. Strangely, there's also a small store on the premises hawking postcards, stamps, used books (?), Yukon souvenirs, and such. Wait a minute: no toilets, but a souvenir shop?

Getting here is fairly easy, once you've made your way to Dawson City. A free ferry spirits you across the river all day and night. Still can't make it to the riverbanks? The hostel offers free pickups from the local airport three times each week.

Our opinion? Primitive as heck, but potentially lots of fun as long as you can stand the pit toilets.

Best bet for a bite: Nancy's

What hostellers say: "Dawson! I mean, awesome!"

Gestalt: Dawson City limits

Hospitality: B

Cleanliness: B

Party index:

How to get there:

By car: From Tok, Alaska, drive west on Highway 2 for 12 km (7 mi.). Turn onto Top of the World Highway (Route 5) and continue east approximately 160 km (100 mi.) to the Dawson River. Hostel is 100 meters (300 feet) before river; look for sign. From Whitehorse, drive along Klondike Highway 525 km (about 325 mi.) to Dawson City. Follow Front Street to ferry landing. Take twenty-four–hour ferry across river. Hostel is 100 meters (about 300 feet) uphill from ferry landing; look for sign.

By plane: Small airport in Dawson City. Hostel makes pickups three times weekly; call hostel for details.

PAUL'S PICKS

THE BEST HOSTELS IN CANADA

FIVE GREAT SKI HOSTELS

EIGHT STRANGE BUT TRUE HOSTELS

ELEVEN CANADIANA HOSTELS

THE BEST HOSTEL CHOW

FIVE HIPPIE HOSTELS

FIVE ROCKIN' GOOD TIME HOSTELS

NINE GREAT FAMILY HOSTELS

. . . AND A HOSTEL WITH A PEACH TREE!

ABOUT THE AUTHOR

Paul Karr is an award-winning journalist and travel writer whose work has appeared in *Sports Illustrated, Sierra, New Age Journal,* and other publications. The co-author of *Hostels U.S.A.* and a tour guide, Paul divides his time between Canada, Europe, and the United States. You can e-mail him directly at:

Atomev@aol.com